STUDY GU

for

The Legal Environment
of Business and
Online Commerce

Henry Cheeseman

Seventh Edition

PEARSON

Boston Columbus Indianapolis New York San Francisco Upper Saddle River
Amsterdam Cape Town Dubai London Madrid Milan Munich Paris Montreal Toronto
Delhi Mexico City Sao Paulo Sydney Hong Kong Seoul Singapore Taipei Tokyo

Executive Editor: Stephanie Wall
Editorial Project Manager: Karen Kirincich
Production Project Manager: Nancy Freihofer
Senior Manufacturing Buyer: Megan Cochran

10 9 8 7 6 5 4 3 2 1

www.pearsonhighered.com

ISBN-10:   0-13-296994-7
ISBN-13: 978-0-13-296994-9

Table of Contents

Chapter 1

LEGAL AND ETHICAL ENVIRONMENT

Why do we stop at red lights or what is the "LAW"?

I. Overview

One of the first objectives of this opening chapter centers around illustrating attempts by great thinkers to answer the unanswerable. How law and ethics are defined by any one individual is ultimately related to his or her personal view of the larger global issues including morality, religion, and philosophy as well as the social sciences. When painting the picture entitled "What is law?" the broadest brush possible must be used. The interweaving of all these disciplines into one area of study, generically called jurisprudence, is what makes law study so formidable, complex, and perplexing. By the same token, those difficulties are what make it so challenging and stimulating. The study of law must start with open channels for new ideas not only from the mind, but also from the heart. Law and its various mechanisms is not just a set of rules of conduct but rather the end product of how society has decided to help or hurt its members. It is no wonder that the fascination with law and law studies is at its zenith today. Students have come to appreciate that law represents the embodiment of the social environment we all live and work in. By analogy, compare the legal environment to the water in which the life of the sea takes place. Big fish may eat little fish and so forth, but if the water itself is contaminated, all its inhabitants suffer. So too must the law be constantly examined for its societal safety. Law must be clean based on solid moral underpinnings and proper ethics. Where it fails, the legal environment may become polluted.

The categorization of schools of jurisprudence starts with a comparison of the old and the new. The traditional schools of thought find their roots in ancient history. The Natural School of jurisprudence is not only a school of thought vis-a-vis law but also finds proponents throughout many religions of the world. It is still considered one of the foundations of legal thinking today and is espoused by many, including Justice Clarence Thomas. The Historical School of jurisprudence was founded in large part by Friedrich Karl von Savigny who felt law was a product of a nation's history. Advocates of a more proactive role for law may find comfort in the Sociological School of jurisprudence. Members of that school see law as a tool to be used in social engineering. Compare that philosophy with the views proffered by members of the Command School of jurisprudence. Advocates of this school are usually members of the ruling class or royalty. Absolute monarchies are an anathema to participatory democracy because such forms of government are really only dictatorships-by-birth.

In spite of the divergent views espoused by the traditional schools of jurisprudence, the schools have a common denominator. They are all rooted on some sort of morality-based foundation. The modern schools of jurisprudence have stepped away from this commonality by finding justification for their points of view in economics, political science, or sociological agendas. The efficacy of these newer theories is untested by the litmus test of time and continues to be a source of spirited and sometimes raucous debate.

One interesting aspect of all schools of jurisprudence is that their proponents try to establish norms of ethical behavior. Ethics is derived from the Latin word *ethicus*, meaning moral. In that sense all these systems represent ways of finding moral foundations upon which a system of law can be built. These moral systems have, in turn, been sought to be identified by a number of notable scholars ranging from

Karl Marx, John Stuart Mill, and Immanuel Kant to John Locke. In all these systems, a methodology is set forth by establishing guideposts for behavior. If these guideposts are universally accepted, the odds are very high that they will no longer be "advisory" but rather "required by law." The process by which moral-based ethical behavior is first *desired*, then *expected*, and finally *mandated* is really the evolution of law. Hopefully with each new generation, the law will evolve in a positive sense, which will best balance the legitimate interests of all parties concerned, both public and private. It is when these interests conflict that sometimes insurmountable problems arise. When the "guideposts" are only advisory and individuals ignore them or interpret them in conflicting ways we find major problems like the ones found in the Enron or WorldCom scandals. How society handles these problems might be relegated to the procedures established under the "law." This might cause discomfort for many individuals, especially employees. What we *should* do as a society might be answered as we proceed through this course.

Your role as a student of law is to try to develop a sensitivity to how complicated the administration of law is in our society today. This course is not designed to act as a substitute for professional law school training. It is designed to help you appreciate the value and importance of law and ethics in both your personal and business behavior. The law is too complex and perplexing, but imagine a world without it. Imagine a world of Cimmerian darkness—a world described by Homer in the Eighth Century B.C. as a region of perpetual gloom.

II. Hypothetical Multi-Issue Essay Question

John Driver is a truck driver for a major office supply company located in Wilmington, DE. His job on this bright Spring day is to deliver computer paper to a large insurance company in Philadelphia, PA. He is to proceed along Interstate 95 to the appropriate exit in Northeast Philadelphia where he is to turn right at the exit and travel three miles along Route 73 to the Insurance Company's main office building. As he gets to the exit along Route 95 he realizes lunchtime is approaching and he decides to pull off the road and take his lunch at a tavern located about six blocks off of Route 73. When he orders his lunch, he decides he is not hungry but is very thirsty. He therefore orders 10 alcoholic beverages which he proceeds to consume in 15 minutes. Before he orders the last two, which are happily served by the bartender on duty, he falls off the bar stool which is clearly seen by the server. He leaves the bar and starts to drive his truck back to the appropriate route when he accidentally hits an elderly woman crossing the street in a marked crosswalk who does recover fully from her injuries but only after much rehabilitation and great costs. She wants to know who she should sue and why. Who should she sue? What does the "law" say? What is the "law" or where do we find it?

III. Outline
What Is Law?

Law consists of rules with binding legal force that regulate the conduct of individuals, businesses, and other organizations within society. It is intended to protect persons and their property from unwanted interference from others. The law must be obeyed subject to sanctions or legal consequences.

Functions of Law
- Facilitating orderly change
- Facilitating planning
- Keeping the peace
- Maintaining the status quo
- Maximizing individual freedom
- Promoting social justice
- Providing a basis for compromise
- Shaping moral standards

Qualities of the Law
Fairness
> The American legal system is one of the most comprehensive, fair, and democratic systems of law ever developed and enforced

Flexibility
> The American legal system is generally responsive to cultural, technological, economic, and social changes

Schools of Jurisprudential Thought
Analytical school—Believes law is shaped by logic

Command school—Believes law is a set of rules developed and enforced by the ruling party

Critical legal studies school—Believes legal rules are unnecessary and that legal disputes should be solved using rules of fairness

Historical school—Believes law is an aggregate of social traditions and customs

Law and economics school—Believes promoting market efficiency should be the central concern of legal decision making

Sociological school—Believes law is a means of achieving and advancing certain sociological goals

Natural school—Believes law is based on what is "correct," law should be based on morality and ethics.

English Common Law
Common law
> Common law is developed by judges who issued their opinions when deciding a case. The principles became precedent for later judges deciding similar cases.

Law court
> A court that developed and administered a uniform set of laws decreed by the kings and queens after William the Conqueror. Legal procedure was emphasized over merits.

Court of Chancery (equity court)
> Court that granted relief based on fairness. Rather than emphasize legal procedure, the chancery court inquired into the merits of a case.

Merchant court
> Courts established to administer the "law of merchants," and were established to administer the rules based upon common trade practices and usage.

Sources of Law
> Codified law—Organization of statutes (written laws from the legislatures).
> Constitutions—Supreme law of the land.
> Executive orders—Order issued by the executive branch.
> Judicial decisions—Individual lawsuit decisions issued by courts.
> Regulations and administrative orders—Rulings and orders of administrative agencies.
> Treaties—Agreements with foreign governments becoming part of the law.
>   ↓   ↓   ↓

Constitutions
> The U.S. Constitution established the structure of the federal government
>> Legislative – (Congress) the power to make the law.
>> Executive – (President) the power to enforce the law.
>> Judicial – (Courts) the power to interpret the law.

The constitution and treaties take precedence over all other laws. State constitutions are valid unless they conflict with the U.S. Constitution or any valid federal law.

Treaties
> A treaty is a compact made between two or more nations

Codified Law
> Statute
>> Written law enacted by the legislative branch of federal and state governments that establishes certain courses of conduct that must be adhered to by covered parties. Federal laws are enacted by the United States Congress, state statutes are enacted by state legislatures.
> Ordinances
>> Laws enacted by local government bodies such as cities and municipalities, counties, school districts, and water districts

Executive Orders
> An executive order is an order issued by a member of the executive branch of government

Administrative Agency Rules and Regulations
> The legislative and executive branches of federal and state governments are empowered to establish administrative agencies to adopt rules and regulations to enforce and interpret statutes enacted by Congress and state legislatures
>> Many agencies regulate business

Judicial Decisions
> A judicial decision is a decision about an individual lawsuit issued by federal and state courts

Doctrine of Stare Decisis
> Based on the common law tradition, past court decisions become precedent for deciding future cases
> Precedent is a rule of law established in a court decision. Lower courts must follow the precedent established by higher courts
> Stare decisis—Latin for "to stand by the decision"—means adherence to precedent

IV. Objective Questions

Terms:

1. That which must be obeyed and followed by citizens subject to its sanction or legal consequences; a body of rules of action or conduct prescribed by controlling authority, and having binding legal force is called _law_.

2. The ___Analytical___ school believes that law is shaped by logic.

3. The Natural School of Law adheres to the position that law should be based on what is correct. This is also referred to as a _____ of law.

4. The _____ school believes that law is a set of rules developed and enforced by the ruling party.

5. The _Historical school_ of jurisprudence believes that the law is an aggregate of social traditions and customs that have developed over the centuries.

6. The school of jurisprudential thought that believes promoting market efficiency should be the central concern of legal decision making is known as the _____ school.

7. Because there were many unfair results due to the limited remedies allowed in the early English Law Courts, a second set of courts called the _____ were established in England.

8. The highest source of law found in the U.S. is found in the _Supreme law_.

9. Under the U.S. Constitution, with the consent of the Senate, the President may enter into _____ with other nations.

10. Adherence to precedent (a rule of law established in court decisions) is known by the Latin term _Stare decisis_, meaning to stand by the decision.

True/False:

1. _F_ One of the functions of the law is to limit [X→maximize] individual freedoms.

2. ____ Under our jury system, the same results will occur in the interpretation of the same criminal statute.

3. _F_ The Analytical School of Jurisprudence maintains that the law is an aggregate of social traditions and customs that have developed over the centuries.

4. ____ The Law and Economics school professes that market efficiency should be the ultimate goal of legal decision making.

5. ____ The Critical Legal Studies movement proposes that rules are enforced by the ruling party rather than a true reflection of society's views.

6. ____ The Court of Chancery provided for only limited law remedies in the early English court system.

7. ____ Equitable orders and remedies of the Court of Chancery took precedence over the legal decisions and remedies of the law courts.

8. ____ The law courts of the English common law could only provide monetary awards for damages.

9. ____ Treaties are classified as having a higher standing in our system of laws than federal, state, or local enactments.

10. ____ Presidential executive orders are expressly provided for in the U.S. Constitution.

11. ____ Stare decisis involves adhering to precedent.

12. ____ Statutes are case decisions issued by the courts.

Multiple Choice:

1. Which of the following would be considered an example of "shaping moral standards," as seen as a function of the law?

A. laws granting freedom of speech and religion
B. laws discouraging drug and alcohol abuse
C. laws providing rights to peaceful protest
D. laws preventing overthrow of the government

2. What function of the law is being served when passing laws that protect the U.S. government from the risk of being forcefully overthrown?

A. maintaining the status quo
B. shaping moral standards
C. facilitating orderly change
D. promoting social justice

3. The Analytical School of jurisprudence maintains that the law should be _____.

A. shaped by logic
B. based on social behavior
C. set by the ruling class
D. based on morality

4 Which school of jurisprudence views law as a sort of evolutionary process, where changing norms of society will be reflected in the law?

A. the Natural Law School of jurisprudence
B. the Sociological School of jurisprudence
C. the Analytical School of jurisprudence
D. the Historical School of jurisprudence

5. What school of jurisprudence bases its principles, for solving legal disputes, on broad notions of "fairness," and subjective decision making by judges?

A. the Natural Law School of jurisprudence
B. the Analytical School of jurisprudence
C. the Critical Legal Studies School of jurisprudence
D. the Sociological School of jurisprudence

6. The _____ School maintains that legal rules are unnecessary and that legal disputes should be solved by applying arbitrary rules based on fairness.

A. Sociological
B. Command
C. Critical Legal Studies
D. Law and Economics

7. The Merchant Court was first established as a separate set of courts in:

A. England.
B. U.S.A.
C. New York City.
D. San Francisco.

8. Which is true with respect to precedent?

A. Lower courts must follow higher court decisions, but may disregard decisions in other   jurisdictions.
B. Lower courts must follow higher court decisions, and also the decisions of other jurisdictions.
C. Higher courts must follow lower court decisions, but may disregard the decisions in other jurisdictions.
D. Higher courts must follow lower court decisions, and also the decisions of other jurisdictions.

9. What led to the creation of the Chancery Courts?

A. the insistence for a court system that emphasized legal procedure rather than the merits of a case
B. the law courts' inability to hear all the cases presented to them
C. the increase in overseas trade and proliferation of piracy
D. the unfair results and limited remedies provided by the law courts

10. What is a judicial decision?

A. a decision issued by the executive branch in a state of emergency
B. a decision about an individual lawsuit issued by a federal or state court
C. a codified law passed by the state legislature
D. a decision issued by the legislative branch to establish courses of conduct that covered parties must adhere to

Matching Question:

Match the following schools of law from the left column to the situations shown in the right column:

(1) Command	(a) Believes promoting market efficiency should be the central concern of legal decision-making.
(2) Critical Legal Studies	(b) Believes law is a set of rules developed and enforced by the ruling party
(3) Historical	(c) Believes law is an aggregate of social traditions and customs.
(4) Law and Ethics	(d) Believes law is a means of achieving and advancing certain sociological goals.
(5) Natural	(e) Believes law is based on "What is correct."
(6) Sociological	(f) Believes legal rules are unnecessary and that legal disputes should be solved using rules of fairness

Answers to Objective Questions:

Terms:

1. law. This is the end product of an evolutionary process which ultimately reflects how a society decides to both help and punish its members. [p. 2]

2. Analytical. This school believes that law is shaped by logic. [p. 7]

3. moral theory. This is still one of the most important schools of jurisprudence and was espoused by Justice Clarence Thomas in his confirmation hearings to the U.S. Supreme Court. [p. 7]

4. Command. This school believes law is a set of rules developed and enforced by a ruling party. [p. 7]

5. Historical School. It believes that changes in the norms of society will gradually be reflected in the law. To these legal philosophers, the law is an evolutionary process. [p. 7]

6. Law and Economics. This school of thought was founded at the University of Chicago and has gained many high profile advocates from both the law profession, such as Judge Richard Posner, and the economics profession, such as Milton Friedman. [p. 8]

7. Chancery Courts. These were the first equity-based courts and were headed by the Lord Chancellor. The early appointees to this position were invariably clerics who were to represent the "King's conscience." [p. 9]

8. Constitution. This is the supreme law of the land and any federal, state, or local law that is found to be in conflict with it is unconstitutional and therefore unenforceable. [p. 11]

9. treaties. Once ratified, treaties become part of the supreme law of the land. Only the federal government may enter into treaties with other nations. [p. 11]

10. stare decisis. When deciding individual lawsuits, federal and state courts issue judicial decisions. [p. 14]

True/False:

1. False. Maximizing individual freedom within the bounds of the needs of the larger society is one of the hallmarks of the U.S. Constitution. [p. 4]

2. False. As illustrated in the text accompanying the case of *Standefer v. United States,* different juries may reach different results under any criminal statute. [p. 5]

3. False. This definition applies to the Historical School of jurisprudence. [p. 7]

4. True. The Law and Economics School is also called the Chicago School, named after the University of Chicago, where it was first developed. [p. 8]

5. False. It proposes that legal rules are unnecessary and are used as an obstacle by the powerful to maintain the status quo. [p. 8]

6. False. It was the limitation on remedies in the law court that led to the creation of the equity-based Court of Chancery. [p. 10]

7. True. The chancellor's remedies were called equitable remedies because they were shaped to fit each situation. [p. 10]

8. True. The only relief available at law courts was a monetary award for damages. [p. 10]

9. True. Once ratified, treaties become part of the supreme law of the land. [p. 12]

10. False. These powers are derived express delegations from the legislative branch and otherwise implied from the U.S. Constitution. [p. 13]

11. True. Promotes uniformity of law within a jurisdiction. [p. 14]

12. False. Statues come from the legislatures. [p. 15]

Multiple Choice:

1. B. Shaping moral standards is one of the functions of law. [p. 4]

2. A. Maintaining the status quo is an important function of law. [p. 4]

3. A. Analytical philosophers believe that results are reached by applying principles of logic to the specific facts of a case. [p. 7]

4. D. The Historical School of jurisprudence believes that the law is an aggregate of social traditions and customs that have developed over the centuries. [p. 7]

5. C. The Critical Legal Studies School proposes that legal rules are unnecessary and are used as an obstacle by the powerful to maintain the status quo. [p. 8]

6. C. The Critical Legal Studies School proposes that legal rules are unnecessary and are used as an obstacle by the powerful to maintain the status quo. [p. 8]

7. A. The rules of the Law Merchant were first administered as a separate court in England. That court was absorbed in the regular law court system in England in the early 1900s. [p. 10]

8. A Based on the common law tradition, past court decisions become precedent for deciding future cases. [p. 14]

9. D. Because of some unfair results and limited remedies available in the law courts, a second set of courts—the Court of Chancery (or equity court)—was established. [p. 10]

10. B. Generally, the power is derived from the Office of the President. [p. 11]

Matching Questions:
1. Command School   B [p. 8]
2. Critical Legal Studies School   F [p. 8]
3. Historical School   C [p. 7]
4. Law and Ethics School   A [p. 8]
5. Natural Law School   E [p. 7]
6. Sociological School   D [p. 7]

Answers to Essay Question

The lady should sue:
1. truck driver – refer to either statute or prior decisions on battery
2. bartender – most states have a statute, Dram Shop Act, which allows recovery for injuries from someone serving alcohol to the party causing the injuries
3. office supply company and/or bar owner – prior cases allow for recovery from employer of the injurer under a doctrine known as "*respondeat superior*"
This case illustrates the application of a number of sources of the law. [p. 11]

Chapter 2

BUSINESS ETHICS AND SOCIAL RESPONSIBILITY

How much of the manufacturing waste should *we dump in the water?*

I. Overview

The novel *Spartacus* was written by the French author Bernard Joseph Saurin in 1760. The novel was named after the Thracian slave who died in 71 B.C. after leading a revolt against the Roman authorities. In this novel, Saurin wrote: "The law often permits what honor forbids." That quote truly encapsulates what the study of ethics vis-à-vis law is all about. While it may have been legal to trade in human misery and subjugation, could it ever be morally acceptable under any of the systems of ethics discussed in this chapter?

The study of ethics revolves around the examination of rules, conduct, and character through a morally-tinted microscope. That law should be grounded in some sort of morality-based foundation is self-evident. Yet painful history has shown us over and over the prices paid when there is an abyss between law and ethics. Sometimes these gaps can only be closed by conflagrations and wars so costly that we are reminded of an old anonymous proverb: "Adam ate the apple, and our teeth still ache."

The goals of all the ethical schools of thought are to seek some sort of morally-based rationale for human behavior. This rationale may be found in outside sources as seen in schools of ethical fundamentalism or in the rule that provides the greatest good to society as illustrated by utilitarianism. Others such as Kant and Rawls have sought to devise formulas of behavior based on universal rules or social contract, respectively. In all these systems, a morally-based methodology is sought as a guidepost for behavior. If these guideposts are universally accepted, the odds are very high that they will no longer be advisory, but rather required by law. The process by which morally-based ethical behavior is first desired, then expected, and finally mandated is really the evolution of law. Note that law is the last stage in this often painful process.

Because so much of our legal and economic activities are conducted in the corporate format, juristic (law-made) business entities cannot ignore this constant and dynamic tug and pull between ethics and law. We have either come a long way or become hopelessly bogged down in political correctness depending on your personal point of view. This dynamic is well illustrated by the differences between the thinking of the court in *Dodge v. Ford Motor Company* in 1919 and today's social audits of corporate citizenship. The bottom line in the study of ethics is ultimately personal. Imagine a world without a concern for law and ethics. As French author Stephanie Félicité Genlis said in 1793, "The man whose probity consists in merely obeying laws cannot be truly virtuous or estimable; for he will find many opportunities of doing contemptible and even dishonest acts, which laws cannot punish."

II. Hypothetical Multi-Issue Essay Question

Taxes are a cost of not only doing business but also an expense of living in a free society. As Justice Oliver Wendell Holmes said in 1927, "Taxes are what we pay for civilized society." But must we pay even in death? The federal government has a long established set of wealth transfer taxes designed to pay back the government for the protection it provided to a decedent during his or her accumulation of wealth. One such tax is the federal estate tax which is imposed on decedents whose estates are valued at over $600,000 at the time of death.

You are a newly graduated associate of the Ras, Ma, and Tas law firm that represents the estate of Dealing Don, the late, great Aspen rental real estate mogul. The fair market value of his rental real estate holdings is over $6 million. Your senior partner finds an Internal Revenue Code section that allows a "use" value for family-owned businesses. This use value is intended to preserve family farm ownership. Should you convert these city rental units to agricultural "use" in order to reduce their reported value to under $600,000?

III. Outline

Law and Ethics—ethics is a set of moral principles or values that governs the conduct of an individual or a group. The law may permit something that would be ethically wrong.

Theories of Ethics
    Ethical fundamentalism—People look to an outside source or central figure for ethical guidelines (20)
    Utilitarianism—People choose the alternative that would provide the greatest good to society
    Kantian ethics—A set of universal rules based on reasoning establishes ethical duties
    Rawls's social justice theory—Moral duties are based on an implied social contract
    Ethical relativism—Individuals decide what is ethical based on their beliefs about right and wrong

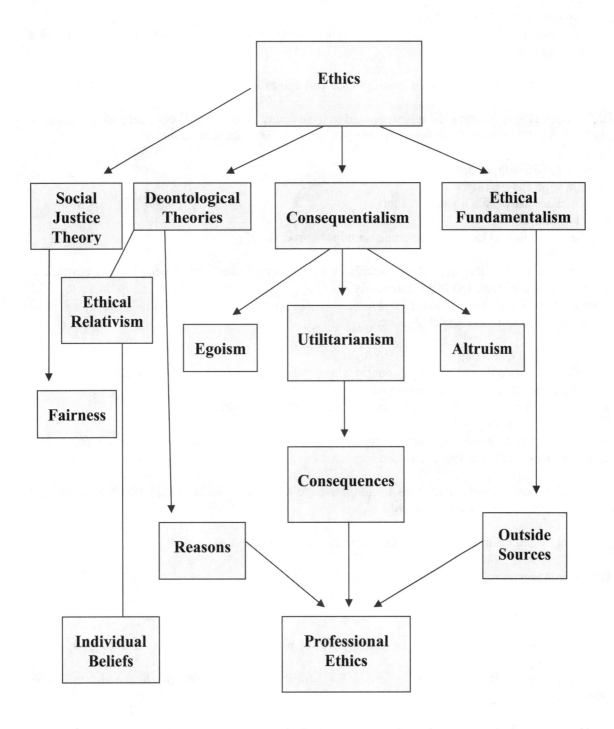

Social Responsibility of Business
Social responsibility of business is a duty owed by businesses to act socially responsible in producing and selling goods and services

Whistleblower Statute – permits private parties to sue companies for fraud on behalf of the government.

Social Contract Theory – each person is presumed to have entered into a social contract with all others in society to obey moral rules that are necessary for people to live in peace and harmony.

Theories of Social Responsibility
Maximize profits
To maximize profits for stockholders
Moral minimum
To avoid causing harm and to compensate for harm caused
Stakeholder interest
To consider the interests of all stakeholders, including stockholders, employees, customers, suppliers, creditors, and local community
Corporate citizenship
To do good and solve social problems

Examples of Ethical Questions
Is it ethical to pay bribes in a foreign country where that is the common business practice?
Is it ethical to use cartoon characters to advertise cigarettes?
Is it ethical to pollute legally if there is another way to handle the problem?
Is insider trading appropriate?
Should working conditions in another country be changed to mimic our standards before we buy products manufactured in these countries?

Sarbanes-Oxley Act prompts companies to adopt a code of ethics, makes certain conduct illegal and establishes criminal penalties for violations.

Corporate social audit – an accounting of the organization's moral health.

IV. Objective Questions:

Terms:

1. _____ is a set of moral principles or values that governs the conduct of an individual or group.

2. When a person looks to an outside source for ethical rules or commands, he or she might be categorized as a _____.

3. A moral theory which dictates that people must choose the action or follow the rule that provides the greatest good to society is called _____.

4. A moral theory which says that people owe moral duties that are based on universal rules is called _____, also known as Kantian ethics.

5. Basing one's behavior on the adage: "Do unto others as you would have them do unto you" is called the _____.

6. _____ permits private parties to sue companies for fraud on behalf of the government.

7. A moral theory that says each person is presumed to have entered into a social contract with all others in society to obey moral rules that are necessary for people to live in peace and harmony is called a _____.

8. _____ is a theory of social responsibility which says that a corporation's duty is to make a profit while avoiding harm to others.

9. A theory of social responsibility that says a corporation must consider the effects its actions have on persons other than its stockholders is called _____.

10. A theory of social responsibility that says a business has a responsibility to do good is called _____.

11. The _____ theory of social responsibility argues that business has a responsibility to do well.

True/False:

1. ____ Law and ethical standards never conflict with one another. If something is a law, it is, by definition, ethical.

2. ____ Under Ethical Fundamentalism, a person looks solely within himself or herself for ethical codes or commands.

3. ____ Utilitarianism is a moral theory that dictates that people must choose the action or rules that provide the greatest good to society.

4. ____ Under Kantian ethics, morality is judged by a person's act or motives.

5. ____ Immanuel Kant supported the Golden Rule.

6. ____ John Locke and Jean Jacques Rousseau supported the Social Contract theory of morality.

7. ____ Ethical Relativism has been widely adopted as a moral theory because of its strict guidelines.

8. ____ Moral Minimum is a theory of social responsibility that says that business is responsible for helping to solve social problems that it did little if anything to cause.

9. ____ A corporation which moves jobs overseas to take advantage of lower pay scales is adhering to the Stakeholder Interest school of corporate ethics.

10. ____ There are no specific governmental laws endorsing a moral minimum of social responsibility on corporations.

Multiple Choice:

1. Literal Larry believes that all ethical standards and rules are set out in a book called *Ethics For All* that was written by a prominent ethical theorist. Larry refers to this book for guidance and rules by which to lead his life. Which of the following moral theories most accurately describes Larry's conduct?

A. Kantian Ethics.
B. Utilitarianism.
C. Ethical Relativism.
D. Ethical Fundamentalism.

2. Societal Sarah believes people should take actions that benefit society as a whole the most. Which of the following moral theories most accurately describes Sarah's beliefs?

A. Kantian Ethics.
B. Utilitarianism.
C. Rawl's Social Justice.
D. Ethical Fundamentalism.

3. Dutiful Daisy always considers how she would feel in another person's place before she takes any action. Then, Daisy only acts in accord with how she would want others to behave in the same circumstances. Which of the following moral theories most accurately describes Daisy's conduct?

A. Kantian Ethics.
B. Ethical Relativism.
C. Ethical Fundamentalism.
D. Utilitarianism.

4. Individual Ingrid firmly believes that each person must look at her own feelings of what is right and wrong to decide what is ethical. Which of the following moral theories most accurately describes Ingrid's beliefs?

A. Utilitarianism.
B. Ethical Fundamentalism.
C. Rawl's Social Justice.
D. Ethical Relativism.

5. Fair Fran believes that fairness is the essence of justice. In addition, Fran believes all people in a society have a contract with one another to obey moral rules. Which of the following moral theories most accurately describes Fran's beliefs?

A. Utilitarianism.
B. Ethical Fundamentalism.
C. Rawl's Social Justice.
D. Ethical Relativism.

6. According to ethical relativism, _____.

A. ethics rely on duties based around universal rules which one is morally bound to follow
B. each person is presumed to have entered into a social contract with all others in society to obey moral rules
C. people must choose an action or follow a rule that provides the greatest good to society
D. there are no universal ethical rules to guide a person's conduct

7. What is "maximizing profits" as a social responsibility theory in business?

A. The theory that a corporation must consider the effects its actions have on persons other than its shareholders.
B. The theory that a corporation's duty is to make a profit while avoiding causing harm to others.
C. The theory that a corporation owes a duty to take actions that increases profits for shareholders.
D. The theory that a business has a responsibility solely to its stakeholders that other than shareholders.

8. C.E.O. Ceo believes her corporation must consider what effects it may have on its employees, suppliers, customers, etc. Which of the following social responsibility theories does Ceo most likely subscribe to?

A. Corporate Citizenship.
B. Stakeholder Interest.
C. Moral Minimum.
D. Maximizing Profits.

9. How are ethical rules established in Rawls's social justice theory?

A. by a set of universal rules based on consistency and reversibility
B. from an original position of a veil of ignorance
C. by the ruling class or people in advantageous positions
D. by following what's best for the society as a whole

10. C.E.O. Crusader believes his corporation can be influential and should be responsible for helping solve many social problems. Crusader believes his corporation should address problems above and beyond those actually caused by the corporation. Which of the following social responsibility theories does Crusader most likely subscribe to?

A. Corporate Citizenship.
B. Stakeholder Interest.
C. Moral Minimum.
D. Maximizing Profits.

V. Answers to Objective Questions:

Terms:

1. Ethics. Ethical standards require more than simply obeying the law. [p. 19]

2. ethical fundamentalist. The Natural Law School of jurisprudence is considered to be one of the oldest, and it is still quite important in the study of law and ethics. [p. 20]

3. Utilitarianism. Many people have difficulty with this theory because of its lack of absolute or bottom line standards. [p. 21]

4. duty ethics. This is traceable to religious doctrines, and also known as Kantian ethics. [p. 21]

5. categorical imperative. The key advocate was Kant. [p. 21]

6. False Claims Act. This statute is also known as the Whistleblower Statute. [p. 21]

7. social contract. Many of the newer schools of jurisprudence are variations on this basic theme. [p. 22]

8. Moral minimum. Under this theory, as long as a business avoids or corrects social injury that it may Cause, it has met its duty of social responsibility. [p. 25]

9. stakeholder interest. The difficulty lies in defining who is a stakeholder. [p. 26]

10. corporate citizenship. This debate has gone on since the inception of the corporate form. [p. 27]

11. corporate citizenship. Business is responsible for helping to solve social problems that it did little, if anything, to cause. [p. 30]

True/False:

1. False. The law may be contrary to a person's ethical standards. [p. 21]

2. False. Under ethical fundamentalism, one looks to an outside source. This source may be from religious or political teachings and the like. [p. 22]

3. True. The moral theory has its origin in the works of Jeremy Bentham and John Stuart. [p. 23]

4. True. The test is based on the categorical imperative. [p. 24]

5. True. The Golden Rule is generally accepted as being based on the categorical imperative preferred by Kant. [p. 24]

6. True. Under this theory, there is an implied contract which states: "I will follow the rules if everyone else does." [p. 25]

7. False. Even though ethics remain an extremely personal decision, few people deny that some universal ethical rules should apply to everyone. [p. 25]

8. False. Moral Minimum is a theory of social responsibility which says that corporate social responsibility is to make a profit while avoiding harm to others. Corporate Citizenship is a theory of social responsibility that says business is responsible for helping to solve social problems that it did little if anything to cause. [p. 28]

9. False. Most proponents of this school of thought would argue that such a move is based on the shareholder's interest alone. [p. 28]

10. False. The legislative and judicial branches of government have established laws that enforce the moral minimum of social responsibility on corporations. [p. 28]

Multiple Choice:

1. D. One of the key criticisms of any form of fundamentalism is that it tends to be too simplistic by trying to answer all questions at all times. [p. 22]

2. B. This approach tends to balance the various interests involved and weigh in favor of the most benefit possible for the least social cost or harm. [p. 23]

3. A. This theory is also often referred to as the Golden Rule. [p. 24]

4. D. Many people have difficulty with this theory because of the lack of outside controls on Ingrid's decisions. [p. 25]

5. C. This theory represents one of the newer schools of jurisprudence. [p. 25]

6. D. Ethical relativism holds that individuals must decide what is ethical based on their own feelings about what is right and wrong. [p. 25]

7. C. The traditional view of the social responsibility of business is that business should maximize profits for shareholders. [p. 26]

8. B. The debate goes on as to how big the stakeholder class should be. [p. 28]

9. B. The principles of justice should be chosen by persons who do not yet know their station in society—thus, their "veil of ignorance" would permit the fairest possible principles to be selected. [p. 28]

10. A. Most corporations have only bought into this theory on a limited basis. [p. 30]

VI. Answers to Essay Question:

A tax law practitioner has a duty to represent his or her client in an ethical manner as prescribed by the professional canons of ethics. For example, candidates for admission to the bar swear to "not counsel or maintain any suit or proceeding which shall appear to be unjust, nor any defense except to be honestly debatable under the law of the land."

The behavior expected here would be to use all *legal* arguments to favor your client's position. This would include any reasonable interpretations of Internal Revenue Code sections that may be applicable in the case at hand.

The law firm should affirm maximum advocacy for its client, but guard against unethical behavior that would pervert the true intention of this code section, i.e., it cannot make white black or vice versa only to save taxes. If there is no plausible way these parcels could be used as agricultural properties, you and the firm should ethically advise your client against using such an IRC code section in this case.

Perhaps, some earlier estate planning should have been done to prevent this problem. In any event, the present tax problem must be ethically dealt with by legitimately arguable positions regarding the code sections involved.

The bottom line rests within ourselves. We all have a duty to pay taxes. These taxes can be avoided legally and ethically. They cannot, however, be evaded by specious claims not based in any sort of reality. In order to help this process an analysis should include reviewing how all the alternative courses of action might affect all the possible stakeholders, including ourselves and society as a whole. In the end, we must develop our best personal instinct to draw the bottom line, but also to do so ethically.

Chapter 3

COURT SYSTEMS AND ADMINISTRATIVE LAW

When can you take a case to court?

I. Overview

You are standing at the window with a friend and your car gets hit. You see it happen and you want to sue. Can you and, if so, where? Your friend saw the same accident. Can he sue? Should you go to Federal Court or State Court and if the latter, which one? For the laymen, these questions might seem easy but they are not.

Additionally, jurisdiction (the power of a court to hear a case) has been complicated by the computer. Where does a transaction take place? Where is the computer? Does it matter? These questions, among others will attempt to be answered in this chapter.

II. Hypothetical Multi-issue Essay Question

Mr. Cav E. At-Emptor is fed up. He has suffered through the ownership of a model XXX Luxmobile auto since he bought it new from Loud and Obnoxious Motors nine months ago. The car has spent more time in the repair shop than on the road and is now out of warranty. Mr. At-Emptor still owes over four years worth of payments on the car and has decided he is tired of paying for the car twice—once to buy it and once again to repair it. He purchased the car in New York but uses it in Colorado. Can he sue L & O Motors in Colorado?

III. Outline
State Court Systems
    Limited-jurisdiction trial courts
        Courts that hear matters of specialized or limited nature
        Sometimes called inferior trial courts
    General-jurisdiction trial court
        Courts that hear cases of a general nature that are not within the jurisdiction of limited-jurisdiction trial courts
        Sometimes called Courts of Record
    Intermediate appellate courts
        Courts that hear appeals from trial courts
        Parties usually file briefs to support their positions
    Highest state court
        The highest court in a state system
        Names may vary by state, but most call it the State Supreme Court

Special Federal Courts
    US Tax Court- cases involving tax laws
    US Claims Court- cases brought against the United States
    US Court of International Trade- cases involving tariffs and international commercial disputes
    US Bankruptcy Court- cases involving bankruptcy law

US District Courts
    These are the federal court system's trial courts of general jurisdiction
    Presently, there are 94 district courts

US Courts of Appeals
    These are the federal court system's intermediate appellate courts
    There are 13 courts of appeals

U.S. Supreme Court
    Created by Article III of the US Constitution
    Highest court in the US
    Located in Washington, D.C.
    Composed of nine justices who are nominated by the President and confirmed by the Senate
    Types of decisions:
        Unanimous- all judges agree on the outcome of the case
        Majority- Most judges agree to the outcome and reasoning of a decision
        Plurality- Most judges agree with the outcome, but differ in reasoning
        Tie- Less than 9 judges sit, and there is a tie decision. In this event, the lower court decision is affirmed.
        Writ of Certiorari is needed for the Supreme Court to hear a case

        Concurring opinion- written by a judge when he/she agrees with the outcome, but not necessarily the reasoning.

        Dissenting opinion- written by a judge that does not agree with the decision.

Limited Jurisdiction of Federal Courts
    (1)   Federal Question- claims arising under the United States Constitution, treaties, federal statutes and regulations.
    (2)   Diversity of Citizenship → amount in question > $75,000 or more and all Plaintiffs citizens of different states than all Defendants

Exclusive jurisdiction- jurisdiction held only by federal courts to hear cases including federal crimes, antitrust matters, bankruptcy, patent, copyright cases, suits brought against the U.S., and most admiralty questions.

Concurrent jurisdiction- jurisdiction shared by two or more courts.

Standing- some stake in the outcome of a lawsuit.

Types of Jurisdiction
- (1) Subject Matter—type of case court can hear
- (2) In Personam—jurisdiction over the person
- (3) In Rem – power from jurisdiction over the property of a lawsuit
- (4) Quasi in Rem- allows a plaintiff who obtains judgment in one state to try to collect by attaching property of the defendant in another state.

Forum selection clause- a clause in a contract that specifies what court will hear the case if there is a dispute.

Choice of law clause- a clause in a contract that specifies what state or country's law will be applied in deciding a dispute.

Long-arm statute- a statute that extends a state's jurisdiction to non-residents who were not served a summons within the state.

Venue- requires lawsuits to be heard by the court that has jurisdiction nearest the location in which the incident occurred or the parties reside.
- - Change of venue
- - Forum shopping

Relevant Court Terms				
Standing	vs	Jurisdiction	vs	Venue
↓		↓		↓
Need a reason to sue		Court's Power to Hear Case		Place within Jurisdiction where case is heard

Jurisdiction of Federal and State Courts				
Exclusive Federal	vs	Concurrent	vs	Exclusive State
↓		↓		↓
Not subject to State jurisdiction		Shared		Not subject to Federal jurisdiction

Administrative Law- a combination of substantive and procedural law.
> Substantive law- law that has been created that the administrative agency enforces.
> Procedural law- establishes the procedures that must be followed by an administrative agency while enforcing substantive administrative law

Administrative agencies
> Federal examples – EEOC, FDA, NLRB
> State examples – corporation departments, State EPA
> Local examples – zoning boards, school boards

Powers of administrative agencies
1. Rule making
2. Judicial authority
3. Executive power
4. Licensing

Administrative Procedure Act (APA) – a federal law that establishes certain administrative procedures that a federal administrative agency must follow in conducting its affairs.

Administrative Law Judge (ALJ)
- A judge who presides over administrative proceedings and decides questions of law and fact concerning a case.

IV. Objective Questions

Terms:

1. The_____ is the highest court in the U.S.

2. A _____ is needed for the Supreme Court to hear a case.

3. The amount in question in a diversity case is _____.

4. _____ means having some stake in the outcome of a lawsuit.

5. A summons served within the territorial boundaries of a state is called _____.

6. A statute that extends a state's jurisdiction to nonresidents who were not served a summons within the state is called a _____.

7. Jurisdiction over property in a lawsuit is known as _____ jurisdiction.

8. _____ is the place within a jurisdiction where a case is heard.

9. _____ is the law that governments enact to regulate industries, businesses, and professionals.

10. Administrative law is a combination of _____ and _____ law.

True/False:

1. ____ Federal Tax Court is a court of general jurisdiction.

2. ____ In a diversity case, all plaintiffs must be citizens of the same states as the defendants.

3. ____ A corporation is only subject to personal jurisdiction in the state in which it is incorporated.

4. ____ State long-arm statutes require that a nonresident have at least minimum contact with the state.

5. ____ Courts will freely grant requests for change of venue if one of the parties makes such a request.

Multiple Choice:

1. In the U.S. Supreme Court, if all the justices voting agree as to the outcome and reasoning used to decide a case, it is a _____ decision.

A. tie
B. plurality
C. majority
D. unanimous

2. Which of the following similarities is observed between tie and plurality decisions reached by the U.S. Supreme Court?

A. the decisions can be appealed against in the U.S. courts of appeals
B. the decisions do not set precedent for later cases
C. the decision of the lower court is affirmed
D. new evidence and testimony is heard before reaching decisions

3. John and Jane have a car accident with Harry. Harry is a friend of John and Jane and decides not to sue. However Harry's girlfriend, Helga, wants to sue John and Jane. Helga cannot sue because she does not have:

A. Standing to sue.
B. Personal jurisdiction.
C. Venue.
D. Subject matter jurisdiction.

4. A plaintiff, by filing a lawsuit, automatically becomes subject to this. However, the defendant must be served a summons to become subject to:

A. Standing.
B. Personal jurisdiction.
C. Venue.
D. Subject matter jurisdiction.

5. Plaintiff Pam obtains a judgment in state Zeon against Defendant Debbie, who lives in state Yalut. Pam tries to collect the judgment by attaching Debbie's property in Yalut. This is known as:

A. *In rem* jurisdiction.
B. A long-arm statute.
C. *Quasi in rem* jurisdiction.
D. writ of certiorari

V. Answers to Objective Questions:

Terms:

1. Supreme Court. The selection process is very important as can be seen from the current political news. [p. 43]

2. writ of certiorari. These are only granted on a selective basis. [p. 45]

3. $75,000. The amount often changes. [p. 7]

4. Standing to sue. An interest in a lawsuit must be more than just secondary or tangential; standing to sue requires a legally recognized stake in the outcome. [p. 50]

5. service of process. Process servers have a high-risk job due to the emotionally charged nature of many court proceedings. [p. 50]

6. long-arm statute. Without such statutes, state boundaries could be used as moats to avoid legal proceedings. [p. 50]

7. *in Rem*. *In Personam* is jurisdiction over the person, *In Rem* is jurisdiction over the property. [p. 51]

8. Venue. This is not used for "forum shopping" but it can be changed. [p. 52]

9. Administrative law. Administrative law is a combination of substantive law and procedural law. [p. 55]

10. substantive; procedural. Substantive law is the underlying cause, procedural law deals with the process. [p. 55]

True/False:

1. False. This is a special federal court. [p. 42]

2. False. They cannot be citizens of the same states. [p. 47]

3. False. A corporation may be subject to personal jurisdiction in the state where it is incorporated, in the state where it has its principal office, and in the state where it is doing business. [p. 50]

4. True. Minimum contacts usually include doing business in the state. [p. 50]

5. False. Courts will usually grant requests for a change of venue if such a change is necessary to avoid prejudice resulting from publicity or some other influence. Courts will not grant a change of venue if the parties are merely forum shopping. [p. 52]

Multiple Choice:

1. D. If all the justices voting agree as to the outcome and reasoning used to decide a case, it is a unanimous decision. Unanimous decisions are precedent for later cases. [p. 45]

2. B. If a majority of the justices agree as to the outcome of a case but not as to the reasoning for reaching the outcome, it is a plurality decision. If there is a tie decision, the lower court decision is affirmed. Such votes are not precedent for later cases. [p. 46]

3. A. Helga cannot sue. To have standing, a party must have a stake in the outcome of a suit. Since Helga was not involved in the accident, she does not have a stake in the suit and cannot sue on behalf of Harry. [p. 50]

4. B. A defendant must be served a summons to be personally subject to the jurisdiction of a court. [p. 50]

5. C. *Quasi in rem* jurisdiction is a means by which a prevailing party in a lawsuit may try to satisfy a judgment. [p. 51]

VI. Answers to Essay Question:

If out-of-court methods do not provide an adequate resolution of the problem, Mr. At-Emptor must initiate a lawsuit in a court having a proper basis for jurisdiction. Here a state court will most likely have jurisdiction over both the subject matter and the parties. Assuming proper service of process is made on the defendants, the lawsuit will have begun. This will often depend on the long-are statute and the amount of contacts L & O has with Colorado.

Once the actual pretrial process has begun, both parties will have their day in court. The defendants may choose to counterclaim based on the contract amounts still due or make pretrial motions to dismiss.

The actual trial will allow both parties to present their sides of the case to the jury in accordance with proper procedures as supervised by the judge. In civil cases, a judge retains the ultimate power to enter the final judgment jury verdict notwithstanding if he or she feels that the jury decision was somehow based on biased, emotional, or inflamed factors.

Because this is a civil case, either party can appeal the judgment rendered by the trial court.

Chapter 4

ALTERNATIVE, JUDICIAL, AND E-DISPUTE RESOLUTION

How does a lawsuit happen?

I. Overview

The judicial process is quite structured. This chapter will focus on the how and when of filing a lawsuit. The process begins with the filing of pleadings, then discovery, and ultimately a trial. What happens if I lose? The appellate process is also discussed. There are many machinations and obstacles to be dealt with along the procedural journey.

Maybe a lawsuit really isn't the answer at all. Alternative dispute resolution may provide viable options to the litigation process. ADR is being revolutionized with the advent of technology as a tool for resolving disputes.

This chapter focuses on the litigation procedural process, alternatives to litigation, and emerging technology that is changing the process.

II. Hypothetical Multi-issue Essay Question

Mork sues Mindy for injuries that he sustained in an automobile accident? He is claiming that Mindy was negligent. Mindy thinks that Mork is responsible for the accident. What pleadings will need to be filed by both parties?

III. Outline

Pretrial Litigation Process
Litigation- the process of bringing, maintaining, and defending a lawsuit

Pleadings
- The paperwork that is filed with the court to initiate and respond to a lawsuit

Complaint and Summons
Plaintiff- the party who files the complaint
Complaint- the document a plaintiff files with the court and serves on the defendant to initiate a lawsuit
Summons- a court order directing the defendant to appear in court and answer the complaint

Answer
The defendant's written response to a plaintiff's complaint that is filed with the court and served on the plaintiff
> Default judgment- can be obtained if a defendant does not answer a complaint
> Cross-Complaint and Reply
>> A document filed by a defendant against the plaintiff to seek damages or some other remedy
>>> Reply- a document filed by an original plaintiff to answer the defendant's cross-complaint
>>>
>>> Intervention- the act of others to join as parties to an existing lawsuit
>>> Consolidation- the act of a court to combine two or more separate lawsuits into one
>>> e-filing- the electronic filing of pleadings, briefs, and other documents related to a contract

Statute of Limitations
A statute that establishes the period during which a plaintiff must bring a lawsuit against a defendant

Discovery
> A legal process during which each party engages in various activities to discover facts of the case from the other party and witnesses prior to trial
>> Deposition- oral testimony given by a party or witness before trial, and under oath
>> Deponent- a party who gives his deposition
>> Interrogatories- written questions submitted by one party to another party
>> Production of documents- a request by one party to another to produce all documents relevant to the case prior to trial
>> Physical or mental examination- a court ordered examination of a party to a lawsuit before trial to determine the extent of the alleged injuries

Dismissal and Pretrial Judgments
> Pretrial motion- a motion a party can make to try to dispose of all or part of a lawsuit prior to trial

Motion for Judgment on the Pleadings
> A motion which alleges that is all the facts presented in the pleadings are taken as true, the party making the motion would win the lawsuit when the proper law is applied to the asserted facts

Motion for Summary Judgment
> A motion which asserts that there are no factual disputes to be decided by the jury and that the judge can apply the proper law to the undisputed facts and decide the case without a jury

Settlement Conference
> A hearing that occurs before a trial in order to facilitate the settlement of a case
> Also called a pretrial hearing

Trial

Trier of fact – the jury in a jury trial; a judge in a non-jury trial

Jury selection

Voir Dire- a process whereby prospective jurors are asked questions by a judge and attorneys to determine whether they are biased in their decisions

The Trial

1. Opening statements
2. Plaintiff's case
   a. Plaintiff has burden of proof
      i. Direct exam
      ii. Cross exam
      iii. Re-direct exam
3. Defendant's case
4. Rebuttal and rejoinder
5. Closing arguments

Verdict and Entry of Judgment

Jury instructions- instructions given by a judge to a jury that informs the jurors of the law to be applied in the case

Jury Deliberations and Verdict

Deliberations- may take minutes or weeks

Verdict- the jury's decision

Entry of judgment

Jury verdict

Judgment not with-standing the verdict

Remittitur

Appeal

The act of asking an appellant court to overturn a decision after the trial courts final judgment has been entered

Appellant- the appealing party

Appellee- the party responding to an appeal

An error of law will result in the reversal of a lower court decision

An appellate court will not reverse a finding of fact

Alternative Dispute Resolution (ADR)

Methods of resolving disputes other than litigation

1. Negotiation

   A procedure whereby the party to a dispute engages in discussions and bargaining to try to reach a voluntary settlement of their dispute

2. Arbitration

   A form of ADR in which the parties choose and impartial third-party to hear and decide the dispute

   Arbitration clause- a clause in a contract that requires disputes arising out of the contract to be submitted to arbitration

   Federal Arbitration Act- a federal statute that provides for the enforcement of most arbitration agreements

Arbitrator's decision
Binding
Non-binding

3. Mediation
A form of ADR in which the parties choose a neutral third-party to act as the mediator of a dispute

Other forms of ADR
Conciliation
Mini-trial
Fact-finding
Judicial reference

E-Dispute Resolution
Use of online ADR services to resolve disputes
e-arbitration- arbitration of a dispute using online arbitration services
e- mediation- mediation of a dispute using online mediation services

IV. Objective Questions

Terms:

1. _____ is the process of bringing, maintaining and defending a lawsuit.

2. _____ is the paperwork filed with the court to initiate and respond to a lawsuit.

3. A _____ is the document a plaintiff files with the court and serves on the defendant to initiate a lawsuit.

4. The act of others joining an existing lawsuit is called _____.

5. The act of a court combining two or more separate lawsuits into one is called _____.

6. An established period of time during which a plaintiff must bring a lawsuit against a defendant is called the _____.

7. Oral testimony given by a party or witness before trial is called a _____.

8. _____ are written questions submitted by one party to another.

9. A _____ occurs before a trial in order to facilitate the resolution of the case.

10. _____ is a process whereby prospective jurors are asked questions by a judge and attorneys to determine whether they would be biased in their decisions.

True/False:

1. ____ If the defendant does not answer the complaint, a default judgment is entered against him or her.

2. ____ A plaintiff can appeal for the extension of the statute of limitations and sue the defendant.

3. ____ The choice of whether to bring or defend a lawsuit should be analyzed like any other business decision

4. ____ Jurors are not paid.

5. ____ The United States Constitution provides that a party to an action at law is guaranteed the right to a jury trial.

6. ____ A defendant bears the burden of proof in a civil action.

7. ____ The appellee is the appealing party in an appeal.

8. ____ An appellate court will reverse a lower court decision if it finds an error of law in the record.

9. ____ A judge may reduce the amount awarded by a jury if she finds the jury was biased, emotional, or inflamed.

10. ____ Mediation is a form of ADR in which the parties choose an impartial third-party to hear and decide the dispute.

Multiple Choice:

1. If a defendant fails to answer a complaint, the court may enter a(n)

A. answer.
B. reply.
C. default judgment.
D. summons.

2. ____ is the act of a court combining two or more separate lawsuits into one lawsuit.

A. Intervention
B. Consolidation
C. Appeal
D. Remittitur

3. ____ are written questions submitted by one party to another party during discovery.

A. Interrogatories
B. Depostions
C. Deponents
D. *Voir Dire*

4. Which of the following statements is true of deposition?

A. A deposition has to be a written statement.
B. A witness' deposition is voluntary and not pursuant to a court order.
C. Deposition is given post trial.
D. A deponent is given a chance to correct his or her deposition.

5. _____ is the process whereby the judge and attorneys ask prospective jurors questions to determine whether they would be biased in their decisions.

A. Consolidation
B. Trial of fact
C. *Voir dire*
D. Intervention

6. What step comes after the presentation of the plaintiff's case in the trial process?

A. Closing arguments
B. Rebuttal
C. Defendant's case
D. Summons

7. ____ is a voluntary private proceeding in which lawyers for each side present a shortened version of their case to the representatives of both sides.

A. Arbitration
B. Mediation
C. Conciliation
D. Mini-trial

8. In which of the following methods of alternative dispute resolution must parties to a case employ a neutral third party to settle their dispute?

A. negotiation
B. fact-finding
C. e-court
D. mini-trial

V. Answers to Objective Questions:

Terms:

1. Litigation. This is also known as "the litigation process." [p. 62]

2. Pleading. Major ones are the complaint, answer, cross-complaint and reply. [p. 62]

3. Complaint. It must name the parties to the lawsuit, allege the facts, and contain a prayer for relief. [p. 63]

4. Intervention. If other persons have an interest in a lawsuit, they may intervene and become parties to the lawsuit. This is called intervention. [p. 64]

5. Consolidation. If several plaintiffs have filed separate lawsuits stemming from the same fact situation against the same defendant, the court can consolidate the cases into one case if doing so would not cause undue prejudice to the parties. This is called consolidation. [p. 64]

6. Statute of limitations. The time-periods vary based upon jurisdiction and the nature of the claim. [p. 66]

7. Deposition. A deposition is given under oath and transcribed. [p. 66]

8. Interrogatories. These must be answered under oath in a prescribed time-period. [p. 67]

9. Settlement conference/ pretrial conference. More than 95% of all cases are settled before they go to trial. [p. 68]

10. *Voir dire.* Biased jurors can be prevented from sitting on a particular case. [p. 69]

True/False:

1. True. A default judgment establishes the defendant's liability. The plaintiff then has only to prove damages. [p. 63]

2. True. If a lawsuit is not filed within the statute of limitations, the plaintiff loses his or her right to sue. [p. 66]

3. True. The choice of whether to bring or defend a lawsuit should be analyzed like any other business decision. This includes performing a cost–benefit analysis of the lawsuit. [p. 68]

4. False. Jurors are paid a minimal fee for service. [p. 69]

5. True. This is pursuant to the Seventh Amendment. [p. 69]

6. False. The plaintiff bears the burden of proof. [p. 70]

7. False. The appellee is the responding party. [p. 71]

8. True. An appellate court will not reverse a finding of fact made by a jury, or if there is no jury then made by a judge, unless such finding is unsupported by the evidence or is contradicted by the evidence. [p. 71]

9. True. This is called remittitur. [p. 71]

10. False. In arbitration, a third-party decides the dispute. [p. 73]

Multiple Choice:

1. C. This establishes liability; the plaintiff must still prove damages. [p. 63]

2. B. This is for the sake of judicial economy, but it must not prejudice a party's rights. [p. 64]

3. A. These questions must be answered under oath in a specific time-frame. [p. 67]

4. D. The deponent is given an opportunity to correct his or her answers prior to signing the deposition. [p. 67]

5. C. Lawyers for each party and the judge can ask prospective jurors questions to determine whether they would be biased in their decisions. [p. 69]

6. C. The defendant's case proceeds after the plaintiff has concluded his or her case. [p. 70]

7. D. The parties get to see the strength and weaknesses of their own case. [p. 75]

8. B. The fact-finder is authorized to investigate the dispute, gather evidence, prepare demonstrative evidence, and prepare reports of his or her findings. [p. 76]

VI. Answers to Essay Question:

Since Mork has already filed the complaint, Mindy will need to file an answer in a timely manner. Her failure to do so could result in a default judgment being entered against her.

Because she believes that Mork is responsible for the accident, she should also file a cross-claim against him. The cross-complaint, in effect, reverses the lawsuit, now making Mork a defendant. Consequently, Mork will need to file a reply to the cross-complaint.

After these pleadings have been filed, the parties will begin the discovery process to ascertain who has the better case.

Chapter 5

CONSTITUTIONAL LAW FOR BUSINESS AND E-COMMERCE

Why can you not run into a crowded theater and yell "fire" when there is no fire?

I. Overview

The scales of justice have long been one of the key symbols of our judicial system. They represent the system's effort to show evenhandedness and give fair weight to the evidence presented by competing parties. This symbol can also be used to illustrate the key learning objective of this chapter. Our founding fathers struggled long and hard to create a balance of power among the three branches of government in much the same way as the justice system attempts to weigh the evidence. This process of balancing among the competing sovereignties of federal, state, and local governments is a process of constant evolution and, like the scale, will constantly shift with the addition and deletion of new political, social, and demographic weights.

What makes this constitutional balancing both fascinating and yet sometimes traumatic is that business people and their entities, represented by all sorts of firms from the smallest sole proprietorship to the largest multinational corporation, are caught in the middle of these sovereign "turf wars." In today's legal environment, there is little doubt about the power of the government to create, regulate, control, and even ban business activities. The real question appears to be which flag to salute--the federal government, the state, the local government, or some combination of all of the above? Where the rules of the game seem to shift almost daily between competing referees, it becomes most difficult for businesses to play the game.

The basic ground rules for business are set out in the U.S. constitutional provisions directly addressed to business, such as the Commerce Clause, and in larger protections accorded to all persons in the Bill of Rights and other key amendments. Many business entities are classified as *juristic* persons (law created entities which are given a limited and controlled legal existence) such as corporations or trusts. Subsequent chapters will go into more detail on how and when these forms of doing business may be used. In the context of constitutional allocation of control over business activity, the most important provision is the Supremacy Clause. Under this clause, the national sovereign can preempt control over any particular form of business it chooses to. This clause, combined with very broad judicial interpretation of the Commerce Clause, has been a part of the process which attempts to create an even playing field for business, i.e., the federal sovereign has long believed that a states power to control commerce under its constitutional police power should be harnessed if it encumbers the national flow of commerce or if it somehow unduly favors local business at the cost of competing political entities such as other cities, states, or even regional interests. The balancing of the scale continues.

What makes this process of setting out the business playing rules even more difficult is that many of our basic rights, set out in the Bill of Rights such as freedom of speech, press, religion, and assembly, have been held by our courts to apply in varying degrees to business enterprises. How, when, where, and to what extent these rights should apply to business continues to be both a source for constant academic debate and a regulatory dilemma for both government and business alike. Law works best where all the players involved have a "bright line" or clear signal to use as a guidepost for their actions. When that line is blurred, all are disserved.

II. Multi-issue Essay Question

Brew Ha Ha Brewery is located in New Salem, California, and is engaged in the business of producing specialized low alcohol products for specifically identified niche markets. It produces diet beers for the overweight crowd, young malts for the young at heart, and aged malts for the over-the-hill yuppie couch potatoes.

Brew Ha Ha's newest product seeks to cash in on the latest craze, a revival of witchcraft! Their new product is named "The Devil Made Me Do It!" The "Devil" beer has the same low alcohol content as all its other products but is designed to look like a steamy caldron of some witch's brew that will conjure up images of the rich and diverse history of occult practices throughout the world.

The Texas State Liquor Control Board took umbrage at this product's motives and felt that it would foster and encourage the practice of witchery in its fair state. It thus decided to ban the sale of "The Devil Made Me Do It!" within the state on the grounds that this product would undermine the morals of its citizens through the practice of witchcraft. The Board claims its actions are allowable under both the U.S. and local constitutions. Brew Ha Ha, in turn, claims its constitutional rights are being violated. What result?

III. Outline

Federalism- federal government shares power with the 50 states.

Separation of Powers
  Article I
    Establishes the legislative branch of government—create federal courts
    This branch is bicameral, consisting of the Senate and House of Representatives, often referred to as Congress.
  Article II
    Establishes the executive branch of government—needs legislative approval for treaties
  Article III
    Establishes the judicial branch of government—reviews acts of other branches for constitutionality
Checks and Balances

Supremacy Clause
  The Supremacy Clause establishes that the federal Constitution, treaties, federal laws, and federal regulations are the supreme law of the land. No state law can conflict with them. See Rowe, Attorney General of Maine, v. New Hampshire Motor Transport Association.

  Preemption Doctrine – federal law takes precedence over state and/or local law.

Commerce Clause
  Grants Congress the power "to regulate commerce with foreign nations, and among the several states, and with Indian tribes"
  Gives the federal government authority to regulate interstate commerce within a state if those activities affect interstate commerce.

State "Police Power"
>   States can enact laws to protect or promote public health, safety, morals, and general welfare
>   State and local laws cannot unduly burden interstate commerce or discriminate against interstate commerce.

>   Dormant Commerce Clause – This is utilized when the federal government chooses not to regulate an area that it is authorized to regulate under Commerce Clause power. A state, under its police power, can enact legislation to regulate that area of commerce.

Bill of Rights
>   Government cannot take away rights without reason. The more fundamental the right, the stronger the reason must be.
>   - Originally the first Ten Amendments to the Constitution
>   - Seventeen other Amendments have been added

Incorporation Doctrine
>   A doctrine that states that most fundamental guarantees contained in the Bill of Rights are applicable to state and local government action.

Freedom of Speech—written, spoken, and symbolic
>   Fully protected speech
>   Speech the government cannot prohibit or regulate due to lack of compelling reasons
>   Limited protected speech
>   Commercial speech—subject to proper time, place, and manner restrictions
>   Offensive speech—subject to proper time, place, and manner restrictions
>   Unprotected speech—no compelling reasons exist to prohibit
>   Dangerous speech
>   Fighting words
>   Speech that incites the violent or revolutionary overthrow of the government
>   Defamatory language
>   Child pornography
>   Obscene speech
>   - Appeals to prurient interest
>   - Depicts sexual conduct in a patently offensive way
>   - Lacks serious literary, artistic, political or scientific value

Freedom of Religion
>   Establishment Clause
>   Prohibits government from establishing a government sponsored religion or promoting one religion over others.
>   Free Exercise Clause
>   Prohibits government from enacting laws that prohibit or inhibit people from participating in or practicing their chosen religion without a compelling reason

Equal Protection Clause
>   Derived from the 14th Amendment
>   Strict scrutiny test or compelling interest test (needs compelling reason)
>   Applied to classifications based on race
>   Intermediate scrutiny test (needs reasonable relation to legitimate government purpose)
>   Applied to classifications based on protected classes other than race (e.g. sex or age) (80)

Rational basis test (needs justifiable reason)
>   Applied to classifications not involving a suspect or protected class

Due Process Clause
>   Contained in the Fifth and Fourteenth Amendments

Substantive due process
>   Requires governmental laws to be clear and not overly broad; the test is whether a reasonable person can understand the law

Procedural due process
>   Requires government to give people proper notice and hearing before depriving them of life, liberty, or property

Privileges and Immunities Clause
>   The clause prohibits states from enacting laws that unduly discriminate in favor of their residents. The clause applies only to citizens, not corporations.

Strict Scrutiny/Compelling Interest Test	Intermediate Test	Rational Basis Test
↓	↓	↓
used for fundamental rights		used for non-fundamental rights
Or	↓	or
Suspect Classes	Special Classes	Non-Suspect Classes
↓	↓	↓
compelling reason needed/narrowest application	fair and substantial relation to important governmental objective	reasonable basis needed
↓	↓	↓
e.g. religion, speech/race, religion discrimination	gender discrimination	education/poverty discrimination

IV. Objective Questions:

Terms:

1. Under the U.S. Constitution, the states delegated certain powers to the federal government. These powers are known as _____ powers.

2. Under the U.S. Constitution, the three branches of government are given different powers. This is known as the doctrine of _____.

3. When a state law conflicts with a federal law, the federal law takes precedent. This concept is known as the _____.

4. The constitutional provision that addresses the issues of a national market and free trade among the states is known as the _____.

5. The power the states retain to regulate private and business activity within their borders is the states' _____.

6. Political Speech is an example of _____.

7. Dangerous speech, defamatory language, and obscene speech are examples of _____.

8. Examples of speech that are not prohibited under the First Amendment, but may be restricted are _____ speech and _____ speech.

9. The First Amendment contains two religion clauses. The _____ prevents a state from establishing or promoting a state religion. The _____ prohibits the government from prohibiting or inhibiting people from participating in their religion.

10. The Fourteenth Amendment's Due Process Clause has two categories of due process; _____ due process and _____ due process.

True/False:

1. ____ The Bill of Rights was part of the U.S. Constitution as originally adopted in 1787.

3. ____ If a state's law is in its best interest, it can preempt any relevant federal law.

2. ____ The federal government has the exclusive right to regulate foreign commerce.

4. ____ All provisions of the Bill of Rights are applicable only to the federal government.

5. ____ The Freedom of Speech Clause extends to protect both speech and conduct.

6. ____ Offensive speech, like obscene speech, can be forbidden under the First Amendment.

7. ____ Commercial speech can never be restricted under the First Amendment.

8. ____ The Establishment Clause guarantees that there will be no state-sponsored religion.

9. ____ The U.S. Supreme Court uses different standards when reviewing equal protection cases, depending on the classification affected.

10. ____ The requirements of the Due Process Clause apply to both state and federal government, but never to private individuals.

11. ____ Substantive due process requires that the government give a person notice and hearing of a legal action before that person can be deprived of life, liberty or property.

Multiple Choice:

1. Which of the following is established by the Supremacy Clause of the U.S. Constitution?

A. The President is the supreme and sovereign head of the United States.
B. The legislative branch of the federal government is the supreme law-making authority in the country.
C. The judiciary is the supreme law-enforcing authority and cannot be influenced by anyone, however powerful, in any manner.
D. The U.S. Constitution and federal treaties, laws, and regulations are the supreme law of the land.

2. The federal government is given the power to set international trade policies in the U.S. Constitution under which doctrine or clause?

A. Doctrine of Separation of Powers.
B. Commerce Clause.
C. Preemption Doctrine.
D. Supremacy Clause.

3. Which of the following statements is true of states' police power?

A. Police power restricts states from regulating inter-state commerce, although it happens within their borders.
B. The states are allowed to regulate army activities within their borders.
C. They are given the authority to enact laws that regulate the conduct of business.
D. The police force of a state is controlled by the federal police department.

4. Which of the following statements is true about the freedom of speech guaranteed by the Bill of Rights?

A. The Freedom of Speech Clause was added to the Constitution in the third amendment.
B. The Freedom of Speech Clause protects speech only, not conduct.
C. There is no provision for fully protected speech in the Constitution.
D. Burning the American flag in protest to a federal government military action is in violation of the Freedom of Speech Clause.

5. If the government believes certain offensive language is inappropriate to air on a television program, the government:

A. Can do nothing; even though it is offensive, it is completely protected by the First Amendment.
B. Can completely ban the speech since offensive language is like obscene language and can be entirely forbidden.
C. Can regulate the language, restricting it to certain times the language can be aired.
D. Can use its discretion to do any of the above.

6. Which of the following is a form of limited protected speech?

A. defamatory language
B. speech that incites the violent or revolutionary overthrow of the government
C. dangerous speech
D. offensive speech

7. A city ordinance prohibits ritual sacrifice of chickens during church services. Most likely, will the ordinance be found to be Constitutional?

A. Yes, the state may regulate such activity by virtue of its police powers.
B. Yes, the state may regulate such activity via the Dormant Commerce Clause.
C. No, the restriction would probably violate the Free Exercise Clause.
D. No, the restriction would probably violate the Establishment Clause.

8. A(n) _____ test is applied to classifications of people based on a suspect class.

A. strict scrutiny
B. intermediate scrutiny
C. rational basis
D. cogent basis

9. Patron Paul is thrown in jail by the police for thirty days without a hearing for allegedly punching Customer Carl at the Big Bear Bar. Have the police violated any constitutional provisions?

A. No, because Carl told the police what happened, so the procedural due process requirement has been met.
B. No, because a reasonable person could understand it is illegal to injure someone else, so the substantive due process requirement has been met.
C. Yes, because procedural due process requires a notice and a hearing.
D. Yes, because a law against punching someone in a bar violates substantive due process.

10. The _____ Clauses in the Constitution collectively prohibit states from enacting laws that unduly discriminate in favor of their residents.

A. Due Process
B. Equal Protection
C. Establishment
D. Privileges and Immunity

Constitution Exercise:

Name the clause from the constitution that is relevant for handling the cases listed below:

1. Arizona statute suspends driver's license for someone who can't pay judgments while Federal Bankruptcy Law exists _____

2. Federal Telecommunication Act of 1996 prohibits state and local governments from blocking entry into telecommunications industry _____

3. Wheat grown by a farmer for home consumption can be regulated by the Federal Government _____

4. Federal Driver's Privacy Protection Act prohibits states from selling personal information without consent _____

5. Maryland statute stated that producers or refiners of petroleum products were not permitted to operate retail service stations in Maryland _____

6. The Telecommunications Act of 1996 requires cable operators not to transmit sexually explicit materials from 6AM to 10PM if signal bleed can occur _____

7. Federal Communications Commission regulations prohibit the broadcast of gambling and lottery information over radio and television _____

8. State high school policy permitting students of the high school to elect a student to give invocations over the public loud speaker at football games _____

9. Alaskan statute requires that owners of Alaskan oil leases must hire Alaskans _____

V. Answers to Objective Questions:

Terms:

1. enumerated. These powers are expressly named or granted to the federal government by the Constitution. [p. 86]

2. separation of powers. Under this doctrine, one branch is not permitted to encroach upon the domains of the other two branches. [p. 86]

3. preemption doctrine. If certain matters are considered of national importance and the federal government has addressed the issue, states may not pass laws that are inconsistent with federal law. Federal law takes precedence over state law. [p. 88]

4. Commerce Clause. This provision is found in Article I, Section 8, Clause 3 of the U.S. Constitution and is the cornerstone of an enormous amount of exclusive legislative and regulatory power over interstate commerce by the federal government. [p. 89]

5. police power. Based on the Tenth Amendment to the U.S. Constitution, the authority to secure the general health, safety, welfare and morals within their boundaries is conferred upon the states. [p. 91]

6. fully protected speech. The government cannot regulate or prohibit the content of fully protected speech. [p. 94]

7. unprotected speech. These are all forms of expression that have been found in varying degrees to be unprotected by the freedom of speech rights guaranteed by the First Amendment to the U.S. Constitution. [p. 96]

8. offensive, commercial. Both of these forms of speech enjoy limited protection under the 1st Amendment. As such, they may not be totally barred, but are subject to restrictions on a case-by-case basis. [p. 96]

9. Establishment Clause, Free Exercise Clause. While not seeking to establish an "official" state religion, our system seeks to strongly protect the individual's right to practice his or her own religious beliefs. [p. 100]

10. substantive, procedural. Substantive goes to content, and procedural goes to application. In both cases, constitutional guarantees are sought to be meaningful in both context and application. They are based on the Fifth and Fourteenth Amendments. [p. 102]

True/False:

1. False. The Bill of Rights was not part of the original Constitution and was not adopted until 1791. [p. 85]

3. False. Under the Supremacy Clause of the U.S. Constitution, federal laws, treaties, and regulations are the supreme laws and may preempt any conflicting state laws. [p. 87]

2. True. The Commerce Clause of the U.S. Constitution grants the federal government the exclusive right to regulate commerce with foreign countries. [p. 90]

4. False. Through the incorporation doctrine, the Supreme Court has held that most provisions of the Bill of Rights apply to the states as well as to the federal government. [p. 93]

5. False. The Freedom of Speech Clause protects oral, written, and symbolic speech, but not conduct. [p. 93]

6. False. Offensive speech can be restricted by the government, but cannot be completely forbidden. [p. 96]

7. False. Commercial speech, like offensive speech, can be subject to certain time, place, and manner restrictions. [p. 96]

8. True. The Establishment Clause prohibits the government from either establishing a government sponsored religion or promoting one religion over another. Thus, it guarantees that there will be no state-sponsored religion. [p. 100]

10. True. Depending on the classification that a given law may impact, the Court may apply a strict scrutiny, intermediate scrutiny, or rational basis test. [p. 100]

9. True. The Due Process Clause imposes no duty on private individuals. [p. 102]

11. False. These are the requirements of procedural due process. [p. 102]

Multiple Choice:

1. D. The Supremacy Clause establishes that the U.S. Constitution and federal treaties, laws, and regulations are the supreme law of the land. [p. 87]

2. B. The Commerce Clause gives the federal government the exclusive power to establish and regulate international trade. [p. 89]

3. C. Police power is the power that permits states and local governments to enact laws to protect or promote the public health, safety, morals, and general welfare. [p. 91]

4. B. The First Amendment's Freedom of Speech Clause protects speech only, not conduct. [p. 93]

5. C. Offensive speech has limited protection under the 1st Amendment. The government cannot forbid such speech, but can restrict it in certain ways. [p. 96]

6. D. The Supreme Court has held that the content of offensive speech may not be forbidden but that it may be restricted by the government under time, place, and manner restrictions. [p. 96]

7. C. The Free Exercise Clause prohibits the government from interfering with the free exercise of religion in the United States. [p. 100]

8. A. Any government activity or regulation that classifies persons based on a suspect class (e.g., race, national origin, citizenship) or involves fundamental rights (e.g., voting) is reviewed for lawfulness using a strict scrutiny test. [p. 101]

9. C. Regardless of the facts of this punching incident, Paul is entitled to notice and a hearing before he is jailed. [p. 102]

10. D. Both Article IV of the Constitution and the Fourteenth Amendment contain Privileges and Immunities Clauses that prohibit states from enacting laws that unduly discriminate in favor of their residents. [p. 102]

Constitution Exercise:

1. Supremacy Clause. Frustrated federal law without the intent to do so. [p. 87]

2. Supremacy Clause. Conflicting laws preempted. [p. 87]

3. Commerce Clause. Wickard v. Filburn, Affects wheat available in interstate commerce. [p. 89]

4. Commerce Clause. Reno v. Condon, Information is an item in interstate commerce. [p. 89]

5. Commerce Clause. Exxon v. Governor of Maryland, Constitutional since no undue burden on commerce or no discrimination. [p. 89]

6. Freedom of Speech. U.S. v. Playboy, Unconstitutional as an overly broad restriction on content-based speech. [p. 93]

7. Freedom of Speech. Greater New Orleans Broadcasting Association, Inc. v. U.S., Rules violate commercial free speech rules since ads are not misleading or about unlawful activities. [p. 93]

8. Establishment Clause. Santa Fe Independent School District v. Jane and John Doe, State affirmatively sponsoring a particular religious practice violates Establishment Clause. [p. 100]

9. Privileges and Immunities Clause. Unconstitutionally bars essential activities without substantial reason. [p. 102]

VI. Answers to Essay Question:

The issue of the regulation and control of the sale of alcoholic products has had a long and controversial history in the U.S. In 1919, Congress passed the Eighteenth Amendment to the U.S. Constitution that banned the manufacture, sale, or transportation of intoxicating liquors in the U.S. After years of futile efforts to enforce this ban, the Eighteenth Amendment was repealed in 1933 by the Twenty-First Amendment to the U.S. Constitution.

As part of the repeal of the Eighteenth Amendment, Section 2 of the Twenty-First Amendment allowed state and local jurisdictions the option to regulate the transportation, importation, or possession of intoxicating liquors within their jurisdictions. Because the Twenty-First Amendment specifically gave states local options over the control and regulation of the sale of intoxicating liquors, it appears that the Texas Liquor Board does have the presumptive power to act on this issue. In addition, traditional police powers to protect the health, safety, and morals of its citizens are also entrusted to state and local authorities.

States have very broad powers regarding the control of intoxicating products, as was seen in the *Capital Cities Cable Case*, but this power is not absolute. There is an expectation by the federal government that any exercise of the local option power of liquor control will be suspect and preempted by the national goals of free commerce required by the Commerce Clause. Thus, even though the state may be the first to act in these types of cases, it may not always have the last word in these matters.

In addition to concerns over power-sharing between national and state governments in cases involving the sale of intoxicating commercial products, we have a possible "larger" issue--that of free speech. Any attempt to limit free speech, albeit by a commercial entity rather than a private person, is always subject to great scrutiny by the courts.

This question was based on a real incident that occurred in Texas in 1991. The Dixie Brewing Co. of New Orleans sought to market a beer in Texas called "Blackened Voodoo Lager." The Texas liquor authorities sought to ban the product because it believed the lager would promote occult practices. It later rescinded the proposed ban for fear of legal challenges.

Those challenges would most likely have been made on the grounds of commercial free speech and interference with the free flow of goods in interstate commerce. At a minimum, the state of Texas would have the burden of proof in showing that the sale of this product would damage the health, safety, morals, and welfare of its citizens as required under the use of its state police powers.

Chapter 6

TORTS AND STRICT LIABILITY

Who can I sue for hurting me?

I. Overview

The word tort is not readily familiar to students who have not yet studied law. Like so many words of art found in the law, it has a special meaning derived from an essentially simple principle. The word is literally derived from the French word for wrong. That French term, in turn, is derived from the Latin phrase *torguere* meaning to twist, or *tortus* meaning to be twisted or wrested aside. When we consider that the odds are high that sooner or later we may be twisted by an auto accident, job-related injury, or some similar event, the term starts to make sense. Injuries of all sorts are an unfortunate fact of life. What makes those injuries actionable, i.e., where a court will recognize legal grounds for bringing a lawsuit, is when someone may have committed a noncontractual wrong for which a court, after appropriate proceedings, may grant a remedy. In other words, sometimes when we get twisted, the law provides an opportunity to correct the situation if the twist is found to be wrongful.

Tort law structure is divided into three main classifications:
1. Intentional torts.
2. Unintentional torts (negligence).
3. Strict liability.

Of these three, the first categories, intentional torts, are the most readily identifiable because they are very often concurrently classified as crimes. A crime is generally defined as an act in violation of a local or national penal statute. The remedy for crimes is sought by governmental authorities on behalf of the victim for all of us because the act is classified as an act against the common welfare of society. The civil remedy for the same act is an action for intentional tort. This lawsuit is brought by the victim directly against the perpetrator of the intentional tort. Damages are paid directly to the victim after proper proceedings are held. The major classifications of intentional torts are acts against the person, and acts against property. Acts against persons include assault, battery, false imprisonment, defamation of character, invasion of privacy, slander, libel, and abuse of the legal process. One recent example of the abuse of legal process was found in Colorado where a group of tax protesters filed liens on the personal assets of government employees as a way to object to government tax collection procedures. An example of an act against property would be intentional trespass upon someone else's land.

The second category, unintentional or negligence torts, is both far more prevalent and more difficult to clearly identify. The first thing to remember is that responsibility can be imposed regardless of intent. This is a consequence-oriented result in the law as compared to the intent-oriented result discussed in the law of intentional torts.

The second major point is that the term negligence is in fact a legal conclusion arrived at only when a special set of sequential circumstances have taken place. These circumstances are generally called elements. Just as the makeup of all physical substances can be broken down into key components, so may many legal doctrines. The doctrine of negligent tort is made up of five key elements. These elements are:
1. A showing of a duty of care owed by the defendant to the plaintiff.
2. A showing of a breach of that duty.

3. A showing of injury to the plaintiff.
4. A showing of causal nexus or connection between the breach of duty and the injury (actual cause).
5. A tying of that actual cause to the legal responsibility for the consequences of the act or omission. This connection between actual and legal cause is referred to as proximate cause.

If all five circumstances are found, and there are no recognized defenses, excuses, or statutory immunities, a legal conclusion of negligence can be reached. An immunity is an exception from liability recognized in the law, usually based on an overriding public policy. Thus the key to the study of negligent torts is the proper identification and use of the elements of negligence. Think of the use of elements as essential building blocks in the construction of a foundation on which a conclusion of negligence can be built. If any of the blocks are missing, the building will not stand.

The third major area of tort law is found in what has generally come to be classified as strict liability torts, i.e., liability without fault. This is not to say that it is automatic liability, but rather that a different set of elements have evolved in certain cases involving special kinds of activities which are considered ultra-hazardous and with regard to the use of certain products. At this juncture, it is important to remember that this doctrine may represent one of the options available to an injured tort victim.

Under all three classifications of tort, the burden of proof remains with the plaintiff to show that he or she has been wronged and that he or she is entitled to some sort of court-ordered remedy from the defendant.

II. Hypothetical Multi-issue Essay Question:

Charles Haney has just been traded from the Clarkcity Trees to the women's team in Clarkcity. Despite the protesting of the women on the team, the league has said that Haney will be permitted to play.

During the first regular season game, Haney found himself not starting but coming off the bench as seventh player. As he drove down the lane for his first lay-up, a 7'0" center from the Western State team steps underneath Haney causing him to fall on his back. While lying on the ground, the 5'0" point guard from Western State remembers Haney's love for women athletes and kicks him in the head. Haney says "thank you" and runs over to the bench where he now thinks he is the trainer.

The team lets Charles act as trainer (Charles had become a certified trainer to handle all of the injuries incurred in his many bar fights), since their doctors were caught in a rare September blizzard in Dallas. Meryl Troops, the shooting guard for the team had come off the floor during the second period due to pain in her neck. Haney looked at her from the end of the bench and told her to take two pain killers and go back into the game. Meryl did just that but was paralyzed when she was hit on the back later during the game. It turned out Meryl's neck had a fracture and she should not have been permitted to go back into the game.

During the game, while President Minton and her husband Dave were seated in the stands, Haney missed a pass from the newly-acquired point guard, Denise Roland. Dave, while not looking, was hit in the head and had to be taken to a hospital. On the way to the ambulance, while Mrs. Minton was stopping for a hot dog, the ceiling over the hot dog counter fell and hit her in the head. She ran around, half crazy, and ended up back on the court where Haney slapped her and told her to stop yelling. She fell and hit her head and ended up with a concussion.

At the end of the night, Haney goes home to his wife where he states that he will never play again. He retires (for the tenth time) only to come out of retirement the next night to start all over again.

REQUIRED: With respect to the above information, answer the following questions:

(a)   Will Haney succeed in a lawsuit filed against the following? (Explain your answers.)
       1. 7'0" center
       2. 5'0" point guard
(b)   Whom should Meryl sue and what will be the likely result? (Include all parties and explain   your answer.)
(c)   Dave Minton wants to sue the arena and Haney. Will he win? Explain.
(d)   Mrs. Minton sues Charles and the arena. Will she win? Explain.

III. Outline

Three Kinds of Torts
       A tort is a civil wrong other than a contract for which the courts provide a remedy
       There are three kinds of torts
              Intentional torts
              Unintentional torts (negligence)
              Strict liability

Intentional	Negligence	Strict Liability
↓	↓	↓
intent	elements: duty, breach, injury, causation, in-fact, proximate cause	no intent, no fault
	↓	
	Defenses: superseding event, assumption of the risk, contributory negligence, comparative negligence	

Tort damages are money damages intended to compensate the injured party.
Punitive damages may be available or intentional torts or strict liability.
       Punitive damages serve the purpose of punishing the defendant.

Product liability- the liability of manufacturers, sellers, and others for injuries caused by defective products.

Intentional Torts against Persons
       Assault—threat of harm
       Battery—contact
       False imprisonment—unauthorized confinement
              Shopkeeper's Privilege- this allows merchants the stop, detain, and investigate suspected shoplifters without liability if there are reasonable grounds, suspects are detained for a reasonable time, and the investigation is conducted in a reasonable manner.
       Misappropriation of right to publicity (appropriation)—misappropriation of a name or likeness
       Invasion of the right to privacy – unwarranted and undesired publicity
       Defamation of character—untrue published statement (public officials-malice)-slander: oral, libel: written
       Intentional misrepresentation (Fraud)- intentionally defrauding a person out of money, property, or something else of value.
       Intentional infliction of emotional distress—extreme and outrageous conduct
       Malicious prosecution- a possible action brought by a defendant when a plaintiff files a frivolous action on one without merit with malice, etc.

Elements of Unintentional Torts (Negligence)
>To be successful in a negligence lawsuit, the plaintiff must prove:
>>The defendant owed a duty of care to the plaintiff
>>The defendant breached this duty of care
>>The plaintiff suffered injury
>>The defendant's negligent act caused the plaintiff's injury (causation in fact and proximate cause)

Problems in making a case for negligence:
>(1) What is duty?
>>-   Reasonable person standard
>(2) Causation:
>>(a) in-fact → Was it the actual cause?
>>(b) Proximate → Is the party in the chain of events legally responsible for the consequences of his/her actions? Was the injury foreseeable?
>>(c) What are damages? → compensatory/punitive

Examples of professional malpractice:
>Professionals, such as doctors, lawyers, architects, accountants, and others owe a duty of ordinary care, called the reasonable professional standard, in providing their services
>A professional who breaches the duty of ordinary care is liable for professional malpractice

Special case—Negligent infliction of emotional distress:
>Negligent infliction of emotional distress is a tort that permits a person to recover for emotional distress caused by the defendant's negligent conduct
>A plaintiff must prove that
>>A relative was killed or injured by the defendant
>>The plaintiff suffered severe emotional distress
>>The plaintiff's mental distress resulted from a sensory and contemporaneous observance of the accident

Special Negligence Doctrines
>Negligence per se—statutory duty
>*Res ipsa loquitur*—presumption of negligence (exclusive control)
>Good Samaritan laws—relief of medical professionals for ordinary negligence
>Assumption of the risk—knowledge and voluntary
>Contributory negligence—no recovery if partially at fault – be careful of the "last clear chance rules"
>Comparative negligence—apportionment of damages

Strict Liability
>Strict liability is liability without fault
>Strict liability doctrine
>>There are certain activities that place the public at risk of injury even if reasonable care is taken
>>The public should have some means of compensation if such injury occurs
>Strict liability was first imposed for abnormally dangerous activities
>>All in the chain of distribution are liable

Common defects creating strict liability
>1. Defect in manufacture
>2. Defect in design
>3. Failure to warn
>4. Defect in packaging

Defenses to Product Liability
- Generally known dangers
- Government contractor defense
- Misuse of product
- Supervening event
- Statute of repose

IV. Objective Questions

Terms:

1. A tort is a civil wrong where an injured individual sues an offending party seeking _____ or monetary compensation.

2. An unintentional tort where the offending party commits an act or omission that a reasonable man would not commit is categorized as a _____ tort.

3. The intentional tort of _____ requires only a reasonable apprehension of immediate harm, whereas the tort of _____ involves harmful or offensive contact with another person.

4. A false statement about a person, which is subsequently intentionally or accidentally published to a third person, is called the tort of _____.

5. A false statement which is spoken to a third person is _____; the name for a false statement which is written in a letter, newspaper, book, etc., or broadcast via movie, video, television show, or radio is _____.

6. If a defendant acts with _____, he makes a false statement knowingly or with reckless disregard of its falsity.

7. A tort in which the violation of a statute or ordinance constitutes the breach of duty of care is called _____.

8. Proving causation for an unintentional tort case requires two elements. The act of the person charged must be both the actual cause or _____, as well as the legal or _____ cause.

9. Under the _____ doctrine, damages are computed according to the fault of the plaintiff as well as the fault of the defendant so that the defendant only pays for the percentage of damage that he caused.

10. The obligation not to cause anyone harm or risk of harm is known as _____ in the law of negligence torts.

True/False:

1. ____ If a magazine publishes a false statement about a public personality, it is liable for invasion of the right to privacy.

2. ____ Assault and battery are mutually exclusive torts that do not occur together.

3. _____ If a newspaper review calls a commercially successful actor talentless, it is liable for defamation of character.

4. _____ Public figures and officials have the same degree of protection under defamation laws as common citizens do.

5. _____ In a lawsuit for malicious prosecution, the original defendant sues the original plaintiff.

6. _____ A threat of future harm or moral pressure is not considered false imprisonment.

7. _____ Under the traditional common law doctrine of contributory negligence, a plaintiff cannot recover damages from a defendant even if the plaintiff was only at fault for a very small part of his own injury.

8. _____ Usually, if certain harm was a foreseeable result of a person's negligent act, the act is said to be the proximate cause of the damages.

9. _____ In determining a person's duty of care under negligence, whether the person acted within the reasonable person standard is determined by that person's subjective intent at the time.

10. _____ Under *res ipsa loquitur*, there is an inference that the defendant was negligent and must therefore bear the burden to prove he was not negligent.

Multiple Choice:

1. Mr. Temper, a 5-foot, 4-inch, 100-pound hothead, tells Mr. Big, a professional wrestler, that he is going to "make him regret he set foot in this bar." At the same time, Temper clenches and raises his fists. Big looks at Temper from head to toe and responds, "Yeah, right."

A. Big can sue Temper only for assault.
B. Big can sue Temper for assault and battery.
C. Big can sue Temper for intentional infliction of emotional distress.
D. Big has no cause of action.

2. Thug approaches Joe, who is standing in line to buy a movie ticket, from behind. Thug plans to hit Joe over the head with a baseball. Completely unaware, Joe bends over to tie his shoe just as Thug swings. Consequently, Thug strikes Ann who was standing in front of Joe, fracturing her skull.

A. Joe can sue Thug for assault; Ann can sue Thug for battery.
B. Joe has no cause of action against Thug; Ann can sue only for battery.
C. Ann can sue Joe for negligence; Joe can sue Thug for contributory negligence.
D. Joe has no cause of action against Thug; Ann can sue for both assault and battery.

3. _____ refers to an attempt by another person to take over a living person's name or identity for commercial purposes.

A. Invasion of the right to privacy
B. Tort of appropriation
C. Defamation of character
D. Disparagement

4. Mr. Gossip tells Ms. Nosy that, "Flashy is a drug dealer. That's how she can afford to drive that Ferrari." Is Gossip liable for defamation of character against Flashy?

A. Yes, because it is a false statement that was told to a third party.
B. Yes, because all that is necessary is that the statement is false.
C. No, because telling only Nosy does not really hurt Flashy.
D. No, because Gossip only said this, but did not write it.

5. Adam said, "My accountant is the worst accountant ever!" Is this statement actionable?

A. Yes, it is defamation of character.
B. Yes, it is disparagement.
C. No, it is a statement of opinion.
D. No, unless the statement was published to a third party.

6. Speedy approaches an intersection in his car, as the light turns yellow. Instead of slowing down, Speedy speeds up and runs a red light. Mr. Walker, a pedestrian waiting to cross the street, yells and waves his fist at Speedy as he drives by. Unfortunately, Walker startles Ms. Precious who is also waiting to cross, and Precious drops the $500 vase she just bought. Is Speedy liable for the damage to the vase?

A. No, because Speedy had no duty to drive carefully.
B. No, because running the light is not a breach of the duty.
C. No, because Speedy's running of the light was not the proximate cause of the broken vase.
D. Yes, because the plaintiff, Precious, suffered injuries.

7. Assume the same facts as in question 5 except that Precious does not notice Walker. After the walk signal illuminates, Precious looks both ways, does not see Speedy, and begins to cross the street. Speedy, however, hits Precious, breaking her leg, as he runs the red light.

A. Speedy is liable for negligence, and Precious can recover damages.
B. Speedy is liable for an intentional tort, and Precious can recover damages.
C. Speedy is not liable for negligence because his acts were not the proximate cause of Precious' injuries.
D. Speedy is not liable for an intentional tort because intentional torts are wrongs against property only.

8. Steve goes to the hospital for a surgical procedure. During the surgery, a surgical instrument is accidentally left in his abdomen. A year later, he later suffers stomach pain and the souvenir is detected. It is unknown which doctor or nurse left the instrument behind. Can he successfully bring a claim?

A. No, the act was accidental and not intentional.
B. No, a patient generally assumes such risk when going into surgery.
C. Yes, the medical staff obviously violated its duty to warn.
D. Yes, under the doctrine of res ipsa loquitur.

9. _____ is a statute that relieves medical professionals from liability for ordinary negligence when they stop and render aid to victims in emergency situations.

A. Good Samaritan law
B. Assumption of the risk
C. Duty of care
D. *Res ipsa loquitur*

10. Which of the following statements is true about the strict liability doctrine?

A. Privity of contract between the injured party and defendant is mandatory.
B. Injured bystanders cannot recover damages under the strict liability doctrine.
C. Parties in the chain of distribution are strictly liable only to the customer who buys the product.
D. Injured bystanders are entitled to the same protection as the consumer or user.

V. Answers to Objective Questions

Terms:

1. damages. The tort must fit into one of the three recognized categories. [p. 109]

2. assault, battery. These acts are also often classified as crimes. [p. 109]

3. defamation of character. Note that publication to a third person is required. [p. 112]

4. slander, libel. Oral and written statements are separately classified. [p. 112]

5. actual malice. Malice is very difficult to prove. [p. 112]

6. negligence. This is the second of the three categories of tort law. [p. 114]

7. duty of care. This is the first element of unintentional (negligence) tort law. [p. 114]

8. causation in fact, proximate. Both elements are required. [p. 116]

9. negligence *per se*. Statutes often establish duties owed by one person to another. [p. 118]

10. comparative negligence. This is a relatively new method as opposed to the old common law rule of contributory negligence. [p. 120]

True/False:

1. True. Threats of future harm are not actionable. [p. 109]

2. False. Assault and battery often occur together, although they do not have to. [p. 110]

3. False. A false statement that appears in writing or other fixed medium is libel. [p. 112]

4. False. The publication of opinions is usually not actionable. [p. 112]

5. False. Public figures and officials can only recover for defamation if they prove the defendant made a false statement knowingly, or with reckless disregard for its falsity, i.e., actual malice. [p. 112]

6. True. In the second lawsuit, the defendant becomes the plaintiff and vice versa. [p. 113]

7. False. Under a reasonable person standard, courts determine how an objective, careful person would have acted in a certain situation. The defendant's subjective thoughts or intentions are not considered. [p. 114]

8. True. In determining proximate cause, if a certain event was a foreseeable result of a negligent act that will generally satisfy this part of the causation requirement. [p. 116]

9. True. Because the defendant has superior knowledge and because the evidence suggests there was a negligent act, *res ipsa loquitur* shifts the burden from the plaintiff to the defendant. [p. 118]

10. True. Under contributory negligence, if the plaintiff contributed in any way to his own injuries, he cannot recover from the defendant under the traditional common law. The more modern view is to use comparative negligence doctrines. [p. 120]

Multiple Choice:

1. D. Since Big is obviously not frightened by this threat, he cannot sue for assault. Because Temper never hit Big, there is no harmful or offensive touching, and therefore, no battery. [p. 109]

2. B. Since Joe was never in apprehension of harm, nor actually harmed by Thug's actions, he has no cause of action. Ann can sue for battery since she was harmed, but not for assault since she was not in apprehension of harm. [p. 110]

3. B. Any attempt by another person to appropriate a living person's name or identity for commercial purposes is actionable. [p. 111]

4. A. The elements of defamation of character require both (1) a false statement and (2) the telling or writing of the statement to a third party. [p. 112]

5. C. The publication of an untrue statement of fact is not the same as the publication of an opinion. The publication of opinions is usually not actionable. [p. 112]

6. C. While Speedy's act was certainly negligent, the chain of events from speeding through the light to breaking the vase is very long and unforeseeable. Consequently, since foreseeability is generally the test for proximate cause, Speedy is not liable for the vase. [p. 114]

7. A. Since Speedy owed Precious a duty of care, breached that duty, and caused Precious injury, he was negligent and is liable. [p. 115]

8. D. This doctrine requires a defendant to prove that he/she was not negligent. [p. 118]

9. A. Almost all states have enacted Good Samaritan laws that relieve medical professionals from liability for injury caused by their ordinary negligence in such circumstances. [p. 118]

10. D. Strict liability is a tort doctrine that makes manufacturers, distributors, wholesalers, retailers, and others in the chain of distribution of a defective product liable for the damages caused by the defect, irrespective of fault. [p. 121]

VI. Answers to Essay Question

(a) (1) Haney assumes the risk of actions that are a normal part of the game and, therefore, will not succeed in this lawsuit

(a) (2) This is a battery and intentional tort.

(b) Meryl should sue Charles for medical malpractice. There was a duty to provide a proper exam which he did not do causing injury. She should also sue the team because under the doctrine of "*respondeat superior*" an employer is liable for the torts of an employee committed while within the scope of the working relationship.

(c) This is a normal and expected part of the game and therefore the risk was assumed by Dave.

(d) The arena had a duty to provide safe premises which they did not do causing injury. A negligence lawsuit would be appropriate. Haney can be sued for the intentional tort of battery and will lose unless he did it under self-defense.

Chapter 7

CRIMINAL LAW AND CYBER CRIMES

When are you guilty beyond a reasonable doubt?

I. Overview

One of the most frequently posed questions to members of the legal profession is: "How can you defend someone you know is guilty of a crime?" The answer lies in a simple truth: we are defending not only the accused but also the criminal justice system. Because of this dual role, no other area of law is more ripe with controversy than criminal law and criminal procedure.

The American system of criminal law has been at the center of constant debate since the inception of the republic. On one side, there is a clear duty on the part of the sovereign to protect its populace from the ravages of miscreants whose behavior simply cannot be tolerated. On the other hand, the easier it is for the sovereign to punish, incarcerate, or even condemn its members to death, the less free the entire society is in the end. Our criminal justice system is designed to afford maximum protection for society's members. It is the government's burden of proof to show guilt beyond a reasonable doubt under the law of criminal procedure. The accused is entitled to an entire set of legal protections generically called due process. That phrase is derived from two provisions in the U.S. Constitution: one in the Fifth Amendment pertaining to actions by the federal government and one in the Fourteenth Amendment pertaining to actions by state governments. Under these provisions and the numerous federal, state, and local criminal codes, our system tells the sovereign we are presumed innocent until properly proven guilty according to the rules of the game. What upsets so many people in our society today is a concern that the rules may have been bent too far in favor of the accused.

As students of the legal system and as potential leaders in business, your job is to know what those rules of the game are and to learn how to comply with them as responsible members of society. Failure to do so is not only bad for business; it is bad for everyone.

II. Hypothetical Multi-issue Essay Question

Mergatroyd T. Wheeler has really come up with something. He has found a way in which his newly patented automobile engine could run on alternative energy. That alternative source of energy is found in a secret process that can turn cow pies into horsepower. His tests showed he could get twenty miles per pie (mpp) behind the wheel of his prototype named B.S. Bukaroo.

Mergatroyd took his idea to a large and prestigious investment banking firm, Wee, Cheatum, and Howe, to promote and sell shares in his new company named Go Pies. The financial records of the company were certified by I, Know, and Nothing CPAs. Shares in the new company were publicly sold to investors from all fifty states.

The company failed because the engine would only run on extremely odiferous pies, and now a number of disgruntled investors are pressing to bring RICO actions, at both the criminal and civil levels, against all parties involved. Comment.

III. Outline

Introduction to Criminal Law
-   Person is presumed innocent
-   Burden of proof is on the government
-   Standard of proof is beyond a reasonable doubt
-   Conviction requires a unanimous decision

What Is a Crime?
>   A crime is a violation of a statute for which the government imposes a punishment. A penal code is a collection of criminal statutes. Penalties could include fine, imprisonment or both. Penal code- a collection of criminal statutes

Parties to a Criminal Action
>   Plaintiff
>>   In a criminal lawsuit, the government (not a private party) is the plaintiff
>>   Government is represented by the prosecutor
>   Defendant
>>   The accused is the defendant
>>   Defendant is represented by a private attorney, public defender, or self

Classification of Crimes		
Felonies	Misdemeanors	Violations
↓	↓	↓
most serious	less serious	least serious/fine
↓	↓	↓
imprisonment often over a year	imprisonment of a year or less	imprisonment light if any
↓	↓	↓
possible fine	possible fine	usually fine

>   Felony, Misdemeanor, and Violation
>>   Felony – most serious type of crime
>>>   o   Punishable by imprisonment or death
>>>   o   Includes crimes that are mala in se (inherently evil)
>>   Misdemeanor – less serious crimes
>>>   o   Not inherently evil (*mala prohibita*), but prohibited by society
>>>   o   Punishable by fines and/or imprisonment of one-year or less
>>   Violation – a crime that is neither a felony nor a misdemeanor that is usually punishable by fine

Intent Crimes
Criminal Act (*Actus Reus*)- the guilty act
>>>   o   The performance of a criminal act
Criminal Intent (*Mens Rea*)- the evil intent
>>>   o   Possession of the mind to commit a prohibited act
Specific Intent – the accused purposefully, intentionally, or with knowledge commits a prohibited act
General Intent – a showing of recklessness or a lesser degree of mental culpability

Non-Intent Crimes
>   A crime that imposes criminal liability without a finding of intent (*mens rea*)

Ex. Involuntary manslaughter

Criminal Law	vs	Civil Law
↓		↓
state brings suit		individual brings suit
↓		↓
punishment		damages
↓		↓
beyond a reasonable doubt		preponderance of the evidence

Stages of Pretrial Criminal Procedure
   Arrest—usually warrant with probable cause Bail Bond
   Indictment or information—formal charge by grand jury or magistrate
   Arraignment—formal charge and plea → guilty, not guilty, *nolo contendare*
   Plea bargaining—the deal

Criminal Trial
   All jurors must unanimously agree before the accused is found guilty of a crime
   If even one juror disagrees, the accused is not guilty
   If all jurors agree the accused did not commit the crime, the accused is innocent
   A guilty defendant can appeal not the government.

Common Crimes
   Murder- the unlawful killing of a human being by another with aforethought malice
   Robbery—taking of personal property with fear or force
   Burglary—breaking (sometimes) and entering with felonious intent
   Larceny—wrongful taking of personal property
   Theft—taking of personal property without consent
   Receiving stolen property—with intent to deprive owner
   Arson—burning

White-Collar Crimes
   Forgery—fraudulent making or altering of written document
   Embezzlement—fraudulent conversion of entrusted property
   Bribery—use of bribes
   Extortion—obtaining of property with fear or force
   Criminal fraud—property through deception or trickery
   Mail & Wire fraud—use of mail or wires to defraud
   Money Laundering Control Act – burying of illegal money
   Racketeer Influenced and Corrupt Organizations Act (RICO)—pattern of racketeering activity
   Corporate Criminal Liability- corporations are criminally liable for the acts of managers, agents and employees

Protection Against Unreasonable Search and Seizure
Fourth Amendment – protects from unreasonable search and seizure by governments
   - Search warrants based on probable cause are necessary in most cases
   - Exclusionary rule – evidence obtained from an unreasonable search and seizure can be excluded from a trial or proceeding

Privileges Against Self-Incrimination

Fifth Amendment provides that no person "shall be compelled in any criminal case to be a witness against himself."

   -Miranda Rights- rights that a suspect must be informed of before interrogation to ensure the suspect will not unwittingly give up Fifth Amendment rights.

Attorney Client Privilege and Other Privileges
Attorney cannot be called as a witness against his client

Other Privileges
   Psychiatrist/Psychologist – patient
   Priest/rabbi/minister/imam – penitent privilege
   Spouse-spouse privilege
   Parent-child privilege

Immunity from Prosecution
   - The government's agreement not to use against a person granted immunity any evidence given by that person

   Other Constitutional Protections
   Fifth Amendment protection against double jeopardy and self-incrimination
   Sixth Amendment protection to a public jury trial
   Eighth Amendment protection against cruel and unusual punishment

IV. Objective Questions:

Terms:

1. At a criminal trial, the government's burden of proof requires that it prove _____ that the accused is guilty.

2. Crimes can be divided into three separate classifications: _____, _____, and _____.

3. In a criminal context, the _____ refers to the guilty act, while the _____ refers to the accused's guilty intent.

4. To be found guilty of a crime, the accused must be found to have had the required state of mind. Where the accused purposely commits an act, this is _____ intent. Where the accused acts recklessly, this is _____ intent.

5. To arrest someone, the police must usually obtain a warrant. The warrant must be based on a showing of _____.

6. When a person is formally charged with a crime, he or she is issued either a _____ from a grand jury or a _____ from a magistrate.

7. Forgery, fraud and embezzlement are examples of _____.

8. A federal act that provides for both criminal and civil penalties for racketeering is commonly called _____.

9. The rights that a suspect must be informed of before interrogation to protect his Fifth Amendment rights are called _____.

10. _____ is a rule that says a client can tell his or her lawyer anything about the case without fear that the attorney will be called as a witness against the client.

True/False:

1. ____ The case against the accused is dismissed if neither an indictment nor information statement is issued.

2. ____ If police do not have time to get an arrest warrant against a fleeing person, they can arrest the person without probable cause.

3. ____ A grand jury determines a person's guilt in serious crimes such as murder.

4. ____ In a criminal action, the parties are the victim and the defendant.

5. ____ If a defendant is found not guilty in a criminal case, the government can retry the case with a new jury.

6. ____ If the accused enters a plea of *nolo contendere*, the government has the option of accepting the plea or requiring the defendant to plead either guilty or innocent.

7. ____ In a criminal trial, all jurors must unanimously find the accused guilty beyond a reasonable doubt for a conviction.

8. ____ Larceny is the taking of personal property from another's home or type of building.

9. ____ Under RICO, to prove a pattern of racketeering, no less than two predicate acts must be committed within a ten-year period.

10. ____ Persons injured by a RICO violation have a private civil action against a violator for treble damages.

11. ____ The exclusionary rule prevents illegally obtained evidence from being used against the person searched.

12. ____ The Eighth Amendment protects the right to a public trial by jury.

Multiple Choice:

1. A collection of criminal statutes is referred to as a(n) _____.

A. bill
B. constitution
C. penal code
D. charter

2. Who is the plaintiff in a criminal lawsuit?

A. the government
B. the respondent
C. a private party
D. the victim

3. _____ crimes require that the perpetrator either knew or should have known that his or her actions would lead to harmful results.

A. Nonintent
B. Specific intent
C. General intent
D. Explicit intent

4. _____ is defined as the substantial likelihood that a person either committed or is about to commit a crime.

A. Probable cause
B. Reasonable doubt
C. Preponderance of evidence
D. Reasonable suspicion

5. What is nolo contendere in legal proceedings?

A. a plea by which the defense attorney sets out reasons as to why the case should not go to trial
B. a plea where the accused agrees to the imposition of a penalty but does not admit guilt
C. a plea by which the defense attorney exhibits evidences that the defendant is not fit to stand for trial
D. a guilty plea where the defendant does not admit the act and asserts innocence though there is sufficient evidence against the defendant

6. Where is the felony murder rule applied?

A. when the felon in the case was killed while the crime transpired
B. when the murder was committed without intent, while committing another crime
C. when the reason for the death is found to be involuntary manslaughter
D. when the crime involves the intended murder of another person

7. Which of the following crimes is an example of a white-collar crime?

A. battery
B. larceny
C. arson
D. forgery

8. _____ is the fraudulent conversion of property by a person to whom that property was entrusted.

A. Embezzlement
B. Bribery
C. Forgery
D. Extortion

9. Which of the following does the Money Laundering Act prohibit?

A. the use of mails or wires to defraud another person
B. knowingly engaging in a financial transaction involving the proceeds of an unlawful activity
C. obtaining property from another, with his or her consent, induced by wrongful use of actual or threatened force
D. the fraudulent conversion of property by a person to whom that property was entrusted

10. Which of the following would violate the Double Jeopardy Clause?

A. The government reopens a case after new incriminating evidence is found against an acquitted person.
B. A person is tried for a case similar to a case from which he was acquitted earlier.
C. A case reaches a hung jury in court and the government reopens the case with a new jury.
D. The criminal act violates more than one jurisdiction and each jurisdiction tries the accused in turn

V. Answers to Objective Questions

Terms:

1. beyond a reasonable doubt. This does not mean absolute certainty. [p. 132]

2. felonies, misdemeanors, violations. These classifications are set out in statutes. [p. 133]

3. *actus reus, mens rea*. Both elements are necessary to the definition of a crime. [p. 134]

4. specific, general. The statutes describe the type of intent required. [p. 134]

5. probable cause. Case law interpretation of this standard is controversial. [p. 135]

6. indictment, information. Each state has its own detailed rules of criminal procedure. [p. 136]

7. white-collar crimes. These crimes are prone to be committed by businesspersons. [p. 139]

8. RICO. Racketeer Influenced and Corrupt Organizations Act. [p. 142]

9. Miranda rights. The Supreme Court requires that the following warning—colloquially called the Miranda rights—be read to a criminal suspect before he or she is interrogated by the police or other government officials:
• You have the right to remain silent.
• Anything you say can and will be used against you.
• You have the right to consult a lawyer and to have a lawyer present with
you during interrogation.
• If you cannot afford a lawyer, a lawyer will be appointed free of charge to
represent you.. [p. 148]

10. Attorney–client privilege. For the privilege to apply, the information must be told to the attorney in his or her capacity as an attorney and not as a friend or neighbor or such. [p. 148]

True/False:

1. True. If the grand jury determines that there is sufficient evidence to hold the accused for trial, it issues an indictment. [p. 136]

2. False. Even if police do not have time to get an arrest warrant, any arrest must be based on probable cause. [p. 136]

3. False. A grand jury does not determine guilt or innocence. The grand jury decides if there is sufficient evidence to hold the accused for a trial. [p. 136]

4. False. In a criminal trial, the parties are the government and the defendant. The victim does not bring criminal charges, but may have a separate civil action. [p. 137]

5. False. If the jury cannot come to a unanimous decision about the defendant's guilt one way or the other, the government may choose to retry the case before a new judge and jury. [p. 137]

6. True. The government can choose to accept this plea or require the accused to plead either guilty or innocent. [p. 137]

7. True. All jurors must unanimously agree that the government has convinced them beyond a reasonable doubt that the accused is guilty. If even one juror is not so convinced, the jury is considered a hung jury. [p. 137]

8. False. This is the definition of burglary. [p. 138]

9. True. Under RICO, a pattern of racketeering activity can be established by any two predicate acts committed within a ten-year period. [p. 142]

10. True. This is a remedy under RICO. [p. 142]

11. True. Where the search is unreasonable, evidence obtained will not be admissible against the person searched. [p. 144]

12. False. The Sixth Amendment is the correct answer. [p. 150]

Multiple Choice:

1. C. Most states have adopted comprehensive penal codes that define in detail the activities considered to be crimes within their jurisdictions and the penalties that will be imposed for their commission. [p. 132]

2. A. In a criminal lawsuit, the government (not a private party) is the plaintiff. [p. 133]

3. C. The government does not have to prove that the accused intended the precise harm that resulted from her actions. [p. 134]

4. A. Probable cause is the evidence of the substantial likelihood that a person either committed or is about to commit a crime. [p. 135]

5. B. A party may enter a plea of nolo contendere whereby the accused agrees to the imposition of a penalty but does not admit guilt. [p. 137]

6. B. The intent to commit the murder is inferred from the intent to commit the other crime. [p. 138]

7. D. The crime of forgery occurs if a written document is fraudulently made or altered and that change affects the legal liability of another person. [p. 139]

8. A. Embezzlers often try to cover their tracks by preparing false books, records, or entries. [p. 140]

9. B. In order to "wash" the money and make it look as though it was earned legitimately, many criminals purchase legitimate businesses and run the money through those businesses to "clean" it before they receive the money. [p. 141]

10. A. The Double Jeopardy Clause of the Fifth Amendment protects persons from being tried twice for the same crime. [p. 149]

VI. Answers to Essay Question:

The RICO (Racketeer Influenced and Corrupt Organization) statute is a federal statute designed to go after white-collar criminals associated with racketeering activities. Even though it can preempt state and local laws covering similar activities, it can be prosecuted in tandem with those statutes. We will assume only the federal law applies here. The elements called for under the statute are:
  (1) A prohibited pattern of acts, which in this case may involve securities and or mail fraud.
  (2) The specific intent to defraud investors.
  If it can be shown that the accused parties made fraudulent misrepresentations about the performance capabilities of the "cow pie" engine to investors, then this behavior may come under the purview of the RICO statute. There is great controversy over the proper fit between the acts defined in the RICO statute as opposed to the normal business risks that come with investing in new ventures. Many commentators have argued that RICO should not be used as a wedge to recover losses from simple bad judgment.

Assuming that the inventor, the investment bankers, and the CPA firm were all properly warned of their rights and all business records were properly searched, it appears likely that they may be criminally liable for securities fraud.

If any of the procedures were not used properly, the criminal case against the accused would most likely fail based on the exclusionary rule. That rule would keep out tainted evidence. It is interesting to note, however, that even though the criminal case may fail, civil damages may still be imposed in a separate trial. The lower burden of proof coupled with the possibility of nonexclusion of the tainted evidence in that forum only exacerbates the problem for the accused under this broad-reaching statute.

As a matter of public policy, government does need statutes like RICO to go after white-collar crime and racketeering-related activities. As mentioned, the concern of many critics of the law is that it is casting too large a net and dragging in innocent, legitimate business entities.

Chapter 8
INTELLECTUAL PROPERTY AND CYBER PIRACY

What are intellectual property rights?

I. Overview

One of the great debates currently being waged in the halls of the U.S. Congress and state legislatures is to what extent a government entity should act as a partner in the promotion of new business opportunities such as e-commerce. As a matter of public policy and related tax policy, there is no question that government sanctioned jump starts to business can bring long-term benefits to the larger community by way of jobs and additional tax revenues. This chapter focuses on several areas of well accepted legal partnerships, i.e., areas of law with long established rules which provide innovative, creative, and new methods of special business legal protections in the name of the larger public good. These protected areas revolve around the law of patents, copyrights, and trademarks. They are designed not only to reward original effort but also to foster and encourage continued new contributions to the common good by creating an economically protected relationship between the writer, inventor, and others, and the government.

The areas of patent, copyright, and trademark law are all individually complex and call for use of highly specialized law practitioners. They have a common denominator in that each of these areas provides a legally protected mechanism for rewarding the creator of work in the economic marketplace. This reward system revolves around two basic principles:

1. Exclusive use of the economic benefits that result from the protected activity.
2. Legal recourse against those who somehow infringe upon this exclusive economic protection.

Where proper statutory procedures are used, the benefits can be great. For example, once a patent is granted, the inventor can reap the exclusive economic benefits for fourteen or seventeen years depending on the type of patent issued. The protection provided under copyright laws is even longer. Since 1976, U.S. copyright laws have extended protections for authors and other creative persons for their lives plus fifty years. The protection can be even longer for copyrights registered by business entities. In the area of trademarks and related marks, the continued use of the registered mark, coupled with renewals can extend the protections of law indefinitely. The most important caveat in trademark law is: "Use it or lose it." Failure to maintain legal protection of trademarks, service marks, or related marks can lead to a loss of protection for them. If the mark is allowed to become a common term for a product, it may be deemed generic and may no longer be entitled to protections that come with exclusive use of the term. One example of such a generic term is found in the word aspirin. Because the original marketers of the product did not protect the name vigorously enough, the name aspirin has fallen into the generic pool of language used to describe products with those chemical properties found in that product, i.e., aspirin.

The best way for a student to approach these areas of the law is to recognize that each of these legally recognized areas of protection carries with it a benefit/burden dichotomy—the benefits of the protective statute will pass to those who know how to use the statute. Proper use of the statute calls for all the individual elements required under the statute to be complied with. Once that burden has been met, the benefits will follow. Students should, therefore, familiarize themselves with respective steps required to obtain patent, copyright, or trademark exclusive use protection as described in the chapter. The multi-issue essay question will illustrate the process and how it is used to protect intellectual property rights.

II. Hypothetical Multi-issue Essay Question

Ted Huie, Fred Dewie, and Ned Louie are all recent graduates of the prestigious law school, I OWE U, located in scenic Backwater, Massazona. Having all recently passed the tough Massazona State Bar Examination, they decided to forego the riches of Wall Street and start their own law practice in Backyard, which is just down the road from Backwater. Their chosen area of specialization in law practice is patents, copyrights, and trademarks. They want to use their proper surnames in advertising their new law firm but are concerned that the use of the law firm name Huie, Dewie, and Louie may raise a few concerns at Walt Disney Studios, Inc. Walt Disney Studios has long held the copyright to the cartoon duck characters named Huey, Dewey, and Louie, and our newly-admitted law practitioners don't want to start their law careers by running "afowl" of the law! What advice would you give them on this issue?

III. Outline

Introduction to Intellectual Property and Cyber Piracy
>   Intellectual Property Rights
>>   Patents, copyrights, trademarks, trade names, domain names, and other valuable business assets

Trade Secret
>   It is a product formula, pattern, design, compilation of data, customer list or other business secret
>>   A defendant must have obtained the secret through theft, bribery, or industrial espionage
>>   A competitor cannot lawfully discover a trade secret through reverse engineering

>   Civil Law: Misappropriation of Trade Secret
>>   Owner can bring a suit to:
>>>   1. Recover profits
>>>   2. Recover damages
>>>   3. Injunction

>   Criminal Law: Economic Espionage Act of 1966
>>   It is a federal crime for any person to convert a trade secret to his or her benefit or the benefit of others, knowingly or intending that the act would cause injury to the owner of the trade secret

Patent
>   Federal Patent Statute
>>   A 1952 federal statute that establishes the requirements for obtaining a patent and protects patented inventions from infringement

>   Patent Period
>   Inventions (20 years)
>   Design Patents (14 years)
>>   The term begins to run from the date the patent application is filed
>>   The U.S. follows the first to invent rule, rather than the first to file rule
>>   At the termination of the patent period, the invention or design enters public domain

>   Patent Application
>   An application must contain a written description of the invention and be filed with the PTO in Washington, D.C.

Patents receive numbers

Patent pending is the designation after the application is filed but not yet granted

Categories of invention:

1. Machines
2. Processes
3. Compositions of matter
4. Improvements to existing machines, processes or compositions of matter
5. Designs for an article of manufacture
6. Asexually reproduced plants
7. Living material invented by a person
- Abstractions and scientific principles cannot be patented unless they are part of the tangible environment

Requirements for Obtaining a Patent

1. Novel (new)
2. Useful (practical purpose)
3. Non-obvious

One-Year on Sale Doctrine

Also known as the public use doctrine

A patent may not be granted if the invention was used by the public for more than one year

The American Inventor's Protection Act

A federal statute that permits an inventor to file a provisional application with the U.S. Patent and Trademark Office three months before filing the final patent application, among other provisions

Patent Infringement

Unauthorized use of another's patent

A plaintiff can recover:

1. Money damages equal to a reasonable royalty rate
2. Other damages caused by infringement
3. An order requiring destruction of the infringing articles
4. Injunction

Copyright

Copyright Revision Act

A 1976 federal statute that (1) established the requirements for obtaining a copyright and (2) protects copyrighted works from infringement

The act protects the work of authors from unauthorized use of work or materials

Only tangible writings are subject to copyright registration and protection

Examples include:

Books

Poems

Periodicals

Newspapers

Lectures

Sermons

Addresses

Musical compositions

Plays

Motion pictures

Radio and television productions

Maps

Works of art, including paintings, drawings, sculpture, jewelry, glassware, tapestry, and lithographs

Architectural drawings

Photographs

Computer programs

Registration of Copyrights

A copyright is created when a work is produced

Published or unpublished works may be registered with the U.S. Copyright Office

Individuals- copyright for life plus seventy years

Owned by business- the shorter of either 95 years from the first publication or 120 years from the creation

After a copyright term runs, the work enters into public domain

Copyright Infringement

An infringement that occurs when a party copies a substantial and material part of a plaintiff's copyrighted work without permission

Remedies:

1. Profit made by defendant
2. Damages suffered by plaintiff
3. An order requiring the impounding and destruction of the infringing works
4. Injunction

Contributory Copyright Infringement Act

Parties who knowingly contribute to another party's copyright infringement may be assessed secondary liability

File to file sharing

Peer to peer networks

Fair Use Doctrine

This permits limited use of a copyright by someone other than the copyright holder without the permission of the copyright holder

The doctrine allows:

1. Quotation of work for review, criticism, scholarly or technical work
2. Use in parody or satire
3. Brief quotation in a news report
4. Reproduction by teachers or students of a small part of work to illustrate a lesson
5. Incidental reproduction for newscast or reporting
6. Reproduction of a work in a legislative or judicial proceeding

Sampling

Criminal Law: No Electronic Theft Act (NET Act)

A federal statute that makes it a crime for a person to willfully infringe on a copyrighted work that exceeds $1,000 in retail value

Digital Millennium Copyright Act (DMCA)

A federal statute that prohibits unauthorized access to copyrighted digital works by circumventing encryption technology in the manufacture and distribution of technologies designed for the purpose of circumventing encryption protection of digital works

Trademark

Lanham Act

An amended federal statute that (1) established the requirements for obtaining a federal mark and (2) protects marks from infringement

Mark- The collective name for trademarks, service marks, certification marks, and collective marks that can be trademarked

Original registration is good for ten years, and can be renewed for an unlimited number of ten year terms

Marks That Can be Trademarked

1. Trademark- a distinctive mark, symbol, name, word, motto, or device that identifies the goods of a particular business
2. Service mark- a mark that distinguishes the services of the holder from those of competitors
3. Certification mark- a mark that is used to certify that a good or service is of a certain quality originated from a particular geographical area
4. Collective mark- a mark owned by an organization used to identify themselves

What cannot be registered:

1. Flags or coat of arms of the U.S., any state, municipality, or foreign nation
2 Marks that are immoral or scandalous
3. Geographical names standing alone
4. Surnames standing alone
5. Any mark that resembles a mark already registered

Distinctiveness of a Mark

A mark must be:

1. Distinctive (unique or fabricated); or
2. Have acquired a secondary meaning (a brand name that has evolved from an ordinary term or phrase)

Trademark Infringement

Unauthorized use of another's mark

Generic Names

A term for a mark that has become a common term for a product line or type of service and therefore has lost its trademark protection

(Examples provided in Figure 8.2 on page 172)

Federal Dilution Act

A federal statute that protects famous marks from dilution, erosion, blurring or tarnishing

Requirements:

1. The mark must be famous
2. The use by the other party must be commercial
3. The use must cause dilution of the distinctive quality of the mark

Dilution- lessening the capacity of identification or distinguishing characteristic

IV. Objective Questions

Terms:

1. Assets such as inventions, writings, trademarks, etc. that are often a business's most valuable asset include _____ property.

2. A product formula, pattern, design, compilation of data, customer list, or other business secret is a(n) _____.

3. The _____ makes it a federal crime to steal another's trade secrets.

4. To be patented an invention must be _____.

5. A patent may not be granted if the invention was used by the public for more than one year prior to the filing of the patent application. This is known as the _____ doctrine.

6. _____ gives the author of qualifying subject matter, and who meets other requirements established by the pertinent law, the exclusive right to publish, produce, sell, license, and distribute the work.

7. Writings that are capable of visual perception are _____.

8. _____ permits certain limited use of a copyright by someone other than the copyright holder without the permission of the copyright holder.

9. A distinctive mark, symbol, name, word, motto, or device that identifies the goods of a particular business and distinguishes the business and products of the holder from those of its competitors are all ways of identifying a(n) _____.

10. _____ refers to a brand name that has evolved from an ordinary term.

True/False:

1. ____ If the owner of a trade secret does not take all reasonable precautions to protect a trade secret, the secret will no longer be protected under unfair competition laws.

2. ____ Design patents are valid for four years and can be renewed at the end of that time.

3. ____ Copyrights cannot be licensed.

4. ____ Use of the symbol © is mandatory for copyright protection.

5. ____ The fair use doctrine permits copyrighted work to be used in parody or satire.

6. ____ Suits brought under the Federal Patent Statute of 1952, Copyright Revision Act of 1976, and the Lanham Trademark Act are properly brought in federal court, not state court.

7. ____ A trademark registration is valid for ten years and can be renewed at the end of that time.

8. _____ The registration of a trademark is given nationwide effect as notice that the mark is the registrant's property.

9. _____ If the registrant of a trademark does not use the registered trademark symbol, the registrant will lose all protection and have no remedy against infringements.

10. _____ Words that are descriptive but have no secondary meaning cannot be trademarked.

Multiple Choice:

1. Which of the following would be considered to be a part of intellectual property?

    A. Patents
    B. Vehicles
    C. Business contracts
    D. Buildings

2. Intellectual property falls into a category of property known as _____.

    A. tangible property
    B. real property
    C. moveable property
    D. intangible property

3. A _____ is a product formula, pattern, design, compilation of data, customer list, or other covert business information.

    A. copyright
    B. trade secret
    C. trademark
    D. patent

4. A closely guarded formula for a recipe protected by a soft drink manufacturer would be considered as an example of a _____.

    A. trade secret
    B. copyright
    C. patent
    D. trademark

5. What federal statute was enacted by the Congress to protect trade secrets?

    A. Sarbanes-Oxley Act
    B. Lanham Act
    C. Telecommunication Act
    D. Economic Espionage Act

6. A _____ is a grant by the federal government upon the inventor of an invention for the exclusive right to use, sell, or license the invention for a limited amount of time.

    A. copyright
    B. trade secret
    C. patent
    D. trademark

7. A _____ is a patent that protects the functionality of a patent.

    A. utility patent
    B. design patent
    C. process patent
    D. method patent

8. _____ is a legal right that gives the author of qualifying subject matter, and who meets other requirements established by law, the exclusive right to publish, produce, sell, license, and distribute the work. A. Patent
    B. Copyright
    C. Trademark
    D. Trade secret

9. Which of the following is suitable for copyrighting?

    A. Buildings
    B. Business methods
    C. Musical compositions
    D. Product logos

10. In terms of copyright law, the use of copyrighted material in a satire or parody would be an example of _____.

    A. piracy
    B. copyright sharing
    C. copyright infringement
    D. application of the fair use doctrine

V. Answers to Objective Questions

Terms:

1. intellectual. Patents, copyrights, etc., qualify as intellectual property. [p. 157]

2. trade secret. Determine the efforts taken by the company to keep it secret. [p. 158]

3. Economic Espionage Act. [p. 158]

4. novel, useful, and nonobvious. The protection is federal in nature and is valid for 20 years. [p. 161]

5. public use. The rule seeks to impose a duty on the inventor to act in a timely manner. [p. 163]

6. Copyright. Promotes intellectual thought. [p. 164]

7. Tangible writings. As hi-tech evolves, expect this definition to be expanded. [p. 164-165]

8. fair use doctrine. Rights are not absolute as shown with these exceptions. One example is works used in a satire. [p. 166]

9. trademark. In many ways, these have become a new international language of business. [p. 167]

10. Secondary meaning. This meaning often has tremendous value; consider the value of terms like Coke and Pepsi. [p. 170]

True/False:

1. True. The owner of a trade secret is obliged to take all reasonable precautions to prevent that secret from being discovered by others. If the owner fails to take such actions, the secret is no longer subject to protection under state unfair competition laws. [p. 158]

2. False. A design patent is valid for fourteen years. [p. 164]

3. False. Copyrights can be sold or licensed to others, whose rights are then protected by copyright law. [p. 164]

4. False. Registrant is entitled to use it but not mandated. [p. 165]

5. True. The following uses are protected under this doctrine: (1) quotation of the copyrighted work for review or criticism or in a scholarly or technical work, (2) use in a parody or satire, (3) brief quotation in a news report, (4) reproduction by a teacher or student of a small part of the work to illustrate a lesson, (5) incidental reproduction of a work in a newsreel or broadcast of an event being reported, and (6) reproduction of a work in a legislative or judicial proceeding. (166)

6. True. These are federally protected intellectual property enactments. [p. 160, 164, 167]

7. True. The original registration of a mark is valid for ten years, and it can be renewed for an unlimited number of ten-year periods. [p. 168]

8. True. The protection is provided under federal statutes. [p. 168]

9. False. Use of the symbol is not mandatory. However, certain remedies may be lost if the symbol is not used. [p. 168]

10. True. Words that are descriptive but have no secondary meaning cannot be trademarked. [p. 170]

Multiple Choice:

1. A. Intellectual property include patents, copyrights, trademarks, and trade secrets. [p. 157]

2. D. Intellectual property falls into a category of property known as intangible rights, which are not tangible physical objects. [p. 157]

3. B. A trade secret is a product formula, pattern, design, compilation of data, customer list, or other business secret. [p. 158]

4. A. A trade secret is a product formula, pattern, design, compilation of data, customer list, or other business secret. [p. 158]

5. D. The Economic Espionage Act (EEA) is a federal statute that makes it a crime for any person to convert a trade secret for his or her own or another's benefit, knowing or intending to cause injury to the owners of the trade secret. [p. 158]

6. C. A patent is a grant by the federal government upon the inventor of an invention for the exclusive right to use, sell, or license the invention for a limited amount of time. [p. 160]

7. A. A utility patent protects the functionality of an invention. [p. 160]

8. B. Copyright is a legal right that gives the author of qualifying subject matter, and who meets other requirements established by copyright law, the exclusive right to publish, produce, sell, license, and distribute the work. [p. 164]

9. C. Books, periodicals, and newspapers; lectures, sermons, addresses, and poems; musical compositions; plays, motion pictures, etc. qualify for copyright protection. [p. 165]

10. D. The following uses are protected under the fair use doctrine: (1) quotation of the copyrighted work for review or criticism or in a scholarly or technical work, (2) use in a parody or satire, (3) brief quotation in a news report, (4) reproduction by a teacher or student of a small part of the work to illustrate a lesson, (5) incidental reproduction of a work in a newsreel or broadcast of an event being reported, and (6) reproduction of a work in a legislative or judicial proceeding. [p. 166]

VI. Answers to Essay Questions

The use of a company name may be subject to scrutiny under any number of protected areas of the law including patents, copyrights, and/or trademarks or related marks. The most likely areas of concern center around copyright and trademarks. There is already a legally recognized copyright protection accorded to Walt Disney Studios, Inc. for the creative cartoon characters known as Huey, Dewey, and Louie. They have long been very popular with children and adults alike and have been vigorously protected by the owners of the copyright. In addition, trademark law may come into play where the owner of a cartoon character has marketed cartoon-related products using the likeness of the three ducks in question.

Is a surname copyrightable or subject to trademark protection? Normally a surname, standing alone, with no creative work attached thereto or without any secondary distinctive meaning, may not be protected. Here both elements—creative work and secondary distinctive meaning—can be found in the names associated with the cartoon characters. Thus Walt Disney Studios, Inc. would have proper grounds for seeking protection for the continued exclusive use of these names as used for the cartoon characters in the public media and in trade.

Does it accord protection in all situations or can legitimate distinctions be made where there is no dilution of the rights and protections provided for under the statute? Consider *Mead Data Central, Inc. v. Toyota Motor Sales, U.S.A., Inc.,* 875 F.2d 1026 (2nd. Cir 1989). In addition, is it fair use to list one's own surname as a business entity that coincidentally sounds and looks the same as another person's protected intellectual property? The need for specialized professional counsel is readily apparent.

They may well be able to collect money damages for harm caused to the plaintiff's business and reputation. But, what they may really want is injunctive relief that would prevent the defendants from using these "ducky" names!

Chapter 9
FORMATION OF TRADITIONAL AND E-CONTRACTS

Do we have a deal?

I. Overview

A contract is an agreement between two or more parties, which provides not only for performance of duties called for under the agreement, but also for legal remedies in case of breach. Because of the possibility of having to ask a court of law for a remedy, think of a contract as a private arrangement on the surface. The difference between an agreement at the surface and a contract below the surface is the law's recognition that certain requirements, called elements, are in place. If these elements are not properly arrived at between private parties, the larger society, represented by its courts, will enter the fray and enforce the rights and duties called for under the contract.

The first objective of this chapter is to introduce students to the basic elements of contract and some of the terminology that they will be using throughout the remainder of the course. The elements of contract are analogous to the legs on a chair or table. They not only provide support but are also its essence, i.e., a table will not only fall if a leg is missing, it is not even really a table. An agreement with all four elements is elevated in the eyes of the law to the status of contract. Without these legs, the agreement fails legally and will not stand. Thus, even though all contracts are agreements, not all agreements are contracts. To be a contract the agreement must show:

1. Mutual assent.
2. Consideration.
3. Capacity.
4. Legality.

The second major objective of this chapter is to introduce students to key terms and phrases used in the study of contract law. One of the hallmarks of the hi-tech information explosion is techno-babble. Walk into a room of specialists from any given area of endeavor and you will hear them talking in code, using language which is often unintelligible to the layperson. Yet that specialized language provides the key to the body of knowledge. The study of law is no different than any other academic specialty in that sense. Lawyers have been referred to as "word merchants," and the profession's use of words of art has long predated the hi-tech world of today. In spite of the movement to use clearer and more straightforward language in legal documentation, the need to know some basic terms remains essential.

The key terms used here tend to be dichotomous, and you can use that dichotomy as a learning tool. Take for example, the number of parties to a contract. At least two parties are required in all contracts. One of those two parties has to initiate the contract formation process. The person starting the mutual assent process with a promise is the *offeror*, the other person is the *offeree*. Next, look at the dichotomy of the promises being used: is it a promise for a promise (*bilateral*), or is it a promise for an act (*unilateral*)? Have these promises been *expressly* made or can they somehow be *implied* from the circumstances? Does the form that this agreement is taking require certain *formalities* (such as a negotiable instrument), or can it be in any manner chosen by the parties (*informal*) as long as the elements of contract are met?

Once the parties have formed an agreement, are the performance obligations already fully met (*executed*), or are there still remaining performance obligations on the part of one or more of the parties (*executory*)? In addition, you may have to examine issues of enforceability. If all the elements are in place, the agreement is now considered a *valid contract*. If one or more of the essential elements is missing, the agreement is not raised to the status of contract and may be legally *void*. There are also certain situations where a contract is created, yet will not be enforced. If a legal defense is found to be in place, such as a writing requirement, the contract may be an *unenforceable contract*. Sometimes, certain persons are given a legally recognized power to avoid the contract after it has been entered into. These contracts are *voidable*, and examples of this sort of situation will be found in cases involving young people or in cases involving people with limited mental capacity.

One thing that is certain about the law of contracts however is that certain very specific questions must be addressed before the law of contracts can be applied to a potential agreement. It might be helpful if the student will answer the following questions when a contract issue arises:

1. Was there an offer, acceptance, consideration, legal capacity and legal subject matter?
2. If all of the elements are present, are there any defenses to the enforcement of the terms of the agreement?
3. Were there any third parties present who might have some legal interest in the contract?
4. Was the contract performed or were there any reasons to excuse performance?
5. If there was no excused non-performance what are the remedies?

Some of these questions will be addressed in this chapter and some in the chapters to follow.

II. Hypothetical Multi-issue Essay Question

John Smith was the owner of a professional football team who had just lost its fourth league championship game which could have propelled them into its first Super Bowl appearance. While preparing for the next season, John discovered that Tom Jordan, a tall and physical wide-receiver, was available through free agency. John offered Tom $45,000,000 to play for his team for the next two years. Tom, after being hit in the head and knocked unconscious during a practice said that that would work but he wanted to be able to renegotiate the deal at the end of the first season if he exceeded certain expectations. John agreed and a deal was signed. It became obvious halfway through the first season that Tom was playing very well and he went to John and said that he would not play the remainder of the season unless his salary was increased by 50%. John agreed. When the season ended, John refused to pay Tom the extra salary? Is John bound to either deal?

III. Outline

What Is a Contract?
   A contract is an agreement that is enforceable by a court of law or equity

Parties to a Contract
   Offeror—party making the offer
   Offeree—party to whom the offer is made

E-Commerce and E-Contracts
   - The sale and lease of goods, the sale of services, and the licensing of software over the internet

Classifications of Contracts
1. Bilateral- an exchange of promises between the parties
2. Unilateral- the offeror's offer can be accepted only by performance of an act by the offeree
3. Formal- a contract that requires a special form or method of creation
4. Informal- a contract that is not formal
5. Valid- An agreement between the parties; supported by legally sufficient consideration; between parties with contractual capacity; accomplishing a legal object
6. Void- a contract that has no legal effect

7. Voidable- a contract which one or both parties may avoid their contractual obligations
    Ratification – a minor, after reaching the age of majority, accepts a contract while created as a minor
8. Unenforceable- a contract in which the essential elements of a valid contract are present, but there is a legal defense to the enforcement
9. Executory- a contract that has not been fully performed by either or both sides
10. Executed- a contract that has been fully performed on both sides
11. Express- an agreement expressed in writing or oral words
12. Implied in fact- a contract in which agreement between the parties has been inferred by conduct
13. Quasi- (Implied in law) when a court awards money damages to a plaintiff for providing work or services to a defendant, even though no actual contract existed. The purpose is to prevent unjust enrichment and unjust detriment.

Requirements of a Contract
1. Agreement (Offer and Acceptance)
2. Consideration
3. Contractual capacity
4. Lawful object

Offer
- The manifestation of willingness to enter into a bargain, so as to justify another person in understanding that his assent to that bargain is invited and will conclude it.
- Elements
  o Objective intent
  o Definite or reasonably certain
  o Must be communicated
- Special offer: Auctions
  o With reserve- seller retains the right to refuse the highest bid and withdraw goods from sale, unless expressly stated otherwise
  o Without reserve- the seller must accept the highest bid
- Termination of an offer
  o Revocation of the offer
  o Rejection of the offer
  o A counteroffer
  o Operation of law
    ▪ Destruction of the subject matter
    ▪ Death or incompetency
    ▪ Supervening illegality
    ▪ Lapse of time

Acceptance
- A manifestation of assent by the offeree to the terms of the offer in a manner invited or required by the offer as measured by the objective theory of contracts
  o Mirror Image Rule- the offeree must accept the terms as stated in the offer
  o Mailbox Rule- acceptance is effective when it is dispatched, even if lost in transmission

Consideration
-something of legal value given in exchange for a promise
    - legal value- promise suffers a detriment, or promisor receives a benefit
    - bargained for exchange

- Gift promises- unenforceable due to a lack of consideration. They are also called gratuitous promises

Contracts that lack consideration
      Illegal consideration
      Illusory promise
      Moral obligation
      Pre-existing duty
      Past consideration

Capacity to Contract
      Those lacking capacity
- Minors
      o May disaffirm
      o Must pay for necessaries of life
- Insane persons
      o Adjudged insane (void)
      o Insane but not adjudged insane (voidable)
- Intoxicated persons

Exculpatory clause
- A contract provision that relieves one (or both) of the parties to a contract from tort liability for ordinary negligence (a release or waiver)

Unconscionable Contract
- A contract that courts refuse to enforce in part or whole because it is so oppressive or manifestly unfair as to be unjust
      o Elements
            ▪ Unequal bargaining power
            ▪ The dominant party unreasonably used its unequal bargaining power to obtain oppressive or unfair terms
            ▪ The adhering party had no reasonable alternative

Bilateral	vs	Unilateral
?		?
promise for promise		promise for act

Express	vs	Implied in Fact	vs	Implied in Law
?		?		?
outward expression		inferred from conduct		not a real contract
				?
				prevent unjust enrichment

Executed	vs	Executory
?		?
completed		not performed by both sides

Valid	vs	Void	vs	Voidable	vs	Unenforceable
?		?		?		?
all elements		no legal effect		at least one party has option to void		legal defense
?						?
enforceable						may be voluntarily performed

IV. Objective Questions

Terms:

1. A contract entered into by way of exchange of promises of the parties, a "promise for a promise," is called a _____.

2. A contract that has no legal effect because one of the essential elements of a contract is missing is called a _____ contract.

3. A contract where a party has the option to avoid his contractual obligations, and if a contract is avoided, both parties are released from their contractual obligations, is called a _____ contract.

4. A contract that has been fully performed on both sides, a completed contract, is called a _____.

5. An agreement that is expressed in written or oral words is defined as a _____.

6. A contract where agreement between parties has been inferred because of their conduct is a(n) _____.

7. Consideration which is already required of a person is invalid _____.

8. An _____ is a promise looking for a promise or an act.

9. The theory that says the intent to contract is judged by the reasonable person standard is known as the _____.

10. _____ is a doctrine that allows minors to disaffirm (cancel) most contracts they have entered into with adults.

True/False:

1. ____ When parties voluntarily enter into a contract, the terms of the contract become private law between the parties.

2. ____ Under a bilateral contract, there is no contract until the offeree performs the requested act.

3. ____ If an offeree in a unilateral contract has already partially completed performance, the offer cannot be revoked.

4. ____ Actual contracts are always express contracts, and never implied-in-fact contracts.

5. ____ An executory contract is one in which the contact has been performed on both sides.

6. ____ Parties to a contract may voluntarily perform a contract that is unenforceable.

7. ____ A quasi contract is a real contract.

8. ____ For an agreement to be formed, there must first be an offer and acceptance.

9. ____ Under contract law, the subjective intent of the parties is important.

10. ____ Gifts are examples of contracts.

Multiple Choice:

1. Joe is a house painter who offers to paint Jennifer's house for $2000 by May 1. Jennifer promises to pay Joe $2000 for the paint job if he completes it by May 1. This is an:

A. Bilateral contract.
B. Unilateral contract.
C. Voidable contract.
D. Executed contract.

2. On September 1, Max makes an offer to sell his car to Nelson. Nelson tells Max he "needs a few days." On September 5, Nelson tells Max he will buy the car. Which of the following is correct?

A. Max is an offeree.
B. A contract was formed on September 5.
C. A contract was formed on September 1.
D. Nelson may void the contract once it is formed since he accepted the offer and therefore may subsequently reject it.

3. Homeowner Helen tells Neighborhood Kid, "If you mow my lawn, I'll pay you $5." Which of the following is correct?

A. Helen and Kid have a bilateral contract.
B. Helen and Kid have a formal contract.
C. Helen and Kid have a unilateral contract.
D. Helen and Kid have a quasi-contract.

4. What is recognizance?

A. a sealed document that contains a formal contract whose contents are known to both parties and the referee who supervised its signing
B. a party's acknowledgement in court that he or she will pay a specified sum of money if another person does not pay it
C. a party's acknowledgement in court that he or she is not liable to pay any money if a certain event occurs
D. a sealed document that contains an informal contract whose contents are known only to the parties

5. A contract in which the essential elements to create a valid contract are met but there is some legal defense to the enforcement is called:

A. Void
B. Voidable
C. Unenforceable
D. Implied in fact

6. Contracts that have been fully performed by one side but not by the other are classified as _____ contracts.

A. void
B. voidable
C. executory
D. executed

7. Kyle goes to a used-car showroom to buy a sedan. He signs an agreement with the store which bears the name of the car, price, and other details. This is an example of a(n) _____ contract.

A. express
B. unilateral
C. implied-in-law
D. implied-in-fact

8. Hellen wants to order a cup of cafe lattè, but she cannot decide on a single or a double. She is thinking about a single, but holds two fingers up to the clerk when she orders without actually stating which strength she wants. The clerk prepares a double, and Hellen now refuses it, saying she only wanted a single. In deciding the terms of Hellen's order, a court will look at:

A. The objective intent of the offeree.
B. The subjective intent of the offeree.
C. The objective intent of the offeror.
D. The subjective intent of the offeror.

9. Which of the following is true for an auction with reserve?

A. The seller retains the right to refuse the highest bidder.
B. Invitations to make an offer are not allowed.
C. Goods cannot be withdrawn from sale after the offer has been made.
D. A bid once made cannot be withdrawn and is legally binding.

10. Which of the following elements has to be proved for a contract to be deemed unconscionable?

A. that the weaker party did not enter the contract under duress
B. that the parties had equal bargaining power
C. that the dominant party justly used its bargaining power
D. that the adhering party had no reasonable alternative

V. Answers to Objective Questions

Terms:

1. bilateral contract. Most contracts are bilateral rather than unilateral. [p. 184]

2. void contract. No contract is created in the first place. [p. 185]

3. voidable contract. A contract is created but may be avoided by one or both of the parties. [p. 186]

4. executed contract. Full performance discharges the parties from any further obligations. [p. 186]

5. express contract. Express terms are always the first step used in interpretation of a contract. [p. 186]

6. implied-in-fact contract. Often courts are asked to write in the terms based on the behavior of the parties. [p. 187]

7. past consideration. This is not a bargained-for-exchange. [p. 187]

8. offer. This is valid when definite and communicated. [p. 189]

9. objective theory of contracts. This theory is designed to give courts a measure by which to ascertain the intent of the parties. [p. 190]

10. Infancy doctrine. This right is based on public policy, which reasons that minors should be protected from the unscrupulous behavior of adults. [p. 196]

True/False:

1. True. But, that agreement is subject to court review. [p. 183]

2. False. A bilateral contract is formed upon the exchange of promises. No act of performance is necessary to create a bilateral contract. However, under a unilateral contract, no contract is formed until the offeree performs the requested act. [p. 184]

3. True. Equity calls for giving the offeree a fair opportunity to complete the act. [p. 185]

4. False. Actual contracts may be express contracts or implied-in-fact contracts. [p. 186]

5. False. An executed contract is one in which both sides have performed. [p. 186]

6. True. Courts look favorably upon such actions if they are based on good ethics and moral obligations. [p. 186]

7. False. It is implied to prevent unjust enrichment. [p. 188]

8. True. This is the first of the four elements of a contract. [p. 189]

9. False. Contract law is governed by the objective theory of contracts that states that the parties' objective intentions are controlling, not their subjective intentions. [p. 190]

10. False. There is no consideration. [p. 194]

Multiple Choice:

1. A This is a bilateral contract because both parties have engaged in making a promise in exchange for the other's promise. [p. 184]

2. B. A contract is formed when an offeree accepts the offeror's offer. When Nelson agreed to buy the car, there was an agreement. [p. 184]

3. C. Helen has made a promise that is contingent on Kid's performing the act of mowing her lawn. Because the contract does not involve a return promise from Kid, but rather his performance, this is a unilateral contract. [p. 184]

4. B. It is a form of formal contract. [p. 185]

5. C. An example of this would be a contract that would violate the Statute of Frauds. [p. 186]

6. C. A contract that has not been performed by both sides is called an executor contract. [p. 186]

7. A. An express contract is stated in oral or written words. [p. 186]

8. C. The objective intent of the offeror, as reasonably interpreted by the offeree, will prevail. A court will take into account the words, conduct, and surrounding circumstances involved. Hellen's silence, coupled with her two-finger signal show her objective intent to order a double strength cafe lattè. [p. 190]

9. A. Unless otherwise expressly stated, an auction is considered an auction with reserve—that is, it is an invitation to make an offer. [p. 191]

10. D. A contract found to be unconscionable under this doctrine is called an unconscionable contract. [p. 199]

VI. Answer to Essay Question

The analysis would probably have to consider the following:
1. Were the elements to a contract present?
    a. There was an offer by John and an acceptance by Tom but was the offer and acceptance reasonable to fulfill the objective theory of contracts? Even though the amount of the consideration was very large, the offer and acceptance were not done in jest and a reasonable person could think that a deal was intended. There was originally sufficient consideration: services for dollars . The increase in salary was not part of the bargained-for-consideration and is probably not enforceable. The other major problem was the mental capacity. Since the deal had been made after a head injury it could be argued that Tom was temporarily unable to understand what he was doing. This, however, was not confirmed through subsequent actions. There probably was a legitimate contract based on the original deal.
2. Were there any defenses to the enforcement of the contract? (to be answered next chapter)
3. Were any third-parties involved? No.
4. Was there an unexcused breach and, if so, what are the remedies? (to be answered next chapter)

Chapter 10

PERFORMANCE AND BREACH OF TRADITIONAL AND E-CONTRACTS

*Why can't I change the terms of my contract or
extend it without consequences?*

I. Overview

The first set of defenses to the enforcement of contracts in this chapter revolves around the issue of free will. Where free will is compromised, mutual assent is also compromised, and the agreement may not stand as a contract. What makes this area of the law difficult it that courts and juries are asked to exercise 20/20 hindsight when trying to determine what the parties were thinking when they were embarking on the road to contract formation. The subjectivity of measuring intent has always been a troublesome puzzle to unravel; yet without it, the objective facts placed before a court may not show the reality of consent. Because of the potential harshness of a bad contract, courts want to be sure that the assent element of a contract is just that--free and real consent to the agreement.

Factors that mitigate or diminish the genuineness of assent can be tracked on a scale of incremental culpability. At the bottom of the scale is an innocent mistake which can be either unilateral of bilateral. In a contract mistake, one or both of the parties is acting under an erroneous belief about some aspect of the contract. Normally, if only one (unilateral) of the parties is mistaken, there will be no grounds for rescission unless that mistake is coupled with some sort of bad faith or abuse on the part of the nonmistaken party, i.e., one step further up the culpability ladder. Where the mistake is mutual (bilateral), either party may seek rescission if the mistake is considered material, i.e., so important that no real meeting of the minds ever occurred.

The next increment up the slope of culpability is found in the area of misrepresentation or concealment. The shade of gray turns darker when a person is actively seeking to mark the cards or pass them under the table. Here we can see that freedom of assent is even further compromised than in mistake alone. Now the element of *scienter* (guilty mind) enters the picture, and the grounds for rescission are greatly increased. If the misrepresentation is material, known to be so by the maker, made with the intent to deceive, and is justifiably relied upon by an innocent and injured party, then the elements of fraud are in place. With a finding of fraud, the injured party may seek rescission and/or civil damages. In addition, the state may choose to prosecute the wrongdoer under the penal code. Contract fraud not only sits at the top of the culpability scale but can also be found at the top of the charts on the most popular white-collar criminal list. Its many permutations can be found in virtually all aspects of commercial activity, and as with so many areas of criminal behavior, the consumer pays the ultimate cost of these crimes through passed on costs for insurance, credit, and any number of other services undermined by these sorts of activities.

Another highly sensitive area of mutual assent is found in the law of undue influence. Undue influence involves taking away a person's free will through any manner of physical, emotional, or psychological manipulation. It can happen in any relationship, and where it is alleged, the person claiming to be the victim of undue influence has the burden of proof in showing the alleged duress. One important exception to this general rule involves persons who act in a fiduciary role. Fiduciary is a term derived from the Latin word *fides* meaning faith, honesty, confidence, or trust. A person in a fiduciary role is entrusted with acting for the benefit of another. Most professionals in law, accounting, the healing arts, and business find themselves bound by fiduciary rules to one degree or another. As for the fiduciary, the burden of proof is now reversed. In dealing with their respective clients, patients, or beneficiaries, a contract is presumed to be under undue influence, and the burden of proof is on the fiduciary to show that the transaction is at arm's length, i.e., fairly arrived at. Most all of the so-called "learned professions" have codes of conduct and canons of ethics designed to address issues of this sort.

The origins of the writing requirement for certain contracts are found in two roots: one historical and one practical. The historical root goes back to early English common law as developed under William the Conqueror and his successors. Status in that society was almost entirely measured by how much land one had control over. Being Lord of the Manor meant privilege, power, and rank. Thus contracts involving the transfer of land ownership were of utmost importance because of the bearing they had on social status. These important contracts were evidenced by highly ritualized written processes of titled transfers to land. The original title to the land was often traceable to a knight's *fief* or fee for services provided to the sovereign. From this phrase, the highest recognized ownership in land today is still called fee simple absolute.

The second root of the writing requirement is found on a more mundane level, having less to do with knights in shining armor and more with practicality. A writing is considered the best and most neutral evidence of the parties' intent at the time the agreement was entered into. The writing does not lose its memory; it does not take sides. Thus when English lawmakers wrote the Statute of Frauds, they decided the statute would serve them with the best of both worlds--impose a writing requirement on certain contracts to act as the best evidence in a court of law.

The English version of the Statute of Frauds has been carried over to our legal system virtually intact for over three hundred years. All U.S. states have adopted their own versions of the statute, and they are virtually uniform in that they require contracts involving interests in land, consideration of marriage, contracts that cannot be performed within one year, third party guarantees, and others to be in writing. The most significant addition to this list came with the adoption of the Uniform Commercial Code. Under the provisions of the UCC, contracts for the sale of goods for more than $500 need to be in writing. Thus, the first question which needs to be answered is: does the statute cover this contract or not?

Once you have decided the contract is covered, what are the effects of having failed to use a writing? Several possibilities may occur at this juncture. The parties may proceed to voluntarily perform the contract. But if one or both decide to assert the statute, its teeth are found in it being used as a defense to enforcement, i.e., if the party against whom contract enforcement is sought has not signed, it may not be enforced against him or her. There are equity-based exceptions to this general rule based on partial performance and promissory estoppel.

Once the contract is finally reduced to writing, the Parol Evidence Rule takes hold. The rule must be reviewed along with its exceptions. The exclusion face of the rule states that the writing is intended to express the final intent of the parties. All prior or contemporaneous statements must ultimately have been reflected in writing and will remain barred from the interpretation of the instrument. This provision is designed to prevent a fraudulent rewrite of the document after the fact with new evidence.

The converse is found in the exceptions to the parol evidence rule. The exceptions to the parol evidence rule are designed to let in additional information not shown on the original writing in certain limited circumstances. These special circumstances are grounded in public policy and simple practical necessity. Public policy provides an overriding basis in cases involving fraud, misrepresentation, deceit, bad faith, power to avoid based on age or mental capacity, duress, undue influence, and mistake. All these elements are considered in the best interest of public policy and will be allowed into evidence, notwithstanding the statute if the facts warrant it.

The second area of exception to the parol evidence rule involves the explanation of ambiguities. If the contract, as written, contains ambiguous language, parol evidence is allowable to clear the ambiguity as long as it is consistent with the original terms. The nature of the evidence allowable under this rule can range from oral statements made by the parties to entire standards of usage and trade used by a particular industry. This exception is particularly important to contracts covered by the UCC. An underlying theory is prevention of fraud. Fraud can be prevented by either keeping evidence in or out depending on the individual equities knocking at the contract door.

The other objective of this chapter is to examine the basic rules with regard to the discharge of contracts. The rules of performance and breach of contract are rooted in common sense. Most contracts are completed legally when the parties have lived up to their reciprocal obligations under that contract. Conversely, a breach is found when a failure of performance is not somehow excused by law. We are expected to live up to our performance obligations and no more. If those obligations are not met, breach of contract is the result.

The evaluation process of contract performance issues is best broken down into time sequence subparts: precontract, during the contract, and postcontract. In precontract issues, what are the covenants entered into before performance is to be initiated? Were there any conditions that may affect the rights and duties of the parties to contract? Conditions are certain events that have a triggering effect on the obligations of contract. The timing of conditions can be superimposed upon the contract. A precondition or condition precedent calls for the event to take place before the contract goes into effect. For example: "I will buy this car if my mechanic signs off on the engine inspection." A concurrent condition calls for two or more events to coincide in time. Consider an escrow where a third party is used as a holder of property and is instructed to act vis-à-vis that property only upon satisfaction of mutually dependent acts of third parties. This is a common form of property transfer used in the sale of real estate. The escrow holds the deed to the property from the seller until the buyer has delivered the purchase price in a form acceptable to both parties. A condition subsequent is found where performance may be excused by a certain event after the contract was entered into. For example, a parolee is allowed to stay out of prison as long as the conditions of the parole release are met.

There are certain circumstances that will act to excuse nonperformance. These circumstances are also based in common sense. Can it really be reasonable to expect personal service contracts to be enforced after death or disability? Or does it make sense to accept performance after destruction of a unique subject matter of the contract? For example, if you bid millions of dollars for a Van Gogh's "Irises" at an auction, and it was destroyed by lightning, is it reasonable to expect the seller to come up with an exact duplicate? A third form of excuse is found in subsequent illegality. If a contract was legal at the time it was formed, but subsequent events have made its enforcement illegal, courts will no longer enforce its performance covenants based on the new illegality.

In addition to excused nonperformance, there are a number of possible circumstances that may result in a discharge from any further contractual performance. These fall into two main categories: discharge by acts of the parties or by operation of law. Discharge by acts of the parties are voluntary postcontract formation events such as mutual rescission, reformation, accord and satisfaction, a substituted contract, or novation. In all these scenarios, the parties have, in effect, reentered the bargaining and created a new deal.

In an operation of law discharge, something has happened where the court steps in and declares this contract performance obligation can no longer be enforced. Examples of such legal impediments to enforcement would include the running of a statute of limitation or bankruptcy. In both cases, any further performance under the contract has been legally ended. If, however, the contract duty has not been discharged, excused, or performed, and the absolute duty to perform has been breached, one must examine what remedies are available to the nonbreaching party.

In this chapter we will complete the following steps necessary to analyze most contractual issues:

1. Have all the elements of the contract been established?(offer, acceptance, consideration, legal capacity and legal subject matter)
2. Are there any defenses to the enforcement of the agreement?
3. Are any third parties involved and what are their rights?
4. Are there any excuses for nonperformance?
5. If a breach has occurred what remedies are available?

II. Hypothetical Multi-Issue Essay Question

Mary Cheers is a pop singer who has been employed by the NFL franchise in Podunk to sing the national anthem at the football stadium before the weekly games for the next ten years. The contract is in writing with the terms mentioned above included. She is to be paid 1% of the ticket revenue for each game. This is also in the written agreement.

Mary arrives at the stadium fifteen minutes before the scheduled starting time for the first game only to find that there are no fans. She tries to call the team officials but they are unavailable. Not knowing what to do, she goes onto the field and sings the Canadian National Anthem. She submits a bill to the team who refuses to pay her. Instead the team sues her for the extra money it cost them to get a replacement for her. It seems that the game went on but at a different stadium. Mary had not known that there were two football stadiums in Podunk. Mary then sues the team for her fee.

What are the legal issues involved in the above set of facts? What are the possible results?

III. Outline

Genuineness of Assent
Mistakes with possible rescission (undoing of the contract)
    Unilateral mistakes—one party is mistaken-rescission possible
    Mutual mistakes—both parties are mistaken-rescission often possible
        Mutual mistakes of a past or existing material fact—rescindable
        Mutual mistake of value—nonrescindable
    Duress
    Undue influence

Misrepresentation
    An assertion that is made that is not in accord with the facts
        Intentional misrepresentation—fraud
        Innocent misrepresentation

Elements of Fraud
    The wrongdoer made a false representation of material fact
    The wrongdoer intended to deceive the innocent party
    The innocent party justifiably relied on the misrepresentation
    The innocent party was injured

Duress
    Occurs where one party threatens to do a wrongful act unless the other party enters into a contract—not enforceable against innocent party
    Economic duress—often changes obligation if no way out

Undue Influence
    A fiduciary or confidential relationship must have existed between the parties
    The dominant party must have unduly used his or her influence to persuade the servient party to enter into a contract
    Voidable by the innocent party

Statute of Frauds

> State statute that requires certain types of contracts to be in writing and signed by the party to be charged to be enforceable
>
> Typical Contracts Generally Required to Be in Writing (more explanation below):
>> Contracts involving interests in land /real property (unless "partly performed")
>> Real estate agents' contracts (equal dignity rule)
>> Contracts that by their own terms cannot possibly be performed within one year
>> Guaranty contracts where a person promises to answer for the debt or duty of another
>
> Contracts for the sale of goods for more than $500

> Further Explanation:
>> Contracts Involving Interests in Land
>> Real property
>>> The land itself as well as buildings, trees, soil, minerals, timber, plants, crops, and other things permanently affixed to the land
>> Fixtures
>>> Personal property that is permanently affixed to the real property, such as built-in cabinets in a house, and becomes part of the real property
>> Transfer of Other Interests in Real Property
>>> Mortgages—interest in real property as security for a loan
>>> Leases—rental
>>> Easements—right to use another's land

One Year Rule

> An executory contract that cannot be performed by its own terms within one year of its formation must be in writing. May not need a writing if there is a possibility of performance.

Guaranty Contracts

> Any secondary contract must be in writing. This does not include primary contracts.

Formality of the Writing

> Formality—contains essential terms of agreement
>
> Required signature of party to be changed
>
> Includes letters, telegrams, invoices, sales receipts, checks, and handwritten agreements on scraps of paper

Parol Evidence Rule

> Parol evidence is any oral or written words outside the four corners of the written contract
>
> If a written contract is a complete and final statement of the parties' agreement, any prior or contemporaneous oral or written statements that alter, contradict, or are in addition to the terms of the written contract are inadmissible in court regarding a dispute over the contract.

Third-party Rights

> Assignment- transfer of contractual rights by an oblige to another party
>> Assignor- an oblige who transfers a right
>> Assignee- a party to whom the right is transferred
>
> Intended beneficiary- a third party who is not in privity of contract, but who has rights under the contract and can enforce the contract against the obligor

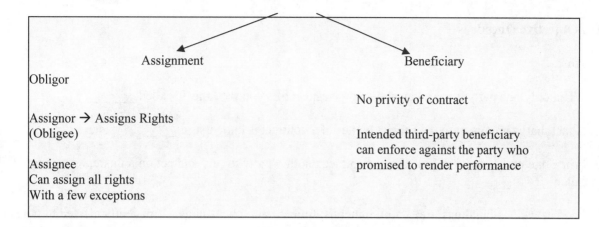

Promises of Performance
   Covenant
      A covenant is an unconditional promise to perform. Nonperformance is a breach.

   Conditions
      A conditional promise only becomes a covenant if the condition is or is not met
            Condition Precedent – no duty until event has occurred
            Condition Subsequent – duty to perform is excused by event occurrence

Discharge of Performance (excuses for nonperformance)
   By agreement
      Mutual rescission—both agree to a new deal
      Novation—agreed substitution of parties
      Accord and satisfaction—compromise by different performance
      Force majeure
      Impossibility of performance—cannot be done

Breach of Contract
   Three types of performance
   1. Complete (Strict)- a party renders performance exactly as required by contract
   2. Substantial Performance (Minor breach)- performance deviates only slightly from complete performance
   3. Inferior Performance (Material breach)- party renders inferior performance of his contractual duties

Money Damages
   Compensatory damages- the loss of the bargain
   Consequential damages- foreseeable damages
   Liquidated damages- the parties agree to the penalty in advance
   Mitigation of Damages- the non-breaching party must avoid or reduce damages caused by the breach, if possible

Equitable Remedies
   Specific performance- orders the breaching party to perform an act
   Reformation- the court may rewrite the contract to express the parties' true intentions
   Injunction- a court order prohibiting a person from doing a certain act

IV. Objective Questions

Terms:

1. When only one party is mistaken about some aspect of a contract, this is called _____.

2. A fact that is important to the subject matter of a contract is known as a _____ fact.

3. When one party consciously decides to induce another party to rely and act on a misrepresentation, this is called _____.

4. Land as well as buildings, trees, soil, minerals, timber, and other things permanently affixed to the land are called _____ property.

5. Contracts for the sale of land must be in writing because of the _____.

6. A rule that says that if a written contract is a complete and final statement of the parties' agreement, any prior or contemporaneous oral or written statements that alter, contradict, or are in addition to the terms of the written contract are inadmissible in court regarding a dispute over the contract is called the _____ rule.

7. The clause in a contract that stipulates that it is a complete integration and the exclusive expression of the agreement and that parol evidence may not be introduced to explain, alter, contradict, or add to the terms of the contract is called a _____ clause.

8. An agreement that substitutes a third party for one of the original contracting parties and makes the new party obligated to perform the contract is called a(n) _____.

9. A _____ is an unexcused nonperformance of a contract.

10. The best excuse for nonperformance of a singing contract where the singer has lost his voice is _____.

True/False:

1. _____ Either party may rescind the contract if there is a mutual mistake in value.

2. _____ Where a party has been fraudulently induced to enter a contract, the innocent party can either rescind the contract or enforce the contract and sue for damages.

3. _____ To be actionable, a fraudulent misrepresentation must be in spoken or written words.

4. _____ A misrepresentation is considered fraud even if it is made without intent to deceive another party.

5. _____ Built-in cabinets in a house are fixtures that become part of the real property.

6. _____ The primary contract is also known as the "guaranty contract" when a person agrees to answer for the debt of another.

7. _____ The Statute of Frauds requires a written contract be signed by the party against whom enforcement is sought.

8. ____ The assignor is the obligee who transfers a right.

9. ____ A condition that requires the occurrence of an event after a party is obligated to perform a duty under a contract is known as a condition precedent.

10. ____ If a professional basketball player refuses to honor his contract and play basketball, the team may avail itself of the remedy of specific performance.

Multiple Choice:

1. On June 1, Farmer Brown contracted to sell a red barn to Rancher Ron. However, unknown to either party, the barn had burned down on May 20. If Ron sues Brown for breach of contract, Brown's best defense is:

A. Fraud.
B. Economic duress.
C. Mutual mistake of fact.
D. Misrepresentation.

2. Ted enticed Fred to enter into a sales contract by intentionally telling Fred certain material facts that Ted knew were untrue. Assume no other relevant facts. On what legal basis can the contract be voided?

A. Voidable because of undue influence, which created no real assent.
B. Voidable because of fraud, where no real assent took place.
C. Voidable because of duress, which prevented real assent.
D. Voidable because of mistake, which did not allow real assent to take place.

3. Ed, an auditor for the IRS, became emotionally involved with Rhonda. At the urging of Rhonda, and fearing that she would sever their relationship, Ed reluctantly waived a tax audit settlement that was grossly unfair to the IRS, Ed's employer's best chance for rescinding this outcome is to show that Ed acted under:

A. A lack of express authority.
B. Duress.
C. Undue influence.
D. There was no consideration.

4. Ann makes a written contract with Betty to sell her car for $5,000. Two days later, Betty asks if Ann will throw in the bike rack with the car. Ann agrees. Which of the following is correct?

A. The sale of the bike rack is enforceable if the contract has a merger clause.
B. The sale of the bike rack is enforceable if the contract is a form contract.
C. The sale of the bike rack is unenforceable under the parol evidence rule.
D. The sale of the bike rack is unenforceable under the equal dignity rule.

5. A written agreement was signed by both parties that was intended to be their entire agreement. The parol evidence rule will prevent the admission of evidence that is offered to:

A. Explain the meaning of an ambiguity in the written contract.
B. Establish that fraud had been committed in the formation of the contract.
C. Prove the existence of a contemporaneous oral agreement that modifies the contract.
D. Prove the existence of a subsequent oral agreement that modifies the contract.

6. A party to whom a right is transferred is called a(n):

A. assignee
B. assignor
C. obligee
D. third-party beneficiary

7. A(n) _____ is an unconditional promise to perform.

A. Condition
B. Covenant
C. Novation
D. Accord and satisfaction

8. Which of the following statements is true of a breach of contract?

A. Strict performance by a party discharges that party's duties under the contract.
B. Inferior performance constitutes a minor breach of contract.
C. Substantial performance constitutes a material breach.
D. The most common remedy for a breach of contract is an award of equitable remedies.

9. _____ is a clause in a contract in which the parties specify certain events that will excuse nonperformance.

A. Approval clause
B. Express condition
C. *Force Majeure*
D. Implied-in-fact condition

10. An award of _____ orders the breaching party to perform the acts promised in a contract.

A. reformation
B. injunction
C. restitution
D. specific performance

V. Answers to Objective Questions

Terms:

1. unilateral mistake. Rescission is allowed only under limited circumstances where the unilateral mistake is tied in with other parties' actual or constructive knowledge of the mistake, where there are clerical or mathematical errors, or where enforcement would lead to an unconscionable result. [p. 207]

2. material. Look at the essential purpose of the contract when trying to identify material facts, i.e., but for this element, would the parties be in this contract at all? [p. 207]

3. fraud. The elements of fraud are intentional false misrepresentation by the wrongdoers coupled with justifiable reliance by the injured innocent party. [p. 208]

4. real property. This classification is based on traditional case law combined with statutory definitions. These issues will be further detailed in the chapters on real and personal property. [p. 211]

5. statute of frauds. This requires that certain contracts, land deals included, must be in writing to be enforceable. [p. 211]

6. parol evidence (rule). The parol evidence rule keeps evidence out unless the evidence qualifies under one of its exceptions based on public policies or clarification of ambiguities. [p. 213]

7. merger. In spite of the wide-spread use of these clauses, they cannot be used to keep out public policy exceptions to the parol evidence rule. [p. 213]

8. novation. This term is derived from the Latin term meaning "new." [p. 217]

9. breach. This gives rise to various remedies. [p. 218]

10. impossibility of performance. The performance is impossible. [p. 218]

True/False:

1. False. Generally, the contract remains enforceable by either party because the identity of the subject matter of the contract is not at issue. [p. 208]

2. True. The innocent party in such a situation has an option of doing either of these things. [p. 208]

3. False. A misrepresentation may occur by the party's conduct. [p. 208]

4. False. To prove fraud, the wrongdoer must have intended to deceive the innocent party. [p. 208]

5. True. Things permanently affixed to real property become part of the real property. [p. 211]

6. False. The second contract is called the guaranty contract. [p. 212]

7. True. The signature of the person who is enforcing the contract is not necessary. [p. 213]

8. True. An obligee who transfers the right to receive performance is called an assignor. [p. 215]

9. False. It requires the occurrence of an event before a party is obligated to perform. [p. 217]

10. False. Specific performance is not available in service contracts. [p. 221]

Multiple Choice:

1. C. Both parties were unaware of a material fact. [p. 207]

2. B. Ted made a false misrepresentation of a material fact with an intent to deceive. Fred detrimentally relied on this representation. Therefore, the elements of fraud are in place. [p. 208]

3. C. Here, the emotional involvement was so overwhelming that the decision was not voluntary and was the product of undue influence. [p. 210]

4. C. The written contract for the sale of the car is the final statement of the parties' agreement. Verbal testimony will not be allowed to alter such a contract except in special circumstances. [p. 213]

5. C. If the contract was intended to be their entire agreement, the rule will not allow evidence to show a contemporaneous oral agreement that modifies the contract. [p. 213]

6. A. The assignee can transfer the right to yet another, unless prohibited by the contract. [p. 215]

7. B. The majority of provisions in contracts are covenants. [p. 216]

8. A. Most contracts are discharged by the complete performance, or strict performance, of the contracting parties. [p. 218]

9. C. A *force majeure* clause usually excuses nonperformance caused by natural disasters such as floods, tornadoes, earthquakes, and such. [p. 218]

10. D. The courts have the discretion to award this remedy if the subject matter of the contract is unique. [p. 221]

VI. Answer to the Essay Question

All of the elements of the contract were present. Additionally since the contract could not be completed within one year it had to be in writing and it was. The problem, however, was that the terms were ambiguous with respect to which stadium and to which anthem was to be sung. The Parol Evidence Rule allows for the introduction of extraneous evidence to clarify an ambiguity. Thus, Mary would be allowed to show that there were ambiguities in the written contract.

Since Mary did not know that there were two stadiums but the team did, she probably would win in a suit with respect to not having appeared at the correct stadium. However, with respect to the anthem, since the game was in the United States, the American National Anthem can be implied. Since she did not go the right stadium and therefore did not perform but through no fault of her own, she probably will not lose the case for compensatory damages. She probably will not be able to collect the fee, however, for the first day since she did not perform but she probably will be able to enforce the remainder of the contract with the corrected terms.

Chapter 11

E-COMMERCE AND DIGITAL LAW

What has the computer done to the law?

I. Overview

The key features of this chapter seek to introduce the student to the basic history of e-commerce and the Internet. The first key objective of this chapter is to describe the most current efforts to tailor the laws of contract, intellectual property, and free speech protections to the realities of cyberspace. The Internet was established in 1969 as a method by which electronic communications were to be used for military and strategic national defense purposes. This basic structure of multiple computers being able to "talk" to each other ended up having many uses beyond its original military origins. Starting in the early 1980's, under the auspices of the National Science Foundation, the Internet was established to facilitate high-speed communications among research and academic centers on a global scale. The efficiencies realized by those centers were not lost on business, and by the late 1990's, the Internet ushered in the Information Age as we know it today.

Among many early legal issues that arose from the widespread use of the Internet were the constitutional interpretations of free speech. An early landmark case on this issue is found in *Reno v. American Civil Liberties Union* (1997) where the U.S. Supreme Court struck down two early attempts to limit or prohibit certain types of speech transmitted over the Internet. The court held that communications transmitted over the Internet were entitled to the same protections as ordinary commercial speech so long as it was not classified as "invasive" in the same sense as radio or television. In addition, the court was concerned about the lack of precision in the statute that sought to limit "indecent" and "patently offensive" communications on the Internet. This decision clearly sent an early signal to users of the Internet that it is a medium of communication in which basic free speech rights will be protected.

With the advent of e-commerce over the Internet, the second key objective of this chapter illustrates how policy makers at all levels of government and industry are seeking to evolve the law to foster and protect commerce while not intruding on basic privacy rights. The Federal Electronic Communications Privacy Act is one such example. That statute makes it a crime to engage in unauthorized interceptions of electronic communications. Other examples of policy-making laws include the intellectual property world of domain names and the Federal Anticybersquatting Consumer Protection Act, which seeks to protect commerce from wrongful or bad faith intrusions of company or individuals' names. These names have enormous value. Such mechanisms such as the Uniform Dispute Resolution Policy established by the Internet Corporation for Assigned Names and Numbers are designed to expedite disputes over domain names. In addition, a number of states are proposing the Uniform Electronic Transactions Act and the Computer Information Transactions Act as models to be used to set up structures for licensing agreements for Internet-based intellectual property and Internet commercial transactions.

What is most interesting about these acts is the fact that they are very heavily patterned after long-existing provisions of the Uniform Commercial Code. Since the early 1950's the U.C.C. has provided the basic model for conducting commerce in this country. It has been adopted, at least in part, by every state in the union. It has been kept up to date by a group known as the National Conference of commissioners on Uniform State Laws. This group is made up of academics, jurists, law and business practitioners and economists. They formulate model laws that are, in turn, proposed to the individual states. Each state may adopt its own particular version of the law, but in the vast majority of cases, the uniform laws are enacted intact. The goal of this process is to create a uniform set of interconnected and common legislation which becomes part of well-functioning and predictable state laws on commerce. It is too early to tell how well these new uniform laws on e-commerce will be received by the respective states. It does seem certain, however, that such laws will be quite necessary to foster and protect the ever-growing scales of commerce now being conducted over the Internet.

Some of the key issues covered in these proposed laws include the electronic formation of contracts, licensing rights and duties, and remedies for breach of electronic commerce contracts. All in all, it is a work in progress that makes this the most exciting time ever to be a student of business law.

II. Hypothetical Multi-Issue Essay Question

Everybody's on Line (Everybody's) provides free e-mail on the World Wide Web. It generates income from pop up ads, paid for by web site advertisers. Currently, there are over five million contracted subscribers to Everybody's service. One of the services provided by Everybody's allows its subscribers to send messages to any other e-mail address in the world.

Spam is defined as unsolicited bulk e-mail. Everybody's is concerned that its subscribers do not use Everbody's facilities and services to spam other e-mail users. Under its "Terms of Service" subscription contract, Everybody's specifically states that subscribers agree not to send spam. Failure to abide by this contract will result in termination of the contract and free e-mail services by Everybody's.

Joe is a subscriber to Everybody's services. He was notified of the "Terms of Service" by way of "shrink-wrap" conditions on the face of his contract and by way of his "point-and-click" consent to those terms every time he logged on to Everybody's web site. Joe likes to think of himself as a free thinker and decided that the whole world should get to see the "real Joe." Joe sent countless nude photos of himself to millions of viewers on web. These photos had no redeeming artistic value and would be classified as pornography. He used Everybody's e-mail return address.

Everybody's is quite upset and comes to you to review its options. What constitutional, intellectual property and contract issues should be taken into account? What remedies does Everybody's have?

III. Outline

Introduction to Cyber Law and E-Commerce
> E-commerce
>> The sale of goods and services by computer over the Internet
> Internet
>> A collection of millions of computers that provide a network of electronic connections between computers

World Wide Web
> An electronic connection of millions of computers that support a standard set of rules for the exchange of information.

Electronic Mail
> Electronic written communication between individuals and businesses using computers connected to the Internet

Internet Service Provider (ISP)
- Companies that provide access to internet communications
- Communications Decency Act of 1996 provides that "No provider or user of an interactive computer service shall be treated as the publisher or speak any of the information provided by another information content provider

Domain Name
> A unique name that identifies an individual's or company's web site
> Domain names can be registered at various sites.
> Anticybersquatting Act specifically aimed at cybersquatters who register Internet domain names of famous companies and people and hold them hostage. The law prohibits cybersquatting if done in bad faith.

E-Contracts (Web-contracts)
> -Contracts entered into over the World Wide Web and by email.
> -E-sign:
>> - Electronic contracts meet the writing requirements of the Statute of Frauds.
>> - Electronic signatures are acceptable.
>> - Electronic Signature in Global and National Commerce Act (E-Sign)

E-Licenses
> Uniform Computer Information Transactions Act (UCITA) is a model state law that creates contract law for the licensing of information technology rights
> Licenses are contracts that transfer limited rights in intellectual property and informational rights as described in the license.
> Licensor
>> The owner of intellectual property or informational rights who transfers rights in the property or information to the licensee.
> Licensee
>> The party who is given limited rights in or access to intellectual property or informational rights owned by the licensor.

Licensing Agreement - a detailed and comprehensive written agreement between a licensor and a licensee that sets forth the express terms of their agreement
> Breach of License → failure to perform a duty as required in the agreement
>> Rights of nonbreaching party:
>>> Refusal of defective tender
>>> Accept the tender
>>> Accept reasonable units and reject the rest
>> Remedies under UCITA:
>>> Cancellation by aggrieved party
>>> Licensor's damages
>>> Licensee's damages
>>> Limitation of remedies

IV. Objective Questions

Terms:

1. _____ is an electronic written communication between individuals using computers connected to the Internet.

2. _____ are companies that provide consumers and businesses with access to the Internet.

3. _____ is a federal statute which provides that Internet service providers (ISPs) are not liable for the content transmitted over their networks by e-mail users and websites.

4. A contract that transfers limited rights in intellectual property and informational rights is called a _____.

5. A detailed and comprehensive written agreement between a licensor and a licensee that sets forth the express terms of their agreement is called a _____.

6. The _____ makes it a crime to intercept an electronic communication at the point of transmission, while in transit, when stored by a router or on a server, or after receipt by the intended recipient.

7. A _____ is a unique name that identifies an individual's or company's website.

8. Sometimes a party will register a domain name of another party's trademarked name or famous person's name. This is called _____.

9. _____ is a federal statute that permits trademark owners and famous persons to recover domain names that use their names where the domain name has been registered by another person or business in bad faith.

10. The ACPA prohibits the act of cybersquatting itself if it is done in _____.

True/False:

1. _____ E-mail contracts need not meet the Statute of Frauds requirements as long as they meet UCITA guidelines.

2. _____ ISPs are not liable for the content transmitted over their networks by e-mail users and websites.

3. _____ Electronic signatures have been held to satisfy the Statute of Fraud's writing requirements in a number of states.

4. _____ Counteroffers are not effective against electronic agents.

5. _____ Voice mail and web page order systems are not electronic agents.

6. _____ Data and software do not constitute intellectual property or information rights.

7. _____ A licensee is a party who is granted limited rights in intellectual property or informational rights owned by another person or company.

8. _____ The Electronic Communications Privacy Act makes it a crime to intercept electronic communications except in cases of law enforcement or permission by the party providing the electronic communication service.

9. _____ A network extension is a unique name that identifies an individual's or company's website.

10. _____ The Internet Corporation for Assigned Names and Numbers is a private court that can adjudicate disputes over domain names with jury trials.

Multiple Choice:

1. Which of the following is true of e-commerce?

A. Lessors cannot use web addresses to lease goods.
B. Intellectual property cannot be explicitly listed for sale on a website.
C. A web-contract is not binding, as opposed to an e-mail contract.
D. Services can be listed for sale on websites.

2. Which federal law regulates the sending of falsified e-mail headers and non-solicited pornography?

A. CAN-SPAM Act
B. Communications Decency Act
C. Electronic Communications Privacy Act
D. Anti-Cybersquatting Consumer Protection Act

3. Which of the following statements is true of e-mail contracts?

A. All e-mail contracts require consideration, capacity and lawful object.
B. E-mail contracts are exempted from the requirements of the Statute of Frauds.
C. E-mail contracts are enforceable even if they don't meet the requirements of a traditional contract.
D. Several e-mails cannot be integrated to determine the parties' agreement.

4. What does the Communications Decency Act of 1996 provide?

A. Businesses can send spam e-mails, as long as they don't lie.
B. ISPs are not liable for the content transmitted over their networks by e-mail users and websites.
C. Businesses are liable for invading the right to privacy if they send unsolicited e-mails.
D. The number of servers an ISP can access in a geographical location is limited.

5. Which law provides that "No provider or user of an interactive computer service shall be treated as the publisher or speaker of any information provided by another content provider?"

A. CAN-SPAM Act
B. Communications Decency Act
C. Electronic Communications Privacy Act
D. Anti-Cybersquatting Consumer Protection Act

6. The _____ recognizes electronic contracts as meeting the writing requirement of the Statute of Frauds for most contracts.

A. Uniform Commercial Code
B. Uniform Computer Information Transactions Act
C. E-SIGN Act
D. Communications Decency Act

7. Which of the following is an example of an e-signature?

A. using a credit card at the supermarket to pay for groceries
B. using a debit card to fill gas as the local gas station
C. ordering Chinese food over the phone and paying with a credit card
D. paying the electric bill online using a smart card

8. The owner of intellectual property rights, that subsequently transfers those rights, is known as a(n):

A. Agent
B. ISP
C. Licensor
D. Licensee

9. An agreement to transfer limited rights to parties for specified purposes and limited duration as defined in Sec. 102(a)(40) of the U.C.I.T.A. is called a:

A. Copyright.
B. Patent.
C. Trademark.
D. License.

10. _____ is the most widely used domain extension in the world.

A. .net
B. .com
C. .biz
D. .org

V. Answers to Objective Questions

Terms:

1. Electronic mail. Using e-mail, individuals around the world can instantaneously communicate in electronic writing with one another. [p. 229]

2. Internet service providers. ISPs provide e-mail accounts to users, Internet access, and storage on the Internet. [p. 231]

3. Communications Decency Act. A provision in the federal Communications Decency Act of 1996 provides: "No provider or user of an interactive computer service shall be treated as the publisher or speaker of any information provided by another information content provider." [p. 231]

4. license. The agreement that is used to transfer limited rights is called a license. [p. 234]

5. licensing agreement. A licensor and a licensee usually enter into a written licensing agreement that expressly states the terms of their agreement. [p. 235]

6. Electronic Communications Privacy Act. The ECPA makes it illegal to access stored e-mail as well as e-mail in transmission. [p. 235]

7. domain name. Most businesses conduct e-commerce by using websites on the Internet. Each website is identified by a unique Internet domain name. [p. 236]

8. cybersquatting. Often the domain name owner will have registered the domain name in order to obtain payment for the name from the trademark holder or the famous person whose name has been registered as a domain name. [p. 238)]

9. Anticybersquatting Consumer Protection Act. The act was specifically aimed at cybersquatters who register Internet domain names of famous companies and people and hold them hostage by demanding ransom payments from the famous company or person. [p. 238]

10. bad faith. The act has two fundamental requirements: (1) The name must be famous and (2) the domain name must have been registered in bad faith. [p. 238]

True/False:

1. False. E-mail contracts usually meet the requirements of the Statute of Frauds, which requires certain contracts to be in writing, such as contracts for the sale of real estate, contracts for the sale of goods that cost $500 or more, and other contracts listed in the relevant Statute of Frauds. [p. 229]

2. True. Internet service providers (ISPs) are companies that provide consumers and businesses with access to the Internet. [p. 230]

5. True. While not yet uniformly decided upon, a number of state courts have upheld electronic signatures as sufficient to satisfy the writing requirements of the Statute of Frauds. [p. 232]

3. True. Most webpages use electronic ordering systems that do not have the ability to evaluate and accept counteroffers or to make counteroffers. [p. 233]

9. False. An electronic agent is any telephonic or computer system that has been established by a seller to accept orders. [p. 233]

4. False. Patents, trademarks, copyrights, trade secrets, data, software programs, and such constitute valuable intellectual property and information rights. [p. 234]

7. True. A licensee is a party who is granted limited rights in or access to intellectual property or informational rights owned by a licensor. [p. 234]

6. True. The Electronic Communications Privacy Act generally makes interceptions of electronic communications illegal except with consent of the owner or for law enforcement purposes. [p. 236]

10. True. A domain name is a unique name that identifies an individual's or company's website. [p. 236]

8. False. The Internet Corporation for assigned Names and Numbers is a corporation under contract with the U.S. government and is responsible for regulating the issuance of domain names in the Internet. It is not a court. [p. 237]

Multiple Choice:

1. D. Electronic commerce is the sale of goods and services by computer over the Internet. [p. 228]

2. A. The Federal Trade Commission (FTC), a federal administrative agency, is empowered to enforce the CAN- SPAM Act. [p. 229]

3. A. E-mail contracts are enforceable as long as they meet the requirements necessary to form a traditional contract. [p. 229]

4. B. Communications Decency Act is a federal statute which provides that Internet service providers (ISPs) are not liable for the content transmitted over their networks by e-mail users and websites. [p. 231]

5. B. Communications Decency Act is a federal statute which provides that Internet service providers (ISPs) are not liable for the content transmitted over their networks by e-mail users and websites. [p. 231]

6. C. One of the main features of the E-SIGN Act is that it recognizes electronic contracts as meeting the writing requirement of the Statute of Frauds for most contracts. [p. 232]

7. D. A digital signature is some electronic method that identifies an individual. [p. 233]

8. C. The licensor is the party who owns the intellectual property or information rights and obligates him- or herself to transfer rights in the property or information to the licensee. [p. 234]

9. D. License. This is a contract that authorizes limited access to and use of informational rights. [p. 234]

10. B. This extension represents the word commercial and is the most widely used extension in the world. [p. 237]

VI. Answer to Essay Question

This case raises numerous possible legal issues and is based, in part, on a famous 1998 case entitled *Hotmail Corp. v. Van$ Money Pie, Inc*. In that case, the defendants were found to be in violation of their subscription contract terms with Hotmail Corp. Specifically, they had engaged in the transmission of pornography spam. Defendants abused Hotmail's "Terms of Service." The U.S. Supreme Court has long held that pornography is not protected speech, and even if it were held to be Joe's copyrighted property, it could not be used in this manner.

Because of the harm done to the plaintiff's reputation, goodwill, and commercial computer facilities by Joe's practices, the court will most likely follow the precedent set in the Hotmail case and issue an injunction against Joe. His actions are in breach of his contract with Everybody's and his speech will not be protected in this case.

Chapter 12

UCC SALES AND LEASE CONTRACTS AND WARRANTIES

Why are "goods" contracts different?

I. Overview

Let us begin this chapter with the word "ditto." Specifically all of the rules we have discussed for traditional contracts in the prior chapters apply to contracts for the sale of goods EXCEPT… It is with these exceptions that this chapter is involved.

Goods are the backbone of business. We buy. We sell. We trade. Often we involve services but without goods, society would probably not survive. And these goods have been traded since the time of the cavemen. This trading activity has necessitated various conventions between the traders and these conventions allow business to flow with minimum interruption. Disputes, however, arose that could not be answered by the common law. Thus was born Article 2 (and 2A) of the Uniform Commercial Code. Its main purpose was to help solve the disputes without disrupting normal business operations. Thus many typical business practices became law.

There are, therefore, some major questions that must be answered when dealing with the sale of goods and leases. This chapter attempts, among other things, to answer the following:

1) What is a good and when does the U.C.C. apply?
2) What are the differences between the common law of contracts and the U.C.C.?
3) Are there any special rules for performance and remedies in a U.C.C contract?
4) What happens if the product is "bad", cause's injury, or is damaged during delivery?

Remember all the rules we studied earlier apply to contracts for the sale of goods EXCEPT…

II. Hypothetical Multi-Issue Essay Question

Mark Smith, Inc. ordered 1,000 individual navy blue kitchen barstools from Barstool, Inc. to be used in typical kitchen bars in homes. The stools were to be delivered on May 1, 2004. No terms were stated as to the delivery so Barstool shipped them by public carrier. On their way to Smith's warehouse, the truck hit a pothole and 200 of the stools were damaged to the point of not being usable. Additionally, when the carrier arrived on May 11, 2004, it was noted that 100 of the stools were light blue instead of navy. Barstool thought that Smith would just accept them. After Smith refused delivery of the above 300 stools, they took acceptance of the remaining 700. What Smith failed to notice before they sold the stools was that the rotating seats were not bolted to the legs of the stool. Five of these stools were sold to Mary Jones who used the stools and was severely injured when the seats fell off the legs. Who is responsible for the problems stemming from each of the groups of stools mentioned?

III. Outline

Introduction to Sales, Leases and Warranties
> UCC Article 2- Sales
> UCC Article 2A- Leases

Uniform Commercial Code (UCC)
- A model act that includes comprehensive laws that cover most aspects of commercial transactions.

Article 2- Sales
> Sale- the passing of title for goods from a seller to a buyer for a price
> Goods- tangible things that are movable at the time of their identification in a contract
> Mixed sale- a sale that involves the provision of a service and a good in the same transaction

Article 2A (Leases)
> Lease- a transfer of the right to the possession and use of named goods for a set term in return for certain consideration
> Lessor- a person who transfers the right of possession and use of goods under a lease
> Lessee- a person who acquires the right to possession and use of goods under a lease

Formation of Sales and Lease Contracts
- Need an offer and acceptance
- Contract may be made in any manner sufficient to show agreement
> Open terms
>> Gap filling rule- certain open terms are permitted to be "read into" a sales or lease contract
>>> Open price term- UCC 2-305(1)
>>> Open payment term- UCC 2-310
>>> Open delivery term- UCC 2-308
>>> Open time term- UCC 2-309
>>> Open assortment term- UCC 2-311(2)

Firm Offer Rule
- A merchant who (1) offers to buy, sell, or lease goods and (2) gives a written and signed assurance on a separate form that the offer will be held open cannot revoke that offer for the time stated, or, if no time is stated, for a reasonable time

Acceptance
- A contract is created when the offeree sends an acceptance, not when the offeror receives it
> Additional terms rule- a UCC rule that permits an acceptance of a sales contract to contain additional terms and still acts as an acceptance rather than a counteroffer in certain circumstances

Battle of Forms Rule
- A UCC rule that states if both parties are merchants, any additional terms contained in the acceptance become part of the sales contract unless (1) the offer expressly limits acceptance to the terms of the offer, (2) the additional terms materially alter the terms of the original contract, or (3) the offeror notifies the offeree that he or she objects to the additional terms within a reasonable time after receiving the offeree's modified acceptance

UCC Statute of Frauds
- A rule that requires all contracts for the sale of goods costing $500 or more and lease contracts involving payments of $1,000 or more to be in writing

Identification of Goods
- Distinguishing the goods named in a contract from the seller's or lessor's other goods

Passage of Title
- Title – legal, tangible evidence of ownership of goods
  - Shipment contract
  - Destination contract

E-Lease and E-Lease Contracts
- Revised Article 2 (Sales) and Revised Article 2A (Leases)
  - Electronic
  - Electronic agent
  - Electronic record
  - Record
  - E-record or E-signature
  - Electronic communication
  - E-contract enforcement

Risk of Loss
- Unless the parties have a specific agreement concerning the assessment of the risk of loss, the UCC mandates who will bear the risk

Shipping terms
- Free on board (FOB)
- Free alongside ship (FAS)
- Cost, insurance and freights (CIF)
- FOB place of destination
- Ex-ship
- No arrival, No sale contract

Sale of Goods by Non-Owners
- Void title- a situation in which a thief acquires no title to the goods he steals, and the person who purchases stolen goods does not acquire a title to those goods
- Voidable title- a title that a purchaser has if the goods were obtained by (1) fraud, (2) a check that is later dishonored, or (3) impersonation of another person
- Entrustment rule- a rule that states that if an owner of goods entrusts those goods to a merchant who deals in goods of that king and the merchant sells those goods to a buyer in the ordinary course of business, the buyer acquires title to the goods

Performance and Remedies for Breach of Sales and Lease Contracts

Ex. 12-3

Possession of Goods at the Time of the Buyer's or Lessee's Breach	Seller's or Lessor's Remedies
Goods in the possession of the seller or lessor	1. Withhold delivery of the goods [UCC 2-703(a), 2A-523(1)(c)].
	2. Demand payment in cash if the buyer is insolvent [UCC 2-702(1), 2A-525(1)].
	3. Resell or release the goods and recover the difference between the contract or lease price and the resale or release price [UCC 2-706, 2A-527].
	4. Sue for breach of contract and recover as damages either of the following:
	a. The difference between the market price and the contract price [UCC 2-708(1), 2A-528(1)]
	b. Lost profits [UCC 2-708(2), 2A-528(2)]
	5. Cancel the contract [UCC 2-703(f), 2A-523(1)(a)].
Goods in the possession of a carrier or bailee	1. Stop goods in transit [UCC 2-705(1), 2A-526(1)].
	a. Carload, truckload, planeload, or larger shipment if the buyer is solvent.
	b. Any size shipment if the buyer is insolvent.
Goods in the possession of the buyer or lessee	1. Sue to recover the purchase price or rent [UCC 2-709(1), 2A-525(1)].
	2. Reclaim the goods [UCC 2-507(2), 2A-529(1)].
	a. The seller delivers goods in cash sale, and the buyer's check is dishonored.
	b. The seller delivers goods in a credit sale, and the goods are received by an insolvent buyer.

Ex. 12.4

Situation	Buyer's or Lessee's Remedy
Seller or lessor refuses to deliver the goods or delivers nonconforming goods that the buyer or lessee does not want.	1. Reject nonconforming goods [UCC 2-601, 2A-509]. 2. Revoke acceptance of nonconforming goods [UCC 2-608, 2A-517(1)]. 3. Cover [UCC 2-712, 2A-518]. 4. Sue for breach of contract and recover damages [UCC 2-713, 2A-519]. 5. Cancel the contract [UCC 2-711(1), 2A-508(1)(a)].
Seller or lessor tenders nonconforming goods and the buyer or lessee accepts them.	1. Sue for ordinary damages [UCC 2-714(1), 2A-516(1)]. 2. Deduct damages from the unpaid purchase or rent price [UCC 2-714(1), 2A-516(1)].
Seller or lessor refuses to deliver the goods and the buyer or lessee wants them.	1. Sue for specific performance [UCC 2-716(1), 2A-521(1)]. 2. Replevy the goods [UCC 2-716(3), 2A-521(3)]. 3. Recover the goods from an insolvent seller or lessor [UCC 2-502, 2A-522].

Agreements Affecting Remedies

> Liquidated damages- damages that will be paid upon the breach of contract that are established in advance

Warranties

> Caveat emptor- "let the buyer beware"
> Express warranty- is created when a seller or lessor makes an affirmation that the goods he or she is selling or leasing meet certain standards of quality, description, performance or condition
> Statements of opinion do not create an express warranty (puffery)
> Implied warranty of merchantability- unless properly disclaimed, an implied warranty that sold or leased goods are fit for the ordinary purpose for which they are sold or leased, as well as other assurances
> > 1. The goods must be fit for the ordinary purpose for which they are used
> > 2. The goods must be adequately contained, packaged and labeled
> > 3. The goods must be of an even kind, quality and quantity within each unit
> > 4. The goods must conform to any promise or affirmation of fact made on the container or label
> > 5. The quality of the goods must pass without objection in the trade
> > 6. Fungible goods must meet a fair, average or middle range of quality
> Implied warranty of fitness for a particular purpose- a warranty that arises when a seller or lessor warrants that the goods will meet the buyer's or lessee's expressed needs

Warranty Disclaimers

- A statement that negates express and implied warranties
  - o "As is"
  - o Disclaimer of the implied warranty of merchantability

  o Disclaimer of the implied warranty of fitness for a particular purpose

Conspicuous Display of Disclaimer
- A requirement that warranty disclaimers be noticeable to the reasonable person

Magnuson-Moss Warranty Act
- A federal statute that regulates written warranties made in connection with the sale or lease of a consumer product

IV. Objective Questions

Terms:

1. _____ are tangible things that are movable at the time of identification to the contract.

2. All states except _____ have adopted some version of UCC Article 2 (Sales).

3. A _____ is a transfer of the right to the possession and use of the named goods for a set term in return for certain consideration. The _____ transfers the right to the _____.

4. A _____ is a sale that involves the provision of a service and a good in the same transaction.

5. The U.C.C. Statute of Frauds applies to contracts for the sale of goods costing _____ or more and lease contracts involving payments of _____ or more.

6. _____ are created when a seller or lessor affirms that the goods he or she is selling or leasing meet certain standards of quality, description, performance, or condition

7. A _____ is a statement that negates express and implied warranties.

True/False:

1. _____ A book is a good under Article 2 of the U.C.C.

2. _____ In a lease contract, the title of goods is passed from the lessor to the lessee.

3. _____ A lessor is the person who acquires the right to possession and use of goods under a lease.

4. _____ A contract is only created when the offeror receives the offeree's acceptance.

5. _____ The shipping term F.O.B. shipping point indicates that the seller is responsible for losses occurring while goods are in route.

6. _____ A sale by a thief still transfers good title to a good faith purchaser.

7. _____ In an ordinary lease, risk of loss belongs to the lessee.

Multiple Choice:

1. According to U.C.C. Article 2 goods include _____.

A. patents
B. real estate
C. stocks
D. inventory

2. In which of the following does the title to the goods pass from the seller to the buyer?

A. option contract
B. rental agreement
C. lease
D. sale of goods

3. Which of the following does Article 2A of the Uniform Commercial Code govern?

A. mixed sales
B. sale of goods
C. leases
D. letters of credit

4. A contract is created when _____.

A. the acceptance has been received by the offeror
B. an acknowledgement is sent by the offeror to the offeree of receiving an acceptance
C. the offeree dispatches the acceptance
D. a written acceptance has been passed between the offeror and the offeree

5. The Statute of Frauds applies to leases:

A. of $1,000 or more.
B. of $500 or more.
C. never
D. when goods are shipped.

6. A title for goods obtained by a seller through fraud, impersonation, or a dishonored check is referred to as a _____.

A. unenforceable title
B. voidable title
C. conditional title
D. unequivocal title

7. A _____ is a seller's or lessor's express or implied assurance to a buyer or lessee that the goods sold or leased meet certain quality standards.

A. bond
B. caveat emptor
C. warranty
D. collateral

V. Answers to Objective Questions

Terms:

1. Goods. This definition does not include money, stock, bonds or real estate. [p. 246]

2. Louisiana. All states except Louisiana have adopted some version of the UCC. [p. 246]

3. Lease, lessor, lessee. Leases take the place of sale with various advantages to both parties. [p. 247]

4. mixed sale. Article 2 applies to mixed sales only if the goods are the predominant part of the transaction. [p. 247]

5. $500, $1,000. The UCC includes Statute of Frauds provisions that apply to sales and lease contracts. [p. 250]

6. Express warranties. It is not necessary to use formal words such as warrant or guarantee to create an express warranty. [p. 257]

7. warranty disclaimer. Warranties can be disclaimed, or limited. [p. 258]

True/False:

1. True. It is movable when identified to the contract. [p. 245]

2. False. In a lease contract, the lessor is the person who transfers the right of possession and use of goods under the lease. [p. 247]

3. False. The lessor is the person who transfers the right. [p. 247]

4. False. Both common law and the UCC provide that a contract is created when the offeree (i.e., the buyer or lessee) sends an acceptance to the offeror (i.e., the seller or lessor), not when the offeror receives the acceptance. [p. 249]

5. False. In this case the seller's responsibility stops at the point of placing the goods in the carrier's possession. [p. 252]

6. False. A thief cannot transfer any title he does not have. The title to the buyer is therefore void. [p. 253]

7. False. It belongs to the lessor. [p. 253]

Multiple Choice:

1. D. Goods are defined as tangible things that are movable at the time of their identification to a contract [p. 246]

2. D. A sale consists of the passing of title of goods from a seller to a buyer for a price. [p. 246]

3. C. Article 2A (Leases) of the UCC directly addresses personal property leases [UCC 2A-101]. [p. 247]

4. C. A contract is created when the offeree (i.e., the buyer or lessee) sends an acceptance to the offeror (i.e., the seller or lessor). [p. 249]

5. A. $500 applies to sales of goods. [p. 250]

6. B. A seller or lessor has voidable title or voidable leasehold interest to goods if he obtained the goods through fraud, if his check for the payment of the goods or lease is dishonored, or if he impersonated another person. [p. 253]

7. C. Warranties, which are based on contract law, may be either expressly stated or implied by law. [p. 257]

VI. Answer to Essay Question

The risk of loss belongs to the buyer when goods are tendered where no terms are stated so Barstools bears the loss on the 200 damaged stools. The 100 stools were non-conforming and can be rejected by Smith. A buyer can reject some, reject all or accept all. As to the injuries to Mary Jones on the 5 stools not assembled properly, she could sue Smith or Barstools under strict liability since they were unreasonably dangerous and anyone in the chain is liable. Warranty needs privity so only Smith would answer the warranty claims.

Chapter 13

CREDIT, SECURED TRANSACTIONS, AND BANKRUPTCY

Why would anyone want to go bankrupt?

I. Overview

The U.S. economy is a credit economy. Consumers borrow money to make major purchases (e.g., homes, automobiles, appliances) and use credit cards (e.g., Visa, MasterCard) to purchase goods and services at clothing stores, restaurants, and other businesses. Businesses use credit to purchase equipment, supplies, and other goods and services. In a credit transaction, the borrower is the *debtor*, and the lender is the *creditor*.

Because lenders are sometimes reluctant to lend large sums of money simply on the borrower's promise to repay, many of them take a *security interest* in the property purchased or some other property of the debtor. The property in which the security interest is taken is called *collateral*. If the debtor does not pay the debt, the creditor can foreclose on and recover the collateral. If the collateral is personal property, the transaction is a *secured transaction* covered by Article 9 of the Uniform Commercial Code. If the collateral is real property, the transaction is usually called a *mortgage*.

A lender who is unsure whether a debtor will have sufficient income or assets to repay the loan may require another person (surety) to guarantee payment. If the borrower fails to repay the loan, the surety is responsible for paying it. This responsibility is called *suretyship*.

On occasion, borrowers become overextended and are unable to meet their debt obligations. Congress has enacted *federal bankruptcy laws* that provide methods for debtors to be relieved of some or all of their debt and to make arrangements to pay debts in the future. Congress enacted the *Bankruptcy Abuse Prevention and Consumer Protection Act of 2005*, which makes it much more difficult for debtors to escape their debts under federal bankruptcy law. The 2005 act, which has been criticized by consumer groups for being too "creditor friendly," has been praised by many businesses, banks, and credit card issuers.

In many credit transactions, particularly consumer credit transactions, the lender is an institution or a party that has greater leverage than the borrower. In the past, this sometimes led to lenders taking advantage of debtors. To rectify this problem, the federal government has enacted *debtor-protection statutes* that protect debtors from abusive, deceptive, and unfair credit practices.

The basic underlying premise of bankruptcy law is founded on a simple reality: bad things happen to good people. How many of us can really provide ourselves with a safe haven from financial disasters brought on by bad health, economic downturns, financial institution failures, and the like? The early bankruptcy laws of England first recognized that businesses can and do fail in spite of the best good faith efforts of their proprietors. That failure should not, in effect, act as a life sentence in keeping that business or its proprietor from reentering the marketplace. Bankruptcy is really one of the earliest forms of recycling, a recycling of economic opportunity for good faith debtors who deserve a second chance.

As with any legal favor, there are people and business entities that get too greedy in asking for the benefit of the law. Bankruptcy is built on a cornerstone of good faith. Where debtors' actions are motivated by bad faith attempts to avoid legitimate obligations, both the law and the larger societal public policies are subverted. The history of the law of bankruptcy is riddled with cases of clear abuse and creditor victimization that have created a dilemma for legislators who must draft our bankruptcy statutes.

The recent history of federal bankruptcy reforms in the U.S. illustrates Congress's attempts to deal with this dilemma of trying to make the law more humane while trying to curb abuses. The Bankruptcy Act of 1978 provided for sweeping reforms that sought to destigmatize bankruptcy in an economy that had grown too dependent on the availability of credit. Unfortunately, with this liberalization came a number of abuses of the law. Graduates of long and expensive professional studies began their lucrative careers with a bankruptcy discharge of school loans. Many consumers loaded up on all sorts of trinkets on credit and kept them debt free under bankruptcy. Corporations began to use the reorganization provisions of the law as a management wedge to get out from under otherwise binding executory contracts, or even worse, tort judgments. Congress responded with the Bankruptcy Amendments and Federal Judgeship Act of 1984 and other subsequent revisions. This legislation sought to pull in the reins on many of these abuses as outlined in the text.

There was still a great need to further balance the basic dichotomy between relief and prevention of abuse. On one side, the mechanics of bankruptcy law needed to be made more cost efficient. The law should probably provide a larger slice of the economic pie for creditors than is presently available while retaining the fresh start opportunities provided for good faith debtors. At the same time, present loopholes in the law needed to be closed. There are still far too many ways to abuse the system. The losses generated add a colossal weight to the cost of credit borne by all of us.

As a response, Congress enacted the Bankruptcy Abuse and Protection Act of 2005. This act makes it more difficult for debtors to escape from their debts. Sides disagree as to its value. The Act is a main focus of this chapter.

II. Hypothetical Multi-issue Essay Question

Describe the options available under the Bankruptcy Code for an individual (non-farmer or fisherman) with financial difficulties.

III. Outline

Unsecured Credit and Secured Credit

> Creditor – the lender in a credit transaction
> Debtor the borrower in a credit transaction

> Unsecured Credit
>> Credit that does not require any security (collateral) to protect the payment of the Debt
> Secured Credit
>> Credit that requires security (collateral) that secures the payment of the loan

Security Interest in Real Property

> Mortgage- a collateral arrangement in which a property owner borrows money from a creditor, who uses real property as collateral for repayment of the loan
>> Mortgagor- the owner-debtor in a mortgage transaction
>> Mortgagee- the creditor in a mortgage transaction
>>> Note- an instrument that evidences the borrower's debt to the lender
>>> Deed of trust- the instrument that gives the creditor a security interest in the debtor's real property that is pledged as collateral

Recording Statute

> A statute that requires a mortgage or deed of trust to be recorded in the county recorder's office of the county in which the property is located

Mechanic's Lien
A contractor, laborer's and material person's statutory lien that makes the real property to which services or materials have been provided security for the payment of the services and materials
See Contemporary Environment- Mechanic's Lien page 231

Secured Transactions in Personal Property
Tangible
Intangible
Secured transaction – is created when a creditor makes a loan to a debtor in exchange for the debtor's pledge of personal property as security
Revised Article 9 of the UCC- an article of the Uniform Commercial Code that governs secured transactions in personal property

Security Agreement
A written document signed by the debtor that creates a security interest in personal property
Agreement must:
1. Clearly describe the collateral
2. Contain the debtor's promise to pay, including terms
3. Set forth the creditor's rights
4. Be signed by the debtor
Attachment- a situation in which a creditor has an enforceable security interest against a debtor and can satisfy the debt our of the designed collateral

The Floating Lien Concept
A security interest in property that was not in the possession of the debtor when the security agreement was executed
1. After acquired property
2. Sales proceeds
3. Future advances

Perfecting a Security Interest
Perfection establishes the right of a secured creditor against other creditors who claim a security interest in the collateral
Three methods:
1. Filing a financial statement
2. Possession of the collateral
3. Purchase money security interest in consumer goods

Priority of Claims
1. Secured vs. unsecured
2. Competing unperfected security interest
3. Perfected vs. unperfected claims
4. Competing perfected security interest

Buyer in the Ordinary Course of Business
A person who in good faith and without knowledge of another's ownership or security interest in goods buys the goods in the ordinary course of business from a person in the business of selling goods of that kind.

Default and Remedies
1. Repossession- the right granted to a secured creditor to take possession of the collateral upon default by the debtor
2. Deficiency judgment – a judgment that allows a secured creditor to successfully bring a separate legal action to recover a deficiency from the debtor. It entitles the secured creditor to recover the amount from the debtor's other property.
3. Artisan's lien- a statutory lien given to workers on personal property to which they furnish services or materials in the ordinary course of business

E-Secured Transactions

Surety and Guaranty Arrangements
Surety arrangement- an arrangement in which a third-party promises to be primarily liable with the borrower for the payment of the borrower's debt
Guaranty arrangement- an arrangement in which a third-party promises to be secondarily liable for the payment of another's debt

Bankruptcy Courts and Procedure
Bankruptcy law is exclusively federal

Types of Bankruptcy
Chapter 7 – Liquidation
Chapter 11- Reorganization
Chapter 12- Adjustment of Debts of a Family Farmer or Fisherman with Regular Income
Chapter 13- Adjustment of Debts of an Individual with Regular Income

Bankruptcy Procedure
Voluntary petition- a petition of bankruptcy filed by a debtor
Involuntary petition- a petition of bankruptcy filed by creditors of a debtor
Proof of claim- a document required to be filed by a creditor that states the amount of his claim against the debtor
Proof of interest- a document required to be filed by an equity security holder that stats the amount of his interest against the debtor

Automatic Stay
The suspension of certain legal activities by creditors against the debtor or the debtor's property

Bankruptcy Estate
The debtor's property and earnings that comprise the estate of a bankruptcy proceeding
Exempt property- property that may be retained by the debtor pursuant to federal or state law that does not become part of the bankruptcy estate
See federal exemptions on page 238 at Figure 13.3

Voidable Transfers
The bankruptcy court may void certain fraudulent transfers of a debtor's property made within two years of filing a petition for bankruptcy

Personal Bankruptcy

Chapter 7 – Liquidation Bankruptcy

A form of bankruptcy in which the debtor's non-exempt property is sold for cash, the cash is distributed to the creditors, and any unpaid debts are discharged

Chapter 7 Discharge

The termination of the legal duty of an individual debtor to pay all debts that remain unpaid upon the completion of the Chapter 7 proceeding

Median Income Test- debtors who earn less than the median income of their state for the size of their family qualify for Chapter 7 bankruptcy

Means test- if the debtor's family income equals or exceeds the mediate state income, a dollar based means test applies

Abusive filing- a filing by an individual or family with higher disposable income than Chapter 7 allows

Chapter 13- Adjustment of Debts of an Individual with Regular Income

A rehabilitation form of bankruptcy that permits bankruptcy courts to supervise the debtor's plan for the payment of unpaid debts in installments over the plan period

Chapter 13- Plan of Payment

A debtor must file a plan of payment, including a budget of estimated income and expenses during the period of the plan

Chapter 13 Discharge

A discharge of a debtor's unpaid debts in a Chapter 13 case that is granted to a debtor after the debtor's plan of payment is completed (could be 3-5 years)

Business Reorganization Bankruptcy

Chapter 11- a bankruptcy method that allows the reorganization of the debtor's financial affairs under the supervision of the bankruptcy court

Chapter 11- Plan of Reorganization

A plan that sets forth a proposed new capital structure for a debtor to have when it emerges from Chapter 11

Chapter 12- Family Farmer and Family Fisherman Bankruptcy

A form of bankruptcy reorganization permitted to be used by family farmers and fishermen

IV. Objective Questions

Terms:

1. _____ is the extension of a loan from one party to another.

2. A contractor or material person's statutory lien that makes the real property to which services or material have been provided security for the payment of services is called a _____.

3. _____ personal property includes equipment, vehicle, farm products, furniture and such.

4. _____ means that the creditor has an enforceable security interest against the debtor and can satisfy the debt out of the designated collateral.

5. A security interest in property that was not in the possession of the debtor when the security agreement was executed is called a _____.

6. The document by which a bankruptcy proceeding is commenced is known as a _____.

7. The legal representative of the bankrupt debtor's estate is the _____.

8. Property that may be retained by a debtor pursuant to federal or state law that does not become part of the bankruptcy estate is called the _____.

9. _____ includes debtor's property for a bankruptcy petition.

10. A _____ provides for the reduction of debts.

True/False:

1. ____ Credit may be extended on either an unsecured or a secured basis.

2. ____ The creditor is the party owing money.

3. ____ Voluntary bankruptcy proceedings are commenced by the creditor.

4. ____ A continuation statement may be filed up to three months prior to the expiration of the financing statement's five-year term.

5. ____ A creditor who has the only secured interest in the debtor's collateral has priority over unsecured interests.

6. ____ Debtor must file proof of claim.

7. ____ Gifts that a debtor is entitled to receive within 180 days after the petition is filed are part of the bankruptcy estate.

8. ____ A Chapter 13 petition can be involuntary.

9. ____ Student loans are dischargeable.

10. ____ An executory contract refers to a contract or lease that has not been fully performed.

Multiple Choice:

1. When is a creditor referred to as a secured creditor?

A. when the creditor has been guaranteed payment by a trustee
B. when the creditor gives a loan without security
C. when the creditor has been paid back his debt
D. when the creditor has acquired collateral

2. A(n) _____ is an instrument that evidences a borrower's debt to the lender for a real property.

A. note
B. consignment
C. accommodation
D. deed of trust

3. To which of the following type of mortgages does the antideficiency statute apply?

A. foreign currency mortgages
B. home improvement mortgages
C. first purchase money mortgages
D. second purchase money mortgages

4. Which of the following transactions occurs when a seller sells goods to a buyer on credit and retains a security interest in the goods?

A. two-party secured
B. three-party secured
C. perfected
D. attached

5. A(n) _____ refers to a document filed by a secured creditor with the appropriate government office that constructively notifies the world of his or her security interest in personal property.

A. security disclosure
B. financing statement
C. possession statement
D. custodial statement

6. Which of the following has the highest priority of claim?

A. the first party to secure the interest
B. the first party to attach the interest
C. the first party to perfect the interest
D. the first party to file a financing statement

7. A(n) _____ is a statutory lien given to workers on personal property to which they furnish services or materials in the ordinary course of business.

A. super-priority lien
B. floating lien
C. artisan's lien
D. judgment lien

8. _____ is an arrangement in which a third-party promises to be primarily liable with the borrower for the payment of the borrower's debt.

A. A mortgage
B. A guaranty arrangement
C. A surety arrangement
D. An artisan's lien

9. Which of the following is true of a guarantor in a guaranty arrangement?

A. The guarantor is primarily liable the principal debtor's debt when it is due.
B. The guarantor can be approached even if the principal debtor is not in default.
C. The creditor can seek first remedy from a guarantor.
D. The guarantor has full legal rights to possession of the real property in this type of arrangement.

10. Which of the following is true of Chapter 7 liquidation?

A. The debtor is not permitted to keep any of his or her assets.
B. The 2005 bankruptcy act has eased the process of applying for Chapter 7 bankruptcy.
C. The debtor's future income cannot be reached to pay the discharged debt.
D. Petitioning for Chapter 7 liquidation does not permit the debtor to petition for bankruptcy under any other chapter.

V. Answers to Objective Questions

Terms:

1. Credit. The party extending the credit, the lender, is called the creditor. The party borrowing the money, the borrower, is called the debtor. [p. 266]

2. mechanic's lien. Investments are protected by state statutes that permit them to file a mechanic's lien against the improved real property. [p. 269]

3. Tangible. Individuals and businesses purchase or lease various forms of tangible and intangible personal property. [p. 269]

4. Attachment. It is a situation in which a creditor has an enforceable security interest against a debtor and can satisfy the debt out of the designated collateral. [p. 270]

5. floating lien. These include after-acquired property, sales proceeds and future advances. [p. 270]

6. petition. A bankruptcy case is commenced when a petition is filed with the bankruptcy court. [p. 276]

7. trustee. A trustee is the legal representative of the debtor's estate and has the power to sell and buy property, invest money, and such. [p. 276]

8. exempt property. The creditors cannot claim this property. [p. 277]

9. Bankruptcy Estate. It also includes debtor's earnings. [p. 277]

10. composition. The petition must state that the debtor desires to affect an extension or a composition of debts, or both. [p. 278]

True/False:

1. True. In a transaction involving the extension of credit, either unsecured or secured, there are two parties. [p. 266]

2. False. The debtor owes, the creditor is owed. [p. 266]

3. False. The debtor commences voluntary proceedings. [p. 276]

4. False. It may be filed up to six months prior. [p. 271]

5. True. It is determined by the priority of claims by the creditors. [p. 273]

6. False. A creditor must file a proof of claim stating the amount of his or her claim against the debtor. [p. 276]

7. True. Gifts, inheritances, life insurance proceeds, and property from divorce settlements that the debtor is entitled to receive within 180 days after the petition is filed are part of the bankruptcy estate. [p. 277]

8. False. Only voluntary petitions are permitted under Chapter 13. [p. 278]

9. False. This is usually not the case unless it creates a hardship for the student. [p. 279]

10. True. Executory contracts and unexpired leases are contracts or leases that have not been fully performed. [p. 281]

Multiple Choice:

1. D. The collateral secures payment of the loan. This type of credit is called secured credit. [p. 267]

2. A. A note is an instrument that evidences a borrower's debt to the lender. [p. 268]

3. C. Antideficiency statutes usually apply only to first purchase money mortgages. [p. 268]

4. A. A two-party secured transaction occurs, for example, when a seller sells goods to a buyer on credit and retains a security interest in the goods. [p. 269]

5. B. A creditor filing a financing statement in the appropriate government office is the most common method of perfecting a creditor's security interest in such collateral; this is known as perfection by filing a financing statement. [p. 271]

6. D. If two or more secured parties have perfected security interests in the same collateral, the first to perfect (e.g., by filing a financing statement, by taking possession of the collateral) has priority. [p. 273]

7. C. If a worker in the ordinary course of business furnishes services or materials to someone with respect to goods and receives a lien on the goods by statute, this artisan's lien prevails over all other security interests in the goods unless a statutory lien provides otherwise. [p. 274]

8. C. In a strict surety arrangement, a third person—known as the surety, or co-debtor—promises to be liable for the payment of another person's debt. [p. 274]

9. A. In a guaranty arrangement, a third person, the guarantor, agrees to pay the debt of the principal debtor if the debtor defaults and does not pay the debt when it is due. [p. 275]

10. C. The debtor's future income, even if he or she becomes rich, cannot be reached to pay the discharged debt. [p. 277]

VI. Answers to Essay Question:

Chapter 7, 11 or 13 is available if rules are followed. This includes a liquidation, reorganization or adjustment.

Chapter 14

SMALL BUSINESS AND GENERAL AND LIMITED PARTNERSHIPS

What type of business should I choose?

I. Overview

An important objective of this chapter is to introduce students to the law of business entity choices. One of the key roles of attorneys engaged in the practice of modern business law is advising their clients on the selection of the best venue for doing business. What seems like a relatively limited set of options is, in fact, quite extensive. These choices can run the gamut from the simplest lemonade stand set up for a youngster to a multinational publicly-traded corporation.

With each choice, the law provides a list of pros and cons. For example, if a person seeks maximum privacy in his or her financial affairs, a private form of sole proprietorship may be best. Compare, however, the business person who wants to leverage the maximum utilization of other people's money while limiting her personal financial exposure. That person may find the corporate form best suited for her needs.

The law literally has something for everyone. The real issue is first finding out what options are legally available and then choosing the best fit. That fit should be tailored by sound advice from a number of quarters including law, accounting, finance, and business management strategy. It is this constant interdependent equation that makes the practice of business law so difficult yet so interesting. The vast majority of the users of this book may never go to law school. Yet that same majority will be influenced every working day by the business entity law choices made in whatever business pursuits they chose. Many of these choices, like partnerships and corporations, will be explained in the next few chapters.

Take, for example, sole proprietorships, covered in this chapter. It remains the most widely used form of business entity even though it may no longer be the most important in sheer economic terms. With the advent of the so-called "information highway" and more emphasis on entrepreneurial niche marketing of goods and services, this form of business may enjoy a renaissance in the Twenty-First century. As we will see this business choice is easy to form and easy to operate but with several liability disadvantages. See outline below.

One of the key distinctions between the partnership form of doing business and the corporate format is the corporation's ability to have an indefinite or perpetual existence. Under state laws of incorporation, a corporation is allowed to continue its juristic existence in spite of the death of its key players. This is not true with partnerships. A partnership is intrinsically tied to the continuing existence of the partners. Partnerships are literally more personal. When the partner is gone, so is the partnership.

One of the questions students frequently ask is: how is it that multi-national business organizations, such as large accounting or law firms, stay in business as partnerships when they frequently lose partners through death or through changes in partnership associations? The technical answer is that with each of these changes, the partnership is theoretically ended and a new one is created. In fact, a well-crafted partnership agreement should have, as one of its key components, an orderly process of succession in case of death or termination. Where these circumstances are properly planned for, the transition is seamless, and the life of the partnership goes on.

Most partnerships are not, however, large and multi-national in scale. Most are created and operated by individuals who have sought to capitalize on their respective economic or talent contributions by acting together in the legal sense. These business ventures could be set for a short- term, specific goal, such as erecting a building, or extend to a full professional career such as a licensed practitioner of law, medicine, or accounting. Just like a marriage, the best intentions at the legal altar of partnership do not always work, and the rules of partnership should provide a means of graceful dissolution.

Determination of which business form to choose for a specific venture is not an easy decision. As we saw in the previous chapters each business form has advantages and disadvantages. The partnership, whether general or limited, is no different. The major difference between the two is that a limited partner is merely an investor. General partners are the typical partners and usually have all of the following rights: to share proportionately in profits, return of capital and management; to information; and to an accounting. The advantages and disadvantages of a general partnership are similar to those discussed for a sole proprietorship in the previous chapter. They include:

Advantages: 1. ease of formation
                   2. single taxation
Disadvantages: 1. unlimited liability
                   2. poor investment liquidity
                   3. length of life
                   4. sharing of control

II. Hypothetical Multi-Issue Essay Question:

Mike Memory decides to start a computer hardware business by opening a shop in the Large Mall in Pennsylvania. Mike agrees to pay Large $500 per week rent and 5% of the profits. The only restrictions imposed by Large are the time and days of opening and closing. After being in business for seven months, Mike defaults on a loan to Happy Bank. Happy, noting that Mike is now broke, attempts to collect from Large claiming that a general partnership exists therefore extending liability to Large. Does a partnership exist between Mike and Large?

III. Outline

Introduction to Entrepreneurship and Small Business
    Sole proprietorship—single owner
    General partnership—two or more owners carry on a business for profit
    Limited partnership—general and limited partners (investors)
    Limited liability partnership (LLP)—all partners are limited partners
    Limited liability company (LLC)—owned by members-hybrid
    Corporation-separate legal entity owned by stockholders

Entrepreneurship
    Entrepreneur- a person who forms and operates a business either by himself or herself, or with others

Advantages of Sole Proprietorship

Owner is the business; no separate legal entity—can operate under trade name by filing a fictitious business name statement

Easy and inexpensive to form

Owner has right to make all management decisions concerning the business

Sole proprietor owns all of the business and has the right to receive all of the business's profits

Sole proprietorship can be easily transferred and sold at owner's discretion

Sole proprietor only subject to personal tax on income

Disadvantages of Sole Proprietorship

Sole proprietor bears the entire risk of loss of the business

He or she will lose his or her entire capital contribution if the business fails

Sole proprietor has unlimited personal liability

Creditors may recover claims against the business from the sole proprietor's personal assets

General Partnership
- An association of two or more persons to carry on as co-owners of a business for profit
- A general partner is a partner of the general partnership who is liable for the debts and obligations of the general partnership

Formation of a General Partnership
- Can be formed with little or no formality
    o 4 criteria under the UPA
        1. An association of two or more person
        2. Carrying on a business
        3. As co-owners
        4. For profit

The Partnership Agreement
- No writing is necessary, but it is good practice to put the partnership agreement in writing
- Partnerships do not pay federal income taxes, income or loss is reported on personal income tax returns

Rights of Partners
1. Right to participate in management
2. Right to share in profits
3. Right to an accounting

Tort Liability of General Partners

The partnership is liable if the tortious act of a partner or employee or agent of the partnership is committed while the person is acting within the ordinary course of partnership business or with the authority of his or her copartners

A partner may seek indemnification from the partner that committed the wrongful act

Contract Liability of Partners
- Partners are jointly liable for the contracts and debts of the partnership

Liability of Incoming Partners
>A new partner who is admitted to the partnership is liable for the existing debts and obligations of the partnership only to the extent of his or her capital contribution

The new partner is personally liable for debts and obligations incurred by the partnership after becoming a partner

Dissolution – change in relationship of partners. It does not always result in termination.
- Partnership for a term
- Partnership at will
    - Winding up- the process of liquidating a partnership's assets and distributing the proceeds to satisfy claims

>Distribution of Assets
>After the winding-up of a dissolved partnership, the assets of the partnership are distributed in the following order
>Creditors (except partners who are creditors)
>Creditor-partners
>Capital contributions
>Profits

>Limited Partnerships – has both general and limited partners
>Limited partners are investors with no voice in management and no unlimited personal liability.
>They are formed under state statute similar to RULPA by execution of a certificate of limited partnership.

Formation of a Limited Partnership
- Certificate of Limited Partnership – a document that two or more persons must execute and sign that makes a limited partnership legal and binding
    - Must contain
        1. Name of the limited partnership
        2. General character of the business
        3. Address of the principal place of business
        4. Name and address of the agent to receive service of legal process
        5. Name and business address of each general and limited partner
        6. Latest date on which the limited partnership is to dissolve
        7. Amount of cash, property or services contributed by each partner, or to be contributed in the future

Defective Formation
1. Certificate not property filed
2. Defect in the certificate
3. Statutory requirements not met in the creation of the limited partnership
- If defective, it may be treated as a general partnership

Limited Partnership Agreement
- A document that sets forth the rights and duties of general and limited partners

Liability of General and Limited Partners
- General partner has unlimited personal liability
- Limited partner is liable for the debts and obligations of the limited partnership

Participation in Management
- Limited partners have no right in management, or they may be treated as general partners

Dissolution of limited partnership
- Upon dissolution, a certificate of cancellation must be filed with the Secretary of State

Limited Liability Limited Partnership (LLLP)
- Similar to a limited partnership, except general partners are not jointly and severally personally liable for the debts and obligations of the LLLP

IV. Objective Questions

Terms:

1. A business entity that is noncorporate in nature, and that is not considered a separate taxpaying entity for income tax purposes is known as a(n) _____.

2. A(n) _____ is a person who forms and operates a new business.

3. If a sole proprietorship fails in business, the owner is subject to _____ liability for claims against the business.

4. When the relation of the partners changes because a partner ceases to be associated in the carrying on of the business of the partnership, a(n) _____ occurs.

5. A partnership with no fixed duration is called a(n) _____.

6. _____ happens when a partnership ends.

7. The process of preserving and selling the assets of the LLC and distributing the money and property to creditors and members after dissolution is known as _____.

8. When a deceased partner's right in specific partnership property vests in the remaining partners instead of passing to heirs or next of kin, it is known as _____.

9. A(n) _____ partner is only an investor.

True/False:

1. ____ The personal liability of a sole proprietor is limited to the extent of her capital contribution to the business.

2. ____ Sole proprietorships are prohibited by law from operating under a fictitious name.

3. ____ A sole proprietorship is owned by its stockholders.

4. ____ A partnership dissolves automatically by operation of law upon the death of a partner.

5. ____ A partnership that is formed for a specific time or purpose dissolves upon the affirmative vote of a majority of the existing partners following the expiration of the time or accomplishment of the objective.

6. ____ The creation of a limited partnership is a formal process that requires writing.

7. ____ A limited partnership cannot have general partners.

8. ____ Defective formation of a limited partnership occurs when a certificate of limited partnership is not properly filed.

9. ____ The general partners of a limited partnership have limited personal liability for the debts and obligations of the limited partnership.

Multiple Choice:

1. Which of the following is true of a sole proprietorship?

A. A business operated under sole proprietorship cannot be transferred.
B. Large businesses cannot be operated under sole proprietorship.
C. A business operated under sole proprietorship should be owned by one or more people of the same family.
D. Creditors can recover claims against the business from the sole proprietor's personal assets.

2. Why does a sole proprietorship not pay taxes at the business level?

A. It does not have a separate legal personality.
B. It is a small business that is exempted from taxation.
C. It is a not-for-profit organization.
D. It is generally an institution with no business dealings.

3. Which of the following is true of general partnership?

A. A business should make a profit in order to qualify as a general partnership.
B. The general partners need not be the co-owners of the business.
C. General partnerships can be either oral or implied from the conduct of the parties.
D. Charity organizations and schools are mostly formed from general partnerships.

4. Which of the following is true of profits and losses in a general partnership?

A. The proportion of profit shared is equal to the general partner's initial investment.
B. Losses are shared equally by all general partners.
C. The general partner who proposed the idea of the business gets most profit.
D. The proportion of investment governs only the proportion of loss shared and not profit obtained.

5. Ted and Fred entered into a written partnership agreement to operate a retail clothing store. Their agreement was silent as to the duration of the partnership. Ted wishes to dissolve the partnership. Which of the following statements is correct?

A. Ted may dissolve the partnership at any time.
B. Ted may dissolve the partnership only after notice of the proposed dissolution is given to all partnership creditors.
C. Ted may not dissolve the partnership unless Fred consents.
D. Ted must apply to a court and obtain a decree unless Fred consents.

6. _____ is a situation in which a partner withdraws from a partnership without having the right to do so at that time.

A. Winding up
B. Indemnification
C. Wrongful dissolution
D. Proliferation

7. Which of the following is true of the liability of an incoming partner?

A. An incoming partner is liable for the previous debts of the partnership.
B. An incoming partner is equally liable for all existing debts of the partnership.
C. An incoming partner is liable for the debts of the partnership only to the extent of his or her capital contribution.
D. An incoming partner is not liable for the future debts of the partnership.

8. Under partnership law, _____ have the right to manage the affairs of the limited partnership.

A. investors
B. sole proprietors
C. limited partners
D. general partners

9. _____ is said to have occurred if a certificate of limited partnership was not properly filed.

A. Defective formation
B. Illegitimate partnership
C. Void partnership
D. Voidable association

10. Which of the following is true of a limited partnership agreement?

A. It provides that all transactions must be approved by all partners.
B. It does not contain information about dissolution of the partnership as it an agreement of formation.
C. It provides that general and limited partners have equal voting rights.
D. It sets forth the terms and conditions regarding the termination of the partnership.

V. Answers to Objective Questions

Terms:

1. sole proprietorship. Under the tax laws, business income and losses are reported on the individual tax returns of the sole proprietor. Although this has many disadvantages, one major benefit is that the problem of corporate double taxation is avoided. [p. 291]

2. entrepreneur. This business may be started alone or with others. [p. 291]

3. unlimited personal. Because there is no legal distinction between the sole proprietor and his or her business, the liabilities of the business and the proprietor are considered one and the same. [p. 292]

4. dissolution. Per section 29 of the Uniform Partnership Act, a dissolution is defined as "the change in the relationship of the partners caused by any partner ceasing to be associated in the carrying on as distinguished from the winding up of the business." [p. 298]

5. partnership at will. The duration of a partnership can be a fixed term, or until a particular undertaking is accomplished, or it can be an unspecified term. [p. 298]

6. Termination. Not all dissolutions end in termination. [p. 299]

7. winding up. This happens if the business is not continued after a legal dissolution. [p. 299]

8. right of survivorship. The value of the deceased general partner's interest in the partnership passes to his or her beneficiaries or heirs upon his or her death [p. 300]

9. limited. They also have no voice in management and no unlimited liability. [p. 301]

True/False:

1. False. A sole proprietor bears the entire risk of loss of such a business and has unlimited personal liability. [p. 292]

2. False. A sole proprietorship can operate under the name of the sole proprietor or a trade name. If a trade name is used, a fictitious business name statement will probably have to be filed. [p. 292]

3. False. The sole proprietor owns all of the business and has the right to receive all of the business's profits. [p. 292]

4. True. Death of a partner acts as an operation of law dissolution of the partnership. [p. 298]

5. False. Such a partnership dissolves automatically upon the expiration of the time or accomplishment of the objective. [p. 299]

6. True. It requires the filing of a certificate of limited partnership and is much more formal than the creation of a regular general partnership. [p. 301]

7. False. A limited partnership has both general and limited partners. [p. 301]

8. True. If there is a substantial defect in the creation of a limited partnership, persons who thought they were limited partners can find themselves liable as general partners. [p. 302]

9. False. General partners have unlimited liability. [p. 303]

Multiple Choice:

1. D. A sole proprietor has unlimited personal liability with respect to the debts and obligations of the business. [p. 292]

2. A. A sole proprietorship is not a separate legal entity, so it does not pay taxes at the business level. [p. 294]

3. C. The agreement to form a general partnership may be oral, written, or implied from the conduct of the parties. [p. 296]

4. B. Unless otherwise agreed, the UPA mandates that a general partner has the right to an equal share in the partnership's profits and losses. [p. 297]

5. A. A partner has the power to withdraw and dissolve the partnership at any time, whether it is a partnership at will or a partnership for a term. [p. 299]

6. C. The partner is liable for damages caused by the wrongful dissolution of the partnership. [p. 299]

7. C. The incoming partner is personally liable for debts and obligations incurred by the general partnership after becoming a partner. [p. 298]

8. D. General partners invest capital, manage the business, and are personally liable for partnership debts. [p. 301]

9. A. If there is a substantial defect in the creation of a limited partnership, persons who thought they were limited partners can find themselves liable as general partners. [p. 302]

10. D. Where there is no such agreement, the certificate of limited partnership serves as the articles of limited partnership. [p. 302]

VI. Answers to Essay Question

The tests for existence of a partnership include the prima facie criteria of sharing profits, the voices in management of the partners and a community of interests. While the use of the mall may be very loosely considered a voice in management and a community of interests (although probably not so), the fact that the sharing of profits is part of the rental agreement would rebut the presumption of the existence of a partnership. There is probably no partnership here and Happy will have to pursue remedies against Mike.

Chapter 15

LIMITED LIABILITY COMPANIES, LIMITED LIABILITY PARTNERSHIPS, AND SPECIAL FORMS OF BUSINESS

What does limited mean?

I. Overview

Business entity choices are strategic decisions based on a number of factors. These elements include choosing the best options for potential capital investment and financial growth, protection from personal liability, and tax planning. No one-entity format is ideal for all objectives. However, recent trends lead to the use of the limited liability company format as the best vehicle for providing the "best of both worlds." Those worlds are the single-layered conduit taxation of proprietorships and partnerships with the limited personal liability accorded to shareholders of a corporation.

The actual advent of limited liability companies does not begin with U.S. legal history. Many countries have allowed for the formation of limited liability companies for a long time. The limited liability company format was not used in the U.S. until the late 1970s.

Why is it that it took so long for this format to catch on in the U.S.? In 1978, the Internal Revenue Service issued a Revenue Ruling with regard to a new limited liability company statute just enacted the year before in Wyoming. Under that ruling, if certain elements of the corporate format were deemed to be missing from the limited liability company format, it would be taxed as partnership and not a corporation. This tax ruling opened the virtual floodgates. Many state legislators enacted laws similar to the Wyoming statute. They wanted to attract new capital from overseas (where limited liability companies have long been accepted) and also provide an attractive legal infrastructure for start-up companies and the like.

The myriad of business organization formats has grown in recent years throughout the vast majority of states. Thus, it is not surprising that there is a call for more uniformity among the states vis-à-vis the passage of laws creating limited liability companies. The group most responsible is the National Conference of Commissioners on Uniform State Laws. In 1995, this group issued the Uniform Limited Liability Company Act (U.L.L.C.A.). This act takes the traditional precedents created by agency law, the various forms of partnerships, and corporations and marries them to a cohesive set of rules for limited liability companies. The states, in turn, are free to adopt their own variations on the basic themes set out in the U.L.L.C.A. These statutes will be "adjusted" over time, experience, and court decisions. All in all, it is a most interesting time in our legal history. In many ways, we are still playing catch-up with the rest of the world. But given the vitality and ingenuity of the U.S. legal system coupled with the current economic growth in so many new start-up businesses, the horizon for this type of business format looks bright indeed.

II. Hypothetical Multi-Issue Essay Question:

Why would potential business owners consider forming a Limited Liability Company?

III. Outline

Limited Liability Company (LLC)

An unincorporated business that combines the most favorable attributes of general partnerships, limited partnerships, and corporations

An LLC is a separate legal entity—an artificial person—that can own property, sue and be sued, enter into and enforce contracts, etc. They are owned by members, and taxed as partnerships unless they elect to be taxed as corporations.

Members are normally liable for the LLC's debts, obligations, and liabilities only to the extent of their capital contributions. Managers are not personally liable.

The Uniform Limited Liability Company Act codifies law throughout the states but is not law unless adopted by the states. The law dictates LLC formation and operation.

Formation of an LLC

Articles of Organization – files with the secretary of state, and usually contain a name, address, duration and other general management information.

Operating Agreement

An agreement entered into by members that governs the affairs and business of an LLC and the relations among members, managers and the LLC

A certificate of interest is a document that evidence's a members ownership interest

Liability of LLC Members

An LLC is liable for any injury or loss caused to anyone as a result of a wrongful act of a member, a manager, or agent, or an employee of the LLC who commits the wrongful act while acting within the ordinary course of business or with authority of the LLC.

Liability of Managers

No personal liability for the debts, obligations or liability of the LLC.

Member's Limited Liability

Members are not liable to third-parties for the debts, obligations and liabilities of the LLC beyond capital contributions.

Management of an LLC

Member managed- each member has equal rights in the management of the business regardless of size of capital contributions

Manager managed – members and non-members who are designated as managers control the LLC and decisions are made by majority vote of members.

Agency Authority to Bind an LLC to Contracts

Member managed- all members have agency authority to bind to contracts

Manager managed- managers have authority to bind, but non-manager members cannot

Dissolution of an LLC
    For term
    At will
    Wrongful disassociation

Limited Liability Partnership – all partners are limited partners with limited liability. There are no general partners.

Articles of Limited Liability Partnership
    The formal documents that must be filed at the secretary of state's office of the state of organization of an LLP in order to form the LLP
    LLPs have the same benefit of flow-through taxation as other types of partnerships.

Franchise
    A franchise is established when one party licenses another party to use the franchisor's trade name, trademarks, commercial symbols, patents, copyrights, and other property in the distribution and selling of goods and services.

    Parties to a Franchise
Franchisor (licensor)
        The party who does the licensing in a franchise situation
    Franchisee (licensee)
        The party who is licensed by the franchisor in a franchise situation

    Types of Franchises
        Distributorship—franchisor manufacturer licenses retailer to distribute product
        Processing Plant—franchisee manufactures with franchisor's secret formula
        Chain-Style—exclusive geographic area to franchisee
        Area—franchisor authorizes the franchisee to negotiate and sell franchises on behalf of the franchisor

Franchise Agreement
    An agreement that a franchisor and franchisee enter into that sets forth the terms and conditions of a franchise
        Trademarks, service marks, trade secrets

Liability of Franchisors and Franchisees
    Separate legal entities
    Franchisee is usually an independent contractor

License
    A business arrangement that occurs when the owner of intellectual property (licensor) contracts to permit another party (licensee) to use the intellectual property

Global Forms of Business
    1. International franchising
    2. Joint ventures- two or more entities combining resources for a single project or transaction
    3. Strategic alliances- two or more companies agree to ally themselves to accomplish a designated objective

IV. Objective Questions

Terms:

1. In the state of its organization an LLC is known as a _____.

2. Each member has equal rights in the management of the business, irrespective of the size of his or her capital contribution if it is a _____ LLC.

3. An arrangement whereby an owner of a patent, trademark, trade secret, or product grants a license to another to sell products or services using the name of such owner is generally known as a _____.

4. In a franchise setting, one party, known as the _____ licenses another, known as the _____ to use a trade name, trademark, commercial symbol, or the like in the distribution and selling of goods and services.

5. In a franchise arrangement, the franchisee may be allowed to use the trademarks and service marks of the franchisor. In addition, the franchisee may be allowed to use _____, which are certain ideas that make a franchise successful but which do not qualify for a trademark, copyright, or patent.

True/False:

1. _____ An LLC is a separate legal entity, distinct from its members.

2. _____ An LLC is taxed as a corporation, unless it elects to be taxed as a partnership.

3. _____ An LLC is formed by filing articles of incorporation with the secretary of state.

4. _____ Profits and losses from an LLC do not have to be distributed in the same proportion.

5. _____ A member of a member-managed LLC and a manager of a manager-managed LLC do have a limited duty of care which does not include ordinary negligence to the LLC.

6. _____ In a member-managed LLC, all members have the right to manage the entity.

7. _____ A member of manager-managed LLC who is not a manager owes no fiduciary duty of loyalty or care, or duty of good faith and fair dealing, to the LLC or its other members.

8. _____ A limited partnership always has at least one general partner.

9. _____ The remedies for breach of a lawful franchise agreement are based on contract theories for breach of contract.

10. _____ A franchise agreement cannot limit the geographical territory in which the franchisee can operate.

Multiple Choice:

1. Which of the following is true of an LLC?

A. An LLC is a creature of federal law.
B. An LLC is regarded a separate legal entity.
C. An LLC cannot hold title to property.
D. The owners of LLC are called general partners or specific partners.

2. A member's ownership interest in an LLC is called a _____.

A. certificate of interest
B. distributional interest
C. collateral interest
D. creditor's interest

3. Which of the following is true of liabilities of LLCs?

A. Members of the LLC are liable to the extent of their capital contribution.
B. Managers of LLCs are personally liable for the debts, obligations, and liabilities of the LLC.
C. LLCs are not liable for any loss or injury caused by their employees.
D. LLCs are not liable for losses caused due to negligence of their managers during the ordinary course of business.

4. Which of the following is true of a member-managed LLC?

A. The member with the highest capital contribution becomes the de facto manager of the LLC.
B. Each member has equal rights in the management of the business of the LLC.
C. Any matter relating to the business of the LLC is decided by a unanimous vote of the members.
D. Shareholders are not allowed to decide matters relating to the business of the LLC.

5. Which of the following methods are used to appoint a manager of a manager-managed LLC?

A. Appointed by the secretary of state
B. Vote of majority of the members
C. Unanimous vote of members
D. Unanimous vote of shareholders

6. _____ is a duty owed by a member of an LLC to not act adversely to the interests of the LLC.

A. Duty of discharge
B. Duty of restitution
C. Duty of loyalty
D. Duty of resolution

7. In a(n) _____ franchise, the franchisor manufactures a product and licenses a retail dealer to sell the product to the public.

A. processing plant
B. area
C. distributorship
D. chain-style

8. Which of the following is true of a franchise?

A. The franchisor and franchisee are established as separate legal entities.
B. A franchisee does not need a license to use the franchisor's trademark.
C. The franchisee does not have access to the franchisor's knowledge.
D. A franchise is considered as a joint venture.

9. In a _____ franchise, the franchisor licenses the franchisee to make and sell its products or services to the public from a retail outlet serving an exclusive geographical territory.

A. distributorship
B. area
C. processing plant
D. chain-style

10. Which of the following is true of the liabilities of a franchisor and a franchisee?

A. The franchisor is not liable for any tort arising out of the franchise.
B. Both franchisee and franchisor are jointly liable for torts committed by either.
C. Franchisees are only liable on their own contracts.
D. Franchisors are always liable for the torts of the franchisees.

V. Answers to Objective Questions

Terms:

1. Domestic LLC. Under the U.L.L.C.A. there are three classifications based on the location in which an LLC is organized: domestic, foreign, and alien. In the state in which it is organized, it is known as a domestic limited liability company. [p. 312]

2. Member-managed. Under Section 404(a) of the U.L.L.C.A. members have equal say in the management of member-managed limited liability companies. [p. 315]

3. Franchise. This method of doing business has become one of the most important of all. Consider its worldwide implications in such key service industries as food, tourism, and the sale of essential commodities. A growing component of international law involves the interpretation and application of long-term multinational franchise contract agreements. [p. 320]

4. Franchisor, franchisee. These are the basic terms used in this body of law. A franchise is established when one party (the franchisor, or licensor) licenses another party (the franchisee, or licensee) to use the franchisor's trade name, trademarks, commercial symbols, patents, copyrights, and other property in the distribution and selling of goods and services. [p. 320]

5. Trade secrets. The interesting aspect of trade secrets is that they are not registered in the same way as certain kinds of other intellectual property, such as patents. Thus they are not as easy to reverse engineer and the like. But they are still considered to be a property and enjoy the protection of the law. [p. 321]

True/False:

1. True. An LLC is a separate legal entity (or legal person) distinct from its members. LLCs are treated as artificial persons who can sue or be sued, enter into and enforce contracts, hold title to and transfer property, and be found civilly and criminally liable for violations of law. [p. 310]

2. False. Under the Internal Revenue Code and regulations adopted by the Internal Revenue Service (IRS) for federal income tax purposes, an LLC is taxed as a partnership unless it elects to be taxed as a corporation. [p. 311]

3. False. An LLC is formed by delivering articles of organization to the office of the secretary of state of the state of organization for filing. [p. 311]

4. True. Unless otherwise agreed, the ULLCA mandates that a member has the right to an equal share in the LLC's profits and losses. Profits and losses from an LLC do not have to be distributed in the same proportion. [p. 312]

5. True. If a covered member or manager commits an ordinary Negligent Act that is not grossly negligent, he or she is not liable to the LLC. [p. 313]

6. True. In a member-managed LLC the members of the LLC have the right to manage the LLC. [p. 315]

7. True. Under Section 409 (h)(1), a non-manager member of a manager-managed LLC is treated equally to a shareholder in a corporation and does not have these fiduciary duties. [p. 317]

8. True. A limited partnership must have at least one general partner who is personally liable for the obligations of the partnership. An LLC provides limited liability to all members. [p. 318]

9. True. If the franchise agreement is reached, the injured party may sue for rescission of the agreement, restitution, and damages. [p. 321]

10. False. The franchise agreement is a contractual agreement. Therefore, the agreement can contain any reasonable restrictions to which parties agree. [p. 321]

Multiple Choice:

1. B. An LLC is a separate legal entity (or legal person) distinct from its members. [p. 310]

2. B. A member's ownership interest in an LLC is called a distributional interest. A member's distributional interest in an LLC is personal property and may be transferred in whole or in part. [p. 312]

3. A. The general rule is that members are not personally liable to third parties for the debts, obligations, and liabilities of an LLC beyond their capital contribution. Members have limited liability. [p. 313]

4. B. In a member-managed LLC, each member has equal rights in the management of the business of the LLC, regardless of the size of his or her capital contribution. [p. 315]

5. B. In a manager-managed LLC a manager must be appointed by a vote of a majority of the members; managers may also be removed by a vote of the majority of the members. [p. 316]

6. C. A duty owed by a member of a member-managed LLC and a manager of a manager-managed LLC to be honest in his or her dealings with the LLC and to not act adversely to the interests of the LLC. [p. 317]

7. C. In a distributorship franchise, the franchisor manufactures a product and licenses a retail dealer to distribute a product to the public. [p. 320]

8. A. The franchisor and franchisee are established as separate legal entities. The franchisor deals with the franchisee as an independent contractor. [p. 321]

9. D. In a chain-style franchise the franchisor licenses a franchisee to make and sell its products or distribute its services to the public from a retail outlet serving an exclusive territory. [p. 321]

10. C. In a franchise, the franchisor and franchisee are established as separate legal entities. Franchisees are liable on their own contracts and are liable for their own torts. [p. 321]

VI. Answers to Essay Question

An LLC is an unincorporated business combining the most favorable attributes of general partnerships, limited partnerships, and corporations. They can own property, sue and be sued, and enter into contracts. They can choose to be taxed as a partnership and their members are normally liable for the LLC's debts, obligations, and liabilities only to the extent of their capital contributions. [p. 310]

Chapter 16
CORPORATIONS AND THE SARBANES-OXLEY ACT

Is a corporation a legal entity?

I. Overview

Corporations can provide many advantages for business including perpetual existence, limited liability, and numerous tax and other legal opportunities to massage the system. These advantages are not free, nor are they always easily obtained. Corporate law has always been technically intricate and demanding of legal practitioners. Corporations can also be more unforgiving to its users than sole proprietorships or partnerships if mistakes are made in its formation and financing. The stakes are simply greater because over eighty-five percent of business done in the U.S. uses the corporate format. This chapter has several objectives: to illustrate how the corporate form is established legally and to see how it is infused with its financial lifeblood, i.e., money. In addition, the process of establishing the basic ground rules for the key players will be examined.

The formation of a corporation starts with a contracting process initiated by a person called a promoter. A promoter of a new corporation is really the catalyst that brings together the diverse elements of law, finance, entrepreneurial talent, and technical competence that will eventually drive the fortunes of the new business entity. The role of promoter is also tied to the laws of contract, fiduciaries, and agency. He or she is expected to act for the benefit of the eventual corporation and can be expected to be personally liable for contracts entered into on its behalf in the interim.

The promoter's main duties are bifurcated towards two main audiences--the state and potential investors. He or she will be involved in contracts with both of these constituencies. With regard to the state, the actual creation of the new corporate entity is the outgrowth of a document called the charter. This document is the foundation contract between the promoter and the state. The charter takes the form of a certificate of incorporation. This certificate provides the official state-sanctioned ground rules under which the new corporate entity will be allowed to do business. Violation of these ground rules can lead to an eventual corporate death penalty, the revocation of the charter. The second critical task of the promoter is to find legal methods so that the start up of the corporation may be infused with financial lifeblood. The corporate form is unparalleled in its ability to be a fundraiser. These funds are generated by two basic methods--debt and equity financing.

Once the proper procedures for the establishment of the corporation have been complied with and adequate financing has been secured, the next step is to see what the basic ground rules will be for key players in this arena. The leading protagonists will be the board of directors, shareholders, and managers of the corporation. The distinctions between these roles are sometimes blurred when it comes to the formation and management of corporations. Yet failure to honor these distinctions can lead to disastrous consequences.

Erosion is defined as a gradual wearing away or disintegration. The wall of limited liability for corporations and their main protagonists has suffered from steady erosion over the past several decades. The floodwall is still holding, but the holes in the dike seem to get bigger every year. What is interesting about these reductions in limited liability is that they are often initiated at the behest of other members of the same corporate family rather than by outside parties. Disadvantaged shareholders, disgruntled corporate officers, and quixotic directors have all done their share of diminishing the liability immunities once held so sacred in the corporate scheme of things.

There are two basic theories under which most of the limitations to corporate entity and/or corporate participants' liability are restricted or eliminated. First, public policy never has allowed the corporate form to act as a total shield from liability to third parties. From the very inception of corporate law, courts and legislators have clung to the back door option of holding someone personally liable where circumstances deemed it appropriate. A creature of the law should not be allowed to become a tool of circumvention of the law. Thus in the areas of crimes, torts, and generally undesirable behavior, a number of corporate shield-bursting mechanisms have always been in place. These have ranged from piercing the corporate veil to outright revocation of the continued existence of the corporation. In all these cases, the underlying premise is that the corporate form should not allow a person to do something that would otherwise be prohibited by public policy.

The second theory is found in the intracorporate workings of the organization itself. Just as the corporate form should not be allowed to defraud creditors and the like, so too should it not be allowed to be used by various members of corporate organizations to harm each other. The cornerstone of relationships between shareholders, directors, and officers is founded in the law of fiduciaries, loyalty, and mutual support. Even though not all aspects of these interdependent relationships could ever realistically be expected to be harmonious, some common good is expected to be interwoven into their behavior towards each other. Some of the most vociferous battles of all are fought in the confines of the corporate boardrooms around the country.

In both external relationships and intracorporate disagreements, the willingness of the contesting parties to go public with their grievances more frequently than ever has led to more exceptions to the rule of limited corporate liability. Time will tell whether or not this erosion bodes well for the economy. If it means a crippling of the economic engine of corporate vitality relative to comparable overseas entities, it does provide cause for alarm. If, however, it holds real wrongdoers responsible for harm, those whom would otherwise be shielded by the false front of a legal stage set, then it is time for the house of cards to come down.

The world of corporate combinations through mergers and the like has been turned upside down in recent history. Several factors have contributed to the frenzy of activity on the street, not all of it well motivated. As with so many of these sorts of fundamental changes to how society orders its affairs, there is no one underlying motive for it. As with any major shift in economic alignment, arguments pro and con can be heard through the halls of academia, in government agencies, and Wall Street.

The proponents for these changes first argue mergers, takeovers, and consolidation are simply marketplace adjustments that reflect attempts to correct inefficiencies in the marketplace. Where a company is poorly managed, running on "cruise control," and is not sufficiently lean and mean, it should be swallowed up by more efficient competitors. This view adopts the law of the jungle—only the strong survive. A really open marketplace rewards the most efficient in economic terms, and drags on that efficiency are doomed to failure and absorption in the end. The proponents of the law and economics, or "Chicago School" movement, proponents argue that mechanisms of law should not only allow this natural business evolution to take place, but that to stifle it would do harm to society in the end.

On the other side of the coin, a number of commentators have argued that runaway activity in the areas of mergers, acquisitions, buyouts, and the like breed a whole new generation of unethical, short-term thinking financial charlatans, whose only real interest is their personal bank accounts. Critics of the merger phenomenon point to the endless game-playing going on in this arena. They argue that what has been created is a big time casino where the chips are bigger than ever. Out of that gaming mentality, the larger society has had to pay for numerous financial scandals because the original players were not really motivated by the long-term good of society. In addition, long term growth, research, and development of essential business fundamentals has been cast aside in the name of greenmail, corporate spin-offs, tax manipulation, and golden parachutes. The net result of this sort of short term thinking is that while the financial market manipulators are playing high stakes poker, our industrial, financial, and transportation infrastructure has sunk into a quagmire of noncompetitiveness in the world marketplace.

The truth probably lies somewhere in between these poles when it comes to these business combinations. Time will ultimately tell if this recent history has reflected a transition cost to stay competitive as a nation, or if we are frittering away our industrial base at the gaming table. Whatever the outcome, each and every one of us will ultimately share in the processes' ultimate benefit or burden.

II. Hypothetical Multi-Issue Essay Question:

Bob Builder has been a subcontractor all his life and is tired of watching the general contractors make all the money. He decides to become a general contractor and chooses the corporate form of business. He goes through all the proper steps and incorporates as a closely held corporation. To generate cash he invests $100,000 as the sole shareholder and is able to borrow $20,000,000 from the local bank. As part of the business' expenses he decides to pay himself a salary of $500,000 per week. Before too long the business is out of money and he decides to declare bankruptcy. The bank wants its money back so they attempt to pierce the corporate veil and go after the personal assets of Bob. Can they do so?

III. Outline

Introduction to Corporations and Sarbanes-Oxley Act
  Corporation- a fictitious legal entity that is created according to statutory requirements

Advantages	Disadvantages
Limited liability of shareholders	Double taxation
Free transferability of shares	Formality
Perpetual existence	Lack of owner control
Centralized management	

  Nature of the Corporation
    Corporate codes- state statutes that regulate the formation, operation and dissolution of corporations
    A corporation is a separate legal entity for most purposes

Characteristics of Corporations
    1. Free transferability of shares
    2. Perpetual existence
    3. Centralized management
    4. Limited liability of shareholders

Publicly Held and Closely Held Corporations
    Publicly held- usually large, with many shareholders
    Closely held- few shareholders, often family members

Incorporation Procedure
    May be incorporated in only one state
        Domestic- the state of incorporation
        Foreign- in all states other than the state of incorporation
        Alien- a corporation incorporated in another country

Articles of Incorporation
    The basic governing documents of a corporation which must be filed with the secretary of state of the state of incorporation
    May include:

1. Name
2. The number of shares authorized to issue
3. Address of initial registered office and the name of the initial registered agent
4. Name and address of each incorporator
5. Duration
6. Purpose
7. Any limitations or regulations
8. Any provisions that would be contained in the corporate bylaws

Registered agent- a person or corporation that is empowered to accept service of process on behalf of the corporation

Corporate Bylaws

A detailed set of rules adopted by the Board of Directors after a corporation is incorporated that contains provisions for managing the business and the affairs of the corporation

Organizational Meeting

Meetings that must be held by the initial directors of a corporation after the articles of incorporation are filed.

S-Corporation- a corporation that has qualified for and elected to be taxed pursuant to the federal Subchapter S Revision Act

Financing a Corporation

Equity securities- representation of ownership rights to a corporation
   Common stock- a type of equity security that represents the residual value of a corporation
   Preferred stock- a type of equity security that is given certain preference and rights over common stock
      Types:
         1. Dividend preference
         2. Liquidation preference
         3. Cumulative dividend right
         4. Right to participate in profits
         5. Conversion rights
         6. Redeemable preferred stock

Authorized, Issued and Outstanding Shares

Authorized- the number of shares provided for in a corporation's articles of incorporation
Issued- shares that have been sold by a corporation
Outstanding- shares that are in shareholder hands
Treasury- shares that have been repurchased by the corporation

Debt Securities

Securities that establish a debtor-creditor relationship in which the corporation borrows money from an investor, to whom a debt is issued
   1. Debenture- a long-term unsecured debt instrument
   2. Bond- a long-term debt security that is secured by collateral
   3. Note- a debt security with a maturity of five years or less
   4. Indenture agreement- a contract between a corporation and a holder that contains the terms of a debt security

Shareholders

Persons or entities that own shares of a corporation

Shareholder's Meeting

Annual- a meeting of the shareholders of a corporation that must be held by the corporation to elect directors and to vote on other matters

Special- meetings of shareholders that may be called to consider and vote on important or emergency issues, such as a proposed merger or amending the articles of incorporation

Proxy- a written document that a shareholder signs, authorizing another person to vote his or her shares at the shareholder's meeting in case of absence

Quorum and Voting Required

Quorum of shares- the required number of shares that must be represented in person or by proxy to hold a shareholder meeting

Look to the bylaws, articles of incorporation, or the RMBCA

Straight voting- shareholders vote the number of shares owned

Cumulative voting- a shareholder is entitled to multiply the number of shares owned times the number of directors to be elected and cast the accumulated number for a single candidate

Dividends

A distribution of profits of a corporation to shareholders

Piercing the Corporate Veil

If a shareholder dominates a corporation and uses it for improper purposes, a court of equity can disregard the corporate entity and hold the shareholder personally liable for the corporation's debts and obligations. This is also called the "alter ego doctrine." Reasons include: undercapitalization or not treating the corporation as a separate entity.

Board of Directors

A panel of decision makers, the members of which are elected by the shareholders

Inside director- a member of the BOD who is also an officer of the corporation

Outside director- a member of the BOD who is not an officer of the corporation

Meetings of the Board of Directors

Regular – established in bylaws

Special

Quorum- the number of directors necessary to hold a meeting and transact business

Corporate Officers

Employees of a corporation who are appointed by the BOD to manage the day-to-day operations of the corporation

Fiduciary Duty of Corporate Directors and Officers

Duty of care

Duty to use care and diligence when acting on behalf of the corporation. Under business judgment rule, honest mistakes of judgment are not the subject of liability.

Duty of loyalty

Duty to subordinate personal interests to those of the corporation and its shareholders

The Business Judgment Rule

Directors and officers are not liable to the corporation or shareholders for honest mistakes of judgment

Sarbanes-Oxley Act
  A federal statute that establishes far-reaching rules to improve corporate governance, eliminate conflicts of interest, and instill confidence in investors of public companies
  See the Ethics Spotlight on page 300

Mergers and Acquisitions
  Merger- a situation in which one corporation is absorbed into another and ceases to exist

Dissolution of a Corporation
  Voluntary
  Administrative
  Winding up and liquidation- assets are collected, liquidated and distributed to creditors, shareholders and other claimants

Multinational Corporations
  A corporation that operates in two or more countries
    Parent
    Subsidiary

IV. Objective Questions

Terms:

1. The articles of incorporation must identify the _____ of the corporation, which is the person empowered to accept service of process on behalf of the corporation.

2. _____ are repurchased shares awaiting ultimate disposition.

3. _____ are unsecured debt.

4. A corporation is generally either a C corporation or a(n) _____ corporation.

5. Shares that are in shareholder hands are called _____.

6. These documents must be filed with the secretary of state of the state of incorporation to effectuate a voluntary dissolution; they are known as the _____.

7. A _____ is a debt security with a maturity of five years or less.

True/False:

1. _____ Publicly held corporations generally have very few shareholders.

2. _____ A corporation must be incorporated in each state in which it chooses to do business.

3. _____ The purpose for which a corporation is formed must be specific and must be stated in the articles of incorporation.

4. _____ A debenture is a long-term debt security that is secured by some form of collateral.

5. _____ More than half of all publicly traded corporations are incorporated in the state of Nevada.

Multiple Choice:

1. _____ are corporations that have many shareholders and whose securities are often traded on national stock exchanges.

A. Closely held corporations
B. Non-profit corporations
C. Publicly held corporations
D. Shore-up corporations

2. Which of the following is a definition of a foreign corporation?

A. A corporation with incorporations in multiple states.
B. A corporation in the state in which it is incorporated.
C. A corporation in states other than the one in which it is incorporated.
D. A corporation in the United States which has been incorporated in another country.

3. Which of the following is true for a corporation's incorporation in a state?

A. Domestic corporations can incorporate into only one state.
B. Domestic corporations can incorporate into all states that it conducts business in.
C. Alien corporations can only incorporate into one state.
D. Foreign corporations can incorporate into more than one state.

4. _____ is the basic governing documents of a corporation which must be filed with the secretary of state of the state of incorporation.

A. Debt security
B. Debenture
C. Certificate of authority
D. Articles of incorporation

5. A detailed set of rules adopted by the board of directors after a corporation is incorporated that contains provisions for managing the business and the affairs of the corporation are referred to as _____.

A. ultra vires rules
B. articles of incorporation
C. bylaws
D. corporation codes

6. _____ is a type of equity security that represents the residual value of a corporation.

A. Common stock
B. Preferred stock
C. Cumulative preferred stock
D. Participating preferred stock

7. Which of the following shares have the right to vote?

A. Unissued shares
B. Treasury shares
C. Outstanding shares
D. Liquidated shares

8. _____ are a panel of decision makers who are elected by the shareholders.

A. Registered agents
B. Corporate officers
C. Stakeholders
D. Board of directors

9. A duty that directors and officers have not to act adversely to the interests of the corporation and to subordinate their personal interests to those of the corporation and its shareholders is known as _____.

A. duty of care
B. duty of loyalty
C. duty of obedience
D. self-dealing

10. Dissolution of a corporation that has begun business or issued shares upon recommendation of the board of directors and a majority vote of the shares entitled to vote is known as _____.

A. liquidation
B. judicial dissolution
C. administrative dissolution
D. voluntary dissolution

V. Answers to Objective Questions

Terms:

1. Registered agent. This person is usually an individual attorney or law firm who has an established relationship with the company. When businesses seek to establish themselves out of the jurisdiction in which they are incorporated, most states will request the business to designate a registered agent under its jurisdiction. [p. 333]

2. S-corporation. See the Contemporary Environment section on page 289 for a complete explanation. [p. 335]

3. Treasury shares. These shares were authorized and issued and have been repurchased. [p. 337]

4. Debentures. This is a form of debt financing. [p. 337]

5. Outstanding shares. It does not matter whether the shares are original issue of reissued treasury shares. [p. 337]

6. Note. Notes can be either secured or unsecured. [p. 337]

7 Articles of dissolution. Because the corporate form is created by law, the law allows its existence to come to a voluntary end. [p. 346]

True/False:

1. False. Publicly held corporations have many shareholders. Closely held corporations generally have few shareholders. [p. 332]

2. False. A corporation can only be incorporated in one state even though it can do business in all other states in which it qualifies. [p. 333]

3. False. Although the purpose must be stated in the articles of incorporation, a corporation can be formed for any lawful purpose, and no specific purpose need be stated. [p. 333]

4. False. This is the definition of a bond. [p. 337]

5. False. They are really incorporated in Delaware! [p. 338]

Multiple Choice:

1. C. Publicly held corporations have many shareholders. Often, they are large corporations with hundreds or thousands of shareholders, and their shares are usually traded on organized securities markets. [p. 332]

2. C. A corporation is a domestic corporation in the state in which it is incorporated. It is a foreign corporation in all other states and jurisdictions. [p. 333]

3. A. A corporation can be incorporated in only one state, even though it can do business in all other states in which it qualifies to do business. [p. 333]

4. D. Articles of incorporation is the basic governing documents of a corporation, which must be filed with the secretary of state of the state of incorporation. [p. 333]

5. C. Either the incorporators or the initial directors can adopt the bylaws of the corporation. The bylaws are much more detailed than are the articles of incorporation. They do not have to be filed with any government official. The bylaws govern the internal management structure of a corporation. [p. 334]

6. A. Common stock is an equity security that represents the residual value of a corporation. Common stock has no preferences. [p. 336]

7. C. The shares that are in shareholder hands, whether originally issued or reissued treasury shares, are called outstanding shares. Only outstanding shares have the right to vote. [p. 337]

8. D. The board of directors of a corporation is elected by the shareholders of the corporation. The board of directors is responsible for formulating policy decisions that affect the management, supervision, control, and operation of the corporation. [p. 341]

9. B. Directors and officers of a corporation owe a fiduciary duty to act honestly. This duty, called the duty of loyalty, requires directors and officers to subordinate their personal interests to those of the corporation and its shareholders. [p. 344]

10. D. A corporation can be voluntarily dissolved if the board of directors recommends dissolution and a majority of shares entitled to vote (or a greater number, if required by the articles of incorporation or bylaws) votes for dissolution as well. [p. 346]

VI. Answers to Essay Question

This is a clear example of undercapitalization. The bank should be able to pierce the corporate veil and go after Bob's personal assets since he is the only stockholder. [p. 341]

Chapter 17

INVESTOR PROTECTION, E-SECURITIES, AND WALL STREET REFORM

What's wrong with insider trading?

I. Overview

Assume a sporting event were to be contested under the following conditions:
1. All the players were well trained.
2. The rules of the game were fully explained to the players.
3. Those rules are fairly and evenhandedly applied to all participants.
4. An even playing field is used as a site for the contest.

With all these suppositions in place, can you rest assured your team will win? Or can you, at best, hope that, win or lose, your team was engaged in a fair contest?

In the broadest sense, the buying and selling of securities is indeed similar to an athletic event. Each participant goes into the game with his or her own self-interest in mind. And all the fair rules in world will not change one essential truth of these or any other contests--there will be winners and there will be losers. That reality must always be kept in mind from the outset by anyone seeking to make his or her fortune through the sale or purchase of securities. Risk is inherent to the nature of this activity, and anyone who fails to appreciate that simple fact should not be there in the first place.

It is most difficult for professionals to master the ins and outs of the financial markets, let alone the casual investor. Yet the lure of playing this game is so strong that every year millions of people invest hard-earned money with nothing more than high hopes and a prayer. Securities law was designed to at least give some substance to those hopes and prayers. That substance is public information upon which investment choices can be rationally made. These laws are not designed to assure a win in this high-risk game, but rather to provide a more even playing field.

The great financial stock market crash of 1929 and the ensuing Depression brought on by that calamity brought to the fore the need to create a greater governmental role in securities markets. Prior to that period, the sale of stocks in corporations remained essentially unregulated except for the common law doctrines of fraud and the like. Manipulative and unscrupulous trading practices coupled with a lot of hopes and unrequited prayers all pointed to a need for a better set of ground rules by which this game could be played.

The basic rules of the game go back almost seventy years to the Securities Act of 1933 and the Securities Exchange Act of 1934 that created the Securities and Exchange Commission. The approach is simple. Provide all information that is deemed necessary to market operation and be honest while doing it. The 1933 Act covers initial issuances while the 1934 Act deals with subsequent trading. Over the years, the Commission's role has greatly increased with the advent of new technologies like programmed trading and with the need to expand its regulatory framework into the financial services arena. Because of recent scandals in this sector of the economy, a number of new white-collar crimes have been added to the government's arsenal for dealing with abuses in this area. All in all, it has made the specialized practice of securities law or SEC accounting more difficult, yet more challenging, than ever. As future business leaders, you have more than just a self-survival need to stay abreast of these changing rules of the game. As a nation we cannot afford the losses created by the manipulative abuses recently seen in these critical markets. If we do not watch out, 1929 can be revisited upon us, this time only worse.

II. Hypothetical Multi-issue Essay Question

Mr. Albert Williams was suffering from a common Twenty-First century malaise, working at a good paying job that provided him only with material but not emotional satisfaction. He wanted to break away and engage in his dream occupation – bread making. He has not had any formal training, but he knew what he liked when he tasted it. He decided to start his own chain of bakeries specializing in Italian breads produced from a special family recipe.

He could not afford to capitalize the entire operation himself, so he came up with a novel idea. Why not sell the individual bakeries to "partners"? They would each get his expertise in producing the bread as well as having their names on specialty products.

Mr. Williams convinced several hundred partners to combine with each other to buy one bakery each for $100,000 and proceeded to start up production of the bread. Unfortunately what he didn't tell his partners was that he didn't know if the recipe would be successful or if it would even work. Having failed to master the art of baking, the bread tasted more like dry dough than Italian bread. His partners are upset and look to see if they can get out of this deal. What results?

III. Outline

The Securities Exchange Commission (SEC)
It is the administrative agency that is empowered to administer the federal securities laws.
Major responsibilities:
1. Adopting rules (rules have the force of law)
2. Investigating alleged security violations and bringing enforcement actions against violators.
3. Regulating activities of securities brokers and advisors.

Definition of a Security
An interest or instrument that is common stock, preferred stock, a bond, a debenture, or a warrant
An interest or instrument that is expressly mentioned in securities acts.
An investment contract-investment in common enterprise expecting profits from the significant work of others

Private Transactions Exempt from Registration
Transactions exempt from SEC registration
1. Non-issuer exemption (average investors)
2. Intrastate offering exemption – an exemption from registration that permits local business to raise capital from local investors to be used in the local economy without the need to register with the SEC.
> Rule 147- securities sold pursuant to an intrastate offering exemption cannot be sold to non-residents for a period of nine months.
3. Private placement exemption – an exemption from registration that permits issuers to raise capital from an unlimited number of accredited investors and no more than 35 non-accredited investors without having to register with the SEC.
> Accredited investors are detailed on page 311
4. Small offering exemption – an exemption from registration that permits the sale of securities not exceeding $1 million during a 12-month period.
> Rule 144- provides that securities sold pursuant to the private placement exemption or the small offering exemption must be held for one year from the date the securities were paid for.

The Securities Act of 1933: Going Public

A federal statute that primarily regulates the issuance of securities by corporations, partnerships, associations, and individuals

Issuer- a business of party selling securities to the public

Registration Statement

A document that an issuer of securities files with the SEC that contains required information about the issuer, the securities to be issued, or other relevant information

Registration statements must contain a description of:

1. The securities being offered for sale
2. The registrant's business address
3. The management of the registrant
4. Pending litigation
5. How the proceeds from the offering will be used
6. Government regulation
7. The degree of competition in the industry
8. Any special risk factors

Registration statements usually become effective 20 days after they are filed.

Prospectus

A written disclosure document that must be submitted to the SEC along with the registration statement and given to prospective purchasers of securities.

Sale of Unregistered Securities

It is a violation of the Securities Act of 1933

Investors can rescind their purchase and recover damages.

Regulating and Offer

Regulation A- permits an issuer to sell securities pursuant to a simplified regulation process.

Offering Statement

Small Corporate Offering Registration (SCOR)

Actions for Violations of the Securities Act of 1933

1. Civil liability under Section 12 (Violating Section 5)
2. Civil liability under Section 11 (Fraud)
   a. Due diligence defense- all defendants except the issuer may assert this defense.
3. SEC actions:
   a. Consent order
   b. Injunction
   c. Request for disgorgement of profits
4. Criminal liability under Section 24

The Sarbanes-Oxley Act

Section 501- a law that established rules for separating the investment banking and securities advice functions of securities firms in order to eliminate many conflicts of interests.

The Securities Act of 1934: Trading in Securities

This is a federal statute that primarily regulates trading in securities.

Section 10(b) - a provision of the act that prohibits the use of manipulative and deceptive devices in the purchase or sale of securities in contravention of the rules and regulations proscribed by the SEC.

Rule 10b-5 – A rule adopted by the SEC to clarify the reach of Section 10(b) against deceptive and fraudulent activities in the purchase and sale of securities.

Scienter- intentional conduct (required for a violation of Section 10(b) and Rule 10b-5.

Actions for Violations of the Securities Exchange Act of 1934

1. Civil liability
2. SEC actions

   Insider Trading Act- a federal statute that permits the SEC to obtain a civil penalty of up to three times the illegal benefits received from or losses avoided on insider trading.
3. Criminal liability under Section 32

Insider Trading

A situation in which an insider makes a profit by personally purchasing shares of a corporation prior to public release of favorable information, or by selling shares of a corporation prior to the public disclosure of unfavorable information.

Insiders

   1. Officers, directors, and employees at all levels of the company
   2. Lawyers, accountants, consultants and agents of the company
   3. Others who owe a fiduciary duty to the company

Tipper-Tippee Liability

Tipper- a person who discloses material non-public information to another

   Liable for profits made by Tippee or other remote Tippees

Tippee- a person who receives material non-public information from a Tipper

   Liable for actions on information, or profits made by remote Tippees

Misappropriation Theory

An outsider's misappropriation of information in violation of a fiduciary duty that violates Section 10(b) or Rule 10b-5

Aiders and Abettors

Parties that knowingly provide assistance to successfully complete SEC fraud

Short-Swing Profits

Section 16(a) of the Securities Exchange Act of 1934 defines any person who is an executive officer, a director, or a ten-percent shareholder of an equity security of a reporting company as a statutory insider for Section 16 purposes.

Section 16(b) - requires that any profits made by a statutory insider on transactions involving short-swing profits belong to the corporation.

Short-swing profits- trades involving equity securities occurring within six months of each other.

E-Securities Transactions

Online securities transactions involving disseminating information to investors, trading in securities, and issuing stocks and other securities to the public

   E-Securities Exchanges
   New York Stock Exchange (NYSE)
   NYSE Europe
   National Association of Securities Dealers Automated Quotation System (NADDAQ)

E-SEC EDGAR
The SEC's electronic data and records system, where companies file registration statements, periodic reports, and other forms

E-Public Offerings (E-IPO)
An initial public offering of a company's stock or other securities over the internet

State "Blue-Sky" Laws
State securities laws are often called "Blue-Sky" laws
The Uniform Securities Act has been adopted by many states

IV. Objective Questions

Terms:

1. Two federal statutes designed to require disclosure of information to investors and prevent fraud are known as the _____ and the _____.

2. The federal administrative agency empowered to administer federal securities laws is called the _____.

3. Generally, a _____ is present when an investor invests money in a common enterprise with the expectation of making a profit from the significant efforts of others.

4. A business or party that sells securities to the public is called a(n) _____.

5. A document filed with the SEC that contains information about the issuer, securities to be issued, and other relevant information is called the _____.

6. A written document used as a selling tool by the issuer, which enables prospective purchasers of securities to evaluate certain risks of a particular investment, is known as the _____.

7. A regulation that permits an issuer to sell securities pursuant to a simplified registration process is called _____.

8. In certain situations, employees and advisors of an issuer of securities use material, nonpublic information to make a profit by buying or selling securities of the issuer. This practice is known as _____.

9. When certain insiders buy and sell securities within a six-month period of time, any gains realized are called _____ profits.

10. Each state is entitled to enact its own laws, known as _____ laws, regulating the offer and sale of securities within its borders.

True/False:

1. _____ Registration statements usually become effective ten business days after they are filed.

2. _____ All defendants except the issuer may assert the due diligence defense against the imposition of Section 11 liability.

3. _____ Certain transactions in securities are exempt from the registration requirements of the federal securities laws as are certain types of securities.

4. _____ Securities issued using a private placement exemption may only be sold to 35 investors.

5. _____ Violation of the federal securities laws can result in civil and criminal actions by the SEC as well as private civil actions by individual investors.

6. _____ Certain individuals associated with a securities offering can avoid liability by proving that, after reasonable investigation, they had reasonable grounds to believe, and did believe that at the time the registration statement became effective, the statements therein were true and that there was no omission of a material fact.

7. _____ An insider who trades on public information is subject to prosecution for violating the federal securities laws.

8. _____ A person who discloses material non-public information to another is called a Tippee.

9. _____ If an insider provides nonpublic information to another who knows the information is not public information and who trades the related securities in reliance on that information, both the insider and the trading party have committed violations of the federal securities laws.

10. _____ The Uniform Securities Act has been adopted by many states.

Multiple Choice:

1. The _____ is a federal statute that primarily regulates the issue of securities by companies and other businesses.

A. Securities Act of 1933
B. Securities Exchange Act of 1934
C. Sarbanes-Oxley Act of 2002
D. Dodd-Frank Wall Street Reform and Consumer Protection Act of 2010

2. The _____ is a federal statute primarily designed to prevent fraud in the trading of securities after they are issued.

A. Securities Act of 1933
B. Securities Exchange Act of 1934
C. Sarbanes-Oxley Act of 2002
D. Dodd-Frank Wall Street Reform and Consumer Protection Act of 2010

3. The courts apply the _____ in determining whether an arrangement is an investment contract.

A. Howey test
B. misappropriation theory
C. strict scrutiny test
D. intermediate test

4. _____ requires securities offered to the public through the use of the mails or any facility of interstate commerce to be registered with the SEC by means of a registration statement and an accompanying prospectus.

A. Section 24 of the Securities Act of 1933
B. Section 12 of the Securities Act of 1933
C. Section 5 of the Securities Act of 1933
D. SEC Rule 506

5. Shadee Corporation wishes to sell securities to raise $850,000 for the purpose of financing several corporate expansion projects. The issuance is considered a small offering. Which of the following statements is correct with respect to the transaction?

A. The transaction cannot be completed without registration because Rule 504 only allows the issuance of $750,000 of securities.
B. The securities can be sold to accredited investors only.
C. The securities can be sold to an unlimited number of accredited investors and to 35 unaccredited investors.
D. The securities can be sold to an unlimited number of accredited unaccredited investors.

6. A(n) _____ refers to a document that an issuer of securities files with the SEC that contains required information about the issuer, the securities to be issued, and other relevant information.

A. registration statement
B. operating statement
C. articles of organization
D. certificate of interest

7. Utilities Ltd. decided to go public by an initial public offering. It sold securities, some of which were bought by James Jefferson. Six months later, Mr. Jefferson sold the Utilities shares he had purchased to Martha Graham and Mark Franco. Two years later, Mr. Jefferson bought back the Utilities shares from Ms. Graham and Mr. Franco and made a profit out of both transactions. Who is the issuer in this scenario?

A. Utilities Ltd.
B. James Jefferson
C. Martha Graham
D. Mark Franco

8. Which of the following is true of Section 24 of the Securities Act of 1933?

A. It imposes civil liability on any person who violates the provisions of Section 5 of the act.
B. It imposes criminal liability on any person who willfully violates the 1933 act or the rules or regulations adopted.
C. It imposes civil liability on persons who intentionally defraud investors by making misrepresentations of material facts in the registration statement.
D. It exclusively regulates the sale of securities online.

9. The electronic data and record system of the Securities and Exchange Commission is known as
_____.

A. SPSE
B. NASDAQ
C. MICEX
D. EDGAR

10. A(n) _____ is a person who discloses material nonpublic information to another person.

A. issuer
B. tippee
C. tipper
D. grantor

V. Answers to Objective Questions

Terms:

1. Securities Act of 1933; Securities Exchange Act of 1934. These laws are the two keystones of today's securities law system. [p. 354]

2. Securities and Exchange Commission or SEC. The Securities Exchange Act of 1934 created the Securities and Exchange Commission (SEC) and empowered it to administer federal securities laws. The SEC is an administrative agency composed of five members who are appointed by the president. [p. 354]

3. Security. The definition of securities has expanded to cover more and more sorts of ventures, including some limited partnership offerings. [p. 354-355]

4. Issuer. A business or party selling securities to the public is called an issuer. [p. 355]

5. Registration statement. A document that an issuer of securities files with the SEC that contains required information about the issuer, the securities to be issued, and other relevant information. [p. 355]

6. Prospectus. A prospectus is a written disclosure document that must be submitted to the SEC along with the registration statement. A prospectus is used as a selling tool by the issuer. It is provided to prospective investors to enable them to evaluate the financial risk of an investment. [p. 356]

7. Regulation A. Regulation A permits issuers to sell up to $5 million of securities to the public during a 12-month period, pursuant to a simplified registration process. Such offerings may have an unlimited number of purchasers who do not have to be accredited investors. [p. 356]

8. Insider trading. A situation in which an insider makes a profit by personally purchasing shares of the corporation prior to public release of favorable information or by selling shares of the corporation prior to the public disclosure of unfavorable information. [p. 364]

9. Short-swing. Profits that are made by statutory insiders on trades involving equity securities of their corporation that occur within six months of each other. [p. 366]

10. Blue-sky laws. This is nicknamed after fraudulent sales of securities that had no underlying value beneath the "Blue Sky." State securities laws are often referred to as "blue-sky" laws because they help prevent investors from purchasing a piece of the blue sky. [p. 368]

True/False:

1. False. Registration statements usually become effective (the effective date) twenty business days after they are filed, unless the SEC requires additional information to be disclosed. [p. 356]

2. True. All defendants except the issuer may assert a due diligence defense against the imposition of Section 11 liability. If this defense is proven, the defendant is not liable. [p. 357]

3. True. Certain securities are exempt from registration with the SEC. Once a security is exempt, it is exempt forever. It does not matter how many times the security is transferred. Congress took cost considerations into account when these exemptions were allowed. [p. 359]

4. False. Securities sold using a private placement exemption may be sold to an unlimited number of accredited investors, but may only be sold to 35 non-accredited investors. [p. 361]

5. True. Depending on the violation, a particular action could result in civil and criminal actions. [p. 363]

6. True. Such a due diligence defense is available to a non-expert with respect to that portion of a registration statement prepared by nonexperts. [p. 363]

7. False. If the information is truly "public" in nature, then an insider is free to trade without committing any violations. [p. 364]

8. False. A person who receives material nonpublic information from a tipper is known as a tippee. [p. 364]

9. True. If an insider provides nonpublic information to another who knows the information is not public information and who trades the related securities in reliance on that information, both the insider and the trading party have committed violations of the federal securities laws. [p. 364-366]

10. True. The Uniform Securities Act has been adopted by many states. This act coordinates state securities laws with federal securities laws. [p. 368]

Multiple Choice:

1. A. The securities act of 1933 is a federal statute that primarily regulates the issuance of securities by corporations, limited partnerships, and associations. [p. 355]

2. B. Unlike the Securities Act of 1933, which regulates the original issuance of securities, the Securities Exchange Act of 1934 primarily regulates subsequent trading. [p. 362]

3. A. A Howey test is a test which states that an arrangement is an investment contract if there is an investment of money by an investor in a common enterprise and the investor expects to make profits based on the sole or substantial efforts of the promoter or others. [p. 354-355]

4. C. Section 5 of the Securities Act of 1933 requires securities offered to the public through the use of the mails or any facility of interstate commerce to be registered with the SEC by means of a registration statement and an accompanying prospectus. [p. 355]

5. D. The small offering exemption exempts the sale of up to $1 million of securities during a 12-month period from registration. The securities may be sold to an unlimited number of accredited and unaccredited investors, but general selling efforts to the public are not permitted. [p. 361]

6. A. A registration statement is a document that an issuer of securities files with the SEC that contains required information about the issuer, the securities to be issued, and other relevant information. [p. 355]

7. A. A business or party selling securities to the public is called an issuer. [p. 355]

8. B. Section 24 of the Securities Act of 1933 imposes criminal liability on any person who willfully violates either the act or the rules and regulations adopted there under. A violator may be fined or imprisoned up to 5 years or both. Criminal actions are brought by the Department of Justice. [p. 358]

9. D. The electronic data and record system of the Securities and Exchange Commission (SEC). [p. 359]

10 C. A person who discloses material nonpublic information to another person is called a tipper. [p. 364]

VI. Answers to Essay Question:

Mr. Williams may have a barrel full of real problems on his hands. He must now worry about possibly having run afoul of the Securities and Exchange Commission. Under the 1933 Act, newly issued securities must comply with the registration requirements of the Act unless they fall into specific exemptions. The first issue revolves around the definition of security for purposes of the 1933 Act. Under the court decision of S.E.C. v. Howey, any contract that calls for an investment with the expectation of income from the efforts of a promoter or third person may be deemed to be a security. Here the most likely interpretation is that the sales contracts for bakeries would be declared a security.

Next, look to see how this security was sold. If there is use of any facility of interstate commerce or the mail, it may be covered under the 1933 Act. Here with sales to several hundred people, lawyers would indicate a very likely use of the mail for purposes of selling the securities.

Then decide if any of the exemptions from registration apply. The securities themselves do not fall into any of the exempt categories. It is not a nonprofit organization, nor is this a sale by a governmental entity. It is not a reorganization or stock split. In addition, it does not appear that any of the transaction exemptions apply. It is not stated as only an intrastate offering. Nor does it appear that Mr. Williams tried to qualify the sales as a private placement or a small offering under either Section 504 or 505. Because he failed to comply with the 1933 Act, he may now be subject to both civil and criminal sanctions by the government. In addition, the private parties hurt by these violations may sue him.

In addition to the problems raised by the 1933 Act, there are problems that may arise under the 1934 Act if Mr. Williams engaged in subsequent trading of his partnership interests after they had first been issued. This is particularly a problem for him under Rules 10(b) and 10(b)-5 that are designed to go after fraudulent transfers of securities. These violations could lead to both civil and criminal sanctions against him by both the government and private parties.

Mr. Williams may be liable under the RICO statute or one or more of the newer federal securities laws recently passed as a result of scandals in the securities markets. [p. 357-359]

Are agents hurting professional sports?

I. Overview

Qui facit per alium facit per se. He who acts through another, acts himself. This simple Latin phrase provides the keystone upon which the mutual obligations of agency law rest. Agency is defined by Section 1 of the Second Restatement of Agency as "the fiduciary relation which results from the manifestation of consent by one person to another that the other shall act on his behalf and subject to his control, and consent by the other so to act."

Agency is a legally recognized relationship that allows an attribution of one person's behavior to another. This carryover process is two-sided in that both benefit and burden inure to parties involved in the agency relationship.

Under the basic doctrine of agency, the principal is allowed to reap the beneficial harvest of the agent's actions made in his or her behalf. For example, assume an agent has agreed to be paid a set salary of $100 for selling certain kinds of goods. The principal gets to keep the net profits from that agent's selling activities, be they $100 or $1,000,000. This net gain is what allows the use of agency theory to maximize one's profits through the actions of another. Exponential growth of most any sort of enterprise is almost always directly tied to effective use of the talent of others through agency law. There are some limits on this ability to designate others to act on one's behalf based on uniqueness of personal services or on public policy grounds that forbid use of agents, such as voting or serving a criminal sentence. As a practical matter, business as we know it today simply could not be conducted on any scale beyond sole proprietorship without extensive use of agency relationships.

The benefits of agency are not without counterbalancing detriment. The Latin maxim *respondeat superior* may be familiar to you. It means that, in certain instances, a principal is liable to third parties for the acts of his or her agent. Just as the benefits of agency can be great, so can the burdens. One of the fastest growing areas of management specialization in today's business environment is risk management. This area generally concerns business financial responsibility for exposure to specified contingencies or perils. Included in these perils are the acts of the agents for which the principal may be liable. The ironic aspect of all this is that the very same people who help a business grow can lead that same enterprise to financial ruin.

Every agency liability question having an involvement with third parties has three subquestions that must be answered in order to come to a final resolution of the issues at hand. They are:
1. What are the responsibilities of the principal and agent vis-à-vis each other?
2. What are the responsibilities of the agent vis-à-vis the third party?
3. What are the responsibilities of the principal vis-à-vis the third party?

Invariably a certain pattern of facts emerges. First there is some sort of principal/agent relationship established. This relationship may be based on actual, implied, apparent, or ratified authority. In all events, once that authority line has been drawn, the question of the legal consequences to the principal and agent vis-à-vis each other must be answered. These consequences would include their respective rights and duties to each other.

Once the first subquestion is resolved, the rights, duties, and obligations of the agent and principal respectively, must be examined vis-à-vis the third party. Often there will be some sort of wrongful and unauthorized act committed by the agent. That act will result in probable liability for both the agent and the principal to the third party who was harmed by the act. Think of the three subquestions as a loop that must be closed in order for the whole case to be resolved. A proper legal description always closes at the point where it began. So must an agency issue. It starts with the establishment of the agency relationship. It goes through the rights and duties of third parties. It terminates back where it began, with a determination of the ultimate responsibilities of the principal and agent vis-à-vis each other.

The study of the law of agency is very important to the upcoming study of business organizations. Both partnerships and corporations act through agents as we will see in the next few chapters. Partners are the agents for each other and the partnership, and officers and others are often agents for corporations. Thus careful attention to this subject will pay dividends later.

II. Hypothetical Multi-Issue Essay Question

John Jewelry owns a jewelry store located in a major mall in Iowa. His store is known for selling items worth no less that $5,000 each. Because he owns many other similar stores, he hires Mike Missing to manage this store. John, however, specifically instructs Mike that he is not permitted to buy any items worth more than $10 without his approval. He is to keep this agreement secret between the two of them. Mike has a poor memory and he purchases 100 diamond rings worth $15,000 each. John refuses to pay for the rings. While selling one of these rings, John accidentally trips and injures the customer buying the ring. He tripped because he was trying to balance a cup of coffee on his nose. John asks for some legal help in determining his potential liability stemming from the above facts.

III. Outline

Agency
> Agency relationships are formed by the mutual consent of a principal and an agent (It is a fiduciary relationship)
>> Principal
>>> The party who employs another person to act on his or her behalf
>> Agent
>>> The party who agrees to act on behalf of another
>> Agency
>>> The principal-agent relationship

> Employer-employee
>> A relationship that results when an employer hires an employee to perform some form of physical service
> Principal-agent
>> A relationship that results when an employer hires an employee and gives that employee authority to act and enter into contracts on his or her behalf

Forming the Agency Relationship
> Express agency
>> This is an agency that occurs when a principal and an agent expressly agree to enter into an agency agreement with each other. This is the most common form of agency.
> Implied agency
>> An agency that occurs when a principal and an agent do not expressly create an agency, but it is inferred from the conduct of the parties

Agency by ratification
    Agency that occurs when
        A person misrepresents himself or herself as another's agent when in fact he or she is not, but the purported principal eventually ratifies the unauthorized act
    Apparent agency
        Agency that arises when a principal creates the appearance of an agency that in actuality does not exist

Principal's and Agent's Duties

Duties of Principals
    Principal's duties (P → A)
        Duty of compensation for services provided
        Duty of reimbursement and indemnification → reimburse for costs and indemnify for losses
        Duty of cooperation and assistance
        Duty to provide safe working conditions

Duties of Agents
    Agent's duties (A → P)
        Duty of performance with reasonable care
        Duty of notification to the principal
        Duty of accountability to maintain accurate records
        Duty of loyalty not to act against the principal's interests (self-dealing, competition, dual agency)

Tort Liability to Third Parties

Principal and agent are each personally responsible for their own conduct
    Negligence
        Principals are liable for the negligent conduct of agents acting within their scope of employment
        Vicarious liability/respondeat superior- a rule that says an employer is liable for the tortuous conduct of its employees or agents while they are acting within the scope of its authority
    Frolic and Detour
        A situation in which an agent does something during the course of his employment to further his own interests rather than the principals
        Principals are generally relieved of liability if the agent's frolic and detour is substantial
    Coming and Going Rule
        A rule that says a principal is generally not liable for injuries caused by its agents and employees while they are on their way to and from work
    Dual-Purpose Mission
        An errand or another act that a principal requests of an agent while the agent is on his personal business
        Most jurisdictions hold that both the principal and agent are liable if the agent injures someone while on such a mission
Intentional Tort
        A principal is not liable for the intentional torts of agents and employees that are committed outside of the principal's scope of business
    Misrepresentation Test
        A test that determines whether an agent's motivation in committing an intentional tort is to promote the principal's business; is so, the principal is liable for any injuries caused by the tort

Work-related Test
A test that determines whether an agent committed an intentional tort within a work-related time or space; if so, the principal is liable for any injury caused by the agent's intentional tort
Misrepresentation
Intentional Misrepresentation (Fraud, Deceit)- a deceit in which an agent makes an untrue statement that he knows is not true
Innocent Misrepresentation- when an agent negligently makes a misrepresentation to a third-party
Third-party may:
1. Rescind the contract and recover any consideration paid; or
2. Affirm the contract and recover damages

Contract Liability to Third Parties

Type of Agency	Liability of Agent	Principal
1. Fully disclosed → known existence and identity of principal	No	Yes
2. Partially disclosed → known existence but unknown identity of principal	Yes	Yes
3. Undisclosed → unknown existence and identity of principal	Yes	Yes

Agent Exceeding the Scope of Authority
Implied warranty of authority- a warranty of an agent who enters into a contract on behalf of another that he has the authority to do so
If the agent exceeds the scope of authority, the principal is not liable on the contract
Ratification- a situation in which the principal accepts an agent's unauthorized contract

Independent Contractor
A person who contracts with another to do something for him who is not controlled by the other nor subject to the other's right to control with respect to his physical conduct in the performance of the undertaking
Factors Determining Independent Contractor Status
1. Whether the worker is engaged in a distinct occupation or an independently established business
2. Length of time the agent has been employed by the principal
3. The amount of time that agent works for the principal
4. Whether the principal supplies the tools and equipment
5. Method of payment
6. Degree of skill necessary to complete the task
7. Whether the worker hires employees to assist him
8. Whether the employer has the right to control the manner and means of accomplishing the desired result

Liability for Independent Contractor's Torts
Generally, a principal is not liable for the torts of an independent contractor

Liability for Independent Contractor's Contracts
Principals are bound by the authorized contracts of their independent contractors

Termination of Agency
    By parties:
        Mutual agreement
        Lapse of time
        Purpose achieved
        Occurrence of a specified event
    By operation of law:
        Death
        Insanity
        Bankruptcy of the principal
        Changed circumstances
        Impossibility of performance
        War

Notification Required at the Termination of an Agency
    1. Parties who dealt with the agent (direct notice required)
    2. Parties who have knowledge of the agency (direct notice required)
    3. Parties who have no knowledge (No notice required, but constructive notice can be achieved through publication)

Wrongful Termination of an Agency or Employment Contract
    It is the termination of an agency contract in violation of the terms of the agency contract. The non-breaching party may recover damages from the breaching party.

IV. Objective Questions

Terms:

1. The party who employs another person to act on her behalf is the _____.

2. An agency that occurs when a principal and agent agree to enter into an agency agreement with each other is called a(n) _____ agency.

3. An agency that occurs when a principal and agent do not expressly create an agency, but it is inferred from the conduct of the parties is called a(n) _____ agency.

4. An agency that occurs when (1) a person misrepresents herself as another's agent when in fact she is not and (2) the purported principal ratifies the unauthorized act is called a(n) _____.

5. An agency that arises when a principal creates the appearance of an agency that in actuality does not exist is known as a(n) _____ agency.

6. A rule that says an employer is liable for the tortious conduct of its employees or agents while they are acting within the scope of its authority is called _____.

7. The rule that says a principal is generally not liable for injuries caused by its agents and employees while they are on their way to or from work is called the _____.

8. The test to determine the liability of the principal: if the agent's motivation in committing the intentional tort is to promote the principal's business, then the principal is liable for any injury caused by the tort is known as the _____ test.

9. An agency results if the third party entering into the contract knows (1) that the agent is acting as an agent for a principal and (2) the actual identity of the principal. This is called a _____ agency.

10. A person who contracts with another to do something for him who is not controlled by the other nor subject to the other's right to control with respect to his physical conduct in the performance of the undertaking is known as _____.

True/False:

1. _____ An employee in an employer/employee relationship is not an agent since she cannot enter into contracts for her principal.

2. _____ A power of attorney, which is an express agency agreement, may be established by either an oral or written agreement.

3. _____ A principal's ratification of an unauthorized contract must be by express approval. Implied consent is not sufficient to bind a principal under ratification principles.

4. _____ An agency relationship must be based on consideration. That is, no agency relationship is created if the agent is not paid for his services.

5. _____ A principal is assumed to know what his agent knows.

6. _____ An agent is prohibited from using his agency for personal benefit even if the principal is aware of and consents to such actions.

7. _____ In a partially disclosed agency, both the agent and the principal are liable on any contract that the agent makes.

8. _____ An agent of a fully disclosed principal is liable on a contract if he does not specify the principal's name in signing the contract.

9. _____ Both agents and principals are liable for an agent's breach of the implied warranty of authority.

10. _____ Constructive notice is sufficient to inform parties who dealt with an agent that the agency has been terminated.

Multiple Choice:

1. The _____ is the party who employs another person to act on his or her behalf.

A. agent
B. principal
C. independent contractor
D. employee

2. A(n) _____ is a fiduciary relationship which results from the manifestation of consent by one person to another that the other shall act in his behalf and subject to his control, and consent by the other so to act.

A. assignment
B. garnishment
C. accommodation
D. agency

3. An agency that occurs when a principal and an agent categorically agree to enter into an agency agreement with each other is known as a(n) _____.

A. agency by ratification
B. implied agency
C. apparent agency
D. express agency

4. Which of the following is true of a general power of attorney?

A. A power of attorney can be oral.
B. Only lawyers can be agents of a power of attorney.
C. A power of attorney cannot be claimed once the principal in incapacitated.
D. It allows the agent to sign legal documents on the principal's behalf.

5. An express agency agreement that is often used to give an agent the control to sign legal documents on behalf of the principal is known as a(n) _____.

A. assignment
B. accommodation
C. power of attorney
D. letter of credit

6. An agency by ratification occurs when the principal _____.

A. accepts an unauthorized act created by an unauthorized agent
B. accepts an authorized act created by an authorized agent
C. creates the appearance of an agency that in actuality does not exist
D. accepts an act carried out under the implied authority of an agent

7. What is imputed knowledge?

A. Information collected by a principal prior to engaging in an agency.
B. Information collected by a principal on an agency.
C. Information learned by an agent that is attributed to the principal.
D. Information learned by a principal that is attributed to an agent.

8. Which of the following is a course of action for a principal if an agent is found competing with him or her?

A. The principal can recover damages from the agent if the competition continues after the agency has ended.
B. The principal can recover profits made by the agent.
C. The principal is given an option of buying the agent's competing venture.
D. The principal is not allowed to recover for lost sales due to the agent's competing venture.

9. Which of the following is true of tort liability for principals and agents?

A. A principal is responsible for the tortious conduct of an agent irrespective of the scope of his or her authority.
B. An agent is fully liable for his or her tortious conduct while on duty for the principal.
C. An agent is liable for the principal's tortious conduct if he or she participates in it.
D. An agent and a principal cannot be held responsible for the same tort.

10. Under the _____ test, if the agent committed an intentional tort to promote the principal's business, the principal is liable for any injury caused by the tort.

A. work-related
B. motivation
C. promotional
D. dual agency

V. Answers to Objective Questions

Terms:

1. Principal. A party who employs another person to act on his or her behalf is called a principal. Most principals are known as employers although that has its own set of special characteristics. [p. 377]

2. Express. Express agency is the most common form of agency. In an express agency, the agent has the authority to contract or otherwise act on the principal's behalf, as expressly stated in the agency agreement. [p. 378]

3. Implied. In many situations, a principal and an agent do not expressly create an agency. Instead, the agency is implied from the conduct of the parties. This type of agency is referred to as an implied agency. The extent of the agent's authority is determined from the facts and circumstances. These can include industry custom, prior dealings between the parties, or any other factors the court may deem relevant. [p. 379]

4. Agency by ratification. Agency by ratification occurs when (1) a person misrepresents himself or herself as another's agent when in fact he or she is not and (2) the purported principal ratifies (accepts) the unauthorized act. In such cases, the principal is bound to perform, and the agent is relieved of any liability for misrepresentation. [p. 379]

5. Apparent. This agency is also sometimes called an agency by estoppel. If the agency is established, the principal is estopped from denying the relationship. It is the principal's actions (or lack thereof) that can create an apparent agency. [p. 380]

6. Respondeat superior. A rule that says an employer is liable for the tortious conduct of its employees or agents while they are acting within the scope of the employer's authority. [p. 384]

7. Coming and going rule. A rule that says a principal is generally not liable for injuries caused by its agents and employees while they are on their way to or from work. [p. 385]

8. Motivation. Under the motivation test, if the agent's motivation in committing an intentional tort is to promote the principal's business, the principal is liable for any injury caused by the tort. However, if an agent's motivation in committing the intentional tort is personal, the principal is not liable, even if the tort takes place during business hours or on business premises. [p. 385-386]

9. Fully disclosed. A fully disclosed agency results if a third party entering into a contract knows (1) that the agent is acting as an agent for a principal and (2) the actual identity of the principal.1 The third party has the requisite knowledge if the principal's identity is disclosed to the third party by either the agent or some other source. In a fully disclosed agency, the contract is between the principal and the third party and the agent is not generally liable. [p. 388]

10. Independent contractors. A person who contracts with another to do something for him who is not controlled by the other nor subject to the other's right to control with respect to his physical conduct in the performance of the undertaking [p. 390]

True/False:

1. True. An agent is empowered to enter into contracts for her principal. An employee in an employer/employee relationship does not have this power. [p. 378]

2. False. A power of attorney, which is an express agency agreement, must be established by a written agreement. An oral agreement is not sufficient to establish a power of attorney. [p. 379]

3. False. Implied consent may be shown by the principal's conduct and is sufficient to show the principal's intent to ratify an unauthorized contract. [p. 379]

4. False. An agency relationship may be created even without consideration. Such an agency is known as a gratuitous agency. [p. 381]

5. True. The legal rule of imputed knowledge means that the principal is assumed to know what the agent knows. This is so even if the agent does not tell the principal certain relevant information. [p. 382]

6. False. An agent may personally benefit from his agency if the principal is aware of such conduct and consents to it. [p. 383]

7. True. Since the actual identity of the principal is not known to the third party in a partially disclosed agency, both the agent and the principal are liable on such a contract. [p. 388]

8. True. Even though agents of fully disclosed principals are not usually liable on contracts for the principals, if the agent does not specify the principal's name in signing the contract, he may be held liable on it. [p. 388]

9. False. Only an agent is liable for an agent's breach of the implied warranty of authority. [p. 389]

10. False. Parties who have dealt with an agent must be given direct notice of termination of the agency. Constructive notice is sufficient for parties who have no knowledge of the agency. [p. 393]

Multiple Choice:

1. B. A party who employs another person to act on his or her behalf is called a principal. [p. 377]

2. D. Agency is the principal–agent relationship; the fiduciary relationship which results from the manifestation of consent by one person to another that the other shall act in his behalf and subject to his control, and consent by the other so to act. [p. 377]

3. D. Express agency is the most common form of agency. In an express agency, the agent has the authority to contract or otherwise act on the principal's behalf, as expressly stated in the agency agreement. [p. 378]

4. D. A general power of attorney is a power of attorney in which a principal confers broad powers on the agent to act in any matters on the principal's behalf. [p. 379]

5. C. An express agency agreement that is often used to give an agent the power to sign legal documents on behalf of the principal is known as a power of attorney. [p. 379]

6. A. Agency by ratification occurs when (1) a person misrepresents himself or herself as another's agent when in fact he or she is not and (2) the purported principal ratifies (accepts) the unauthorized act. In such cases, the principal is bound to perform, and the agent is relieved of any liability for misrepresentation. [p. 379]

7. C. Most information learned by an agent in the course of an agency is imputed to the principal. The legal rule of imputed knowledge means that the principal is assumed to know what the agent knows. This is so even if the agent does not tell the principal certain relevant information. [p. 382]

8. B. Agents are prohibited from competing with the principal during the course of an agency unless the principal agrees. The reason for this rule is that an agent cannot meet his or her duty of loyalty when his or her personal interests conflict with the principal's interests. The principal may recover the profits made by the agent as well as damages caused by the agent's conduct, such as lost sales. An agent is free to compete with the principal when the agency has ended unless the parties have entered into an enforceable covenant not to compete. [p. 383]

9. C. A principal and an agent are each personally liable for their own tortuous conduct. The principal is liable for the tortious conduct of an agent who is acting within the scope of his or her authority. The agent, however, is liable for the tortious conduct of the principal only if he or she directly or indirectly participates in or aids and abets the principal's conduct. [p. 384]

10. B. A motivation test is a test that determines whether an agent's motivation in committing an intentional tort is to promote the principal's business; if so, the principal is liable for any injury caused by the tort. [p. 385]

VI. Answers to Essay Question

John is liable for the rings under the theory of apparent authority. Secret limitations between a principal and an agent have no effect when an agent has been held out as such by the principal. Such was the case here since Mike was John's store manager performing his normal managerial duties as far as others could tell.

The doctrine of respondeat superior holds that a principal is liable for the negligent torts of an agent if committed within the scope of the agency. Such seems to be the case here and, thus, John is liable for the customer's injuries. [p. 384]

Chapter 19

EQUAL OPPORTUNITY IN EMPLOYMENT

Why is discrimination wrong?

I. Overview

No single American legal issue is inflamed with more controversy than discrimination in the workplace. The genesis of our nation's heritage is rooted in a diversity of peoples who immigrated to the New World in order to flee the royalist, class, or caste systems that so often predestined their opportunities for social and economic advancement. The U.S. Declaration of Independence, and the government founded on it, was the first major system of self-governance premised on the assumption that all persons are born equal and should be treated equally in the eyes of the law. As we all know, that equality has often been a hope rather than a reality for many.

The same diversity that has been a source of national pride has also been the basis of disparate treatment of persons in the workplace for many years. The term discriminate has within it two distinct and opposite meanings. On the positive side, discrimination is simply a fact of life. We are not all equal in all ways. We have different talents, strengths, levels of training, and abilities. Employers, in turn, should be allowed and expected to seek utilization of these divergent talents and strengths in their own best interests. To discriminate in the positive sense is to reward ability and merit. The positive aspect of discrimination really says that uniqueness should be discerned, differentiated, distinguished, and rewarded in the workplace. In the end, economic marketplace factors are blind to any other factors but job performance. Like it or not, positive discrimination is a simple economic necessity which is no different than the laws of nature and cannot be ignored.

The negative side of discrimination is found in a wrongful process of selection. For a society founded on a premise of equality, we have certainly had more than our share of unequal treatment in the workplace. The negative side of discrimination is inequality of treatment based on wrongful motive, justifications, or rationalizations. Each choice not based on talent, ability, and merit is a step away from the inherent basis of equality before the law. Wrongful discrimination is like cancer. If it is allowed to grow unchecked, it will kill. None of us can afford to look the other way and say: "It's not my problem." Wrongful discrimination against any group is a wrong upon the society at large. Most everyone appreciates that fact intuitively, if not intellectually. Why is discrimination wrong? Yes it is unfair, but in an economic sense it may force us to avoid hiring the best person for the job. This is why businesses must avoid unfair discrimination.

It is difficult to legislate fairness but it has been clear that something must help if diversity is to be fostered. When it is left up to the law, the participants often attempt to find shortcuts. Hiring the best person for the job often gets lost in the shuffle. Yet can we leave such an important issue to individual consciences alone? This is how the concept of affirmative action was born.

Consider the dilemma posed by affirmative action. Past history provides vivid proof that patterns of discrimination have deep roots and will continue unless some sort of corrective social engineering takes hold in the workplace. Yet, is the cure worse than the disease? Can reverse discrimination really be justified? Is it any wonder that every day this quandary seems to get deeper? It is like kicking in quicksand—the more you try to move, the faster you sink.

One element that provides hope for positive change is goodwill. Where people of goodwill cling to the basic rightness of equity before the law, that equity will eventually result in a changed culture. Until then, law and our courts will continue to be the testing grounds for this monumental change in the social order.

II. Hypothetical Multi-issue Essay Question

An item recently appeared on the news wires:

"Major department store says no to Santa!"

A person who had been working for a major New York City department store was seeking to be reinstated into his seasonal job assignment as a Santa for the holidays. He had performed this job satisfactorily for a number of years.

He was denied reinstatement because he tested positive for HIV since the last holiday season. The department store was concerned that the health and safety of children sitting on Santa's lap would be placed in jeopardy. Even if the risk to health was minimal, the department store argued that the fear of parents to bring their children to a person known to have been tested positive for HIV would cost the store much lost business and damage its goodwill.

"Santa" decides to file a complaint with the EEOC. What will be the result?

III. Outline

Introduction to Equal Opportunity in Employment
Equal opportunity includes the right of all employees and job applicants to be treated without discrimination and to be able to sue employers if they are discriminated against

Title VII of the Civil Rights Act of 1964 as amended by the Equal Employment Opportunity Act of 1972.
Five protected classes:
Race, color, religion, sex, national origin
Disparate treatment discrimination
Discrimination against a specific individual because that person belongs to a protected class
Disparate impact discrimination
Discrimination that occurs where a neutral-looking employment rule causes discrimination against a protected class

Intentional Discrimination
A court may award punitive damages in some cases involving intentional discrimination.
The sum of compensatory and punitive damages is capped depending on the size of the employer.

Equal Employment Opportunity Commission (EEOC)
The federal agency responsible for enforcing most federal anti-discrimination laws

Remedies for Violations of Title VII
Back pay
Reasonable attorney fees
Equitable remedies

Retaliation
Title VII prohibits retaliation for filing or participating in a Title VII action.
Acts of retaliation include dismissal, demotion, harassment or any other method of retaliation

Race, Color and National Origin Discrimination

Race discrimination- it is based upon categories, such as, African American, Asian, Caucasian, Native American

Color discrimination- it is based upon the color of a person's skin

National origin discrimination- it is based upon the country of a person's ancestors, a person's cultural characteristics, or a person's heritage

Sex Discrimination and Sexual Harassment

Sex discrimination- discrimination based upon gender

Pregnancy Discrimination – the Pregnancy Discrimination Act forbids discrimination based upon pregnancy, childbirth, or related medical conditions

Quid pro quo discrimination- job related benefits exchanged for sexual favors:
Sexual harassment
May include lewd remarks, touching, intimidation, posting of indecent materials, and other verbal or physical conduct that occurs on the job which creates a hostile work environment
Same-sex Discrimination
Oncale v. Sundowner Offshore Services, Inc. – the U.S. Supreme Court held that same-sex sexual harassment and discrimination in employment are actionable under Title VII

Employer's Defenses to a Charge of Sexual Harassment

Affirmative Defenses
1. The employer exercised reasonable care to prevent or correct the harassing behavior
2. The employee unreasonably failed to take advantage of any preventive or corrective opportunities provided by the employer
Court considerations:
1. Was there an anti-harassment policy?
2. Did the employer have a complaint mechanism?
3. Were employees informed of the policies and procedures?
4. Any other relevant factors

Religious Discrimination

Discrimination against a person because of her religion or religious practices
Must make a reasonable accommodation
The accommodation cannot create an undue hardship on the employer

Defenses to Title VII Action

1. Merit
2. Seniority
3. Bona Fide Occupational Qualification (BFOQ)
Must be job related and a business necessity

Equal Pay Act

A federal statute that protects both sexes from pay discrimination based upon sex.
Jobs of equal skills, effort, responsibility, or similar working conditions are covered
Criteria that justify different wages
1. Seniority
2. Merit
3. Quantity or quality produced
4. Any other factor other than sex

Age Discrimination in Employment Act (ADEA)

The act that prohibits age discrimination practices against employees who are 40 and older

Older Worker Benefit Protection Act (OWBPA) - a federal statute that prohibits age discrimination in employee benefits

American with Disabilities Act (ADA)

A federal statute that imposes obligations on employers and providers of public transportation, telecommunication, and public accommodations to accommodate individuals with disabilities

Qualified Individual with a Disability

A person who can perform the essential functions of the job with or without reasonable accommodations that:

1. Has a physical or mental impairment that substantially limits one or more major life activities;

2. Has a record of such impairment; or

3. Is regarded as having such impairment

Forbidden Conduct

Employers cannot ask applicants about disabilities

Pre-employment medical examinations are forbidden before a job offer

An aggrieved individual must first file a claim with the EEOC.

Affirmative Action

See the Contemporary Environment section on page 365

IV. Objective Questions

Terms:

1. The right of all employees and job applicants (1) to be treated without discrimination and (2) to be able to prosecute employers if they are discriminated against is generally known as _____.

2. The federal agency responsible for enforcing most federal antidiscrimination laws is called the _____.

3. _____ discrimination is the type of discrimination that occurs where a neutral-looking employment rule causes discrimination against a protected class.

4. Protected classes under Title VII include _____.

5. The practice of refusing to hire or promote someone unless she has sex with the manager or supervisor is illegal and is called _____ discrimination.

6. The duty that employers owe employees to accommodate (1) the occurrence of religious practices, observances, or beliefs if it does not cause undue hardship to the employer or (2) a handicapped person's special requirements in the workplace is known as the duty of _____.

7. The selection or promotion qualification that is based on work, educational experience, and professionally developed ability tests is called _____ selection or promotion.

8. Discrimination based on sex, religion, and national origin is permitted if there is a legitimate reason for such discrimination and if it can be shown to be based on _____.

9. A hiring policy that provides that certain job preferences will be given to minority or other protected class applicants when an employer makes an employment decision is called _____.

10. Discrimination against a group that is usually thought of as a majority by a group that is usually thought of as a minority is generally referred to as _____.

True/False:

1. _____ The EEOC will issue a right to sue letter to the complainant even if it does not find a violation upon investigation of the charge.

2. _____ Under Title VII, a private complainant must first file a complaint with the EEOC before bringing suit against the employer.

3. _____ When the EEOC decides to bring suit on behalf of a complainant, it issues a right to sue letter.

4. _____ Only women are protected from sex discrimination under Title VII.

5. _____ Employers are not strictly liable to any of their employees who might have suffered sexual harassment at the workplace.

6. _____ Title VII, like many local ordinances, prohibits discrimination based on a person's sexual preference.

7. _____ Religions are permitted to hire only members of their religions for jobs within their organizations.

8. _____ Back pay, liquidated damages, and overtime pay are all remedies available under the Equal Pay Act.

9. _____ The ADEA is a federal statute that prohibits age discrimination practices against employees who are 40 years and older.

10 _____ Employers are obligated to provide reasonable accommodations to physically challenged employee if they do not incur significant difficulty or expense for the employers.

Multiple Choice:

1. The _____ is the federal agency responsible for enforcing most federal antidiscrimination laws.

A. EEOC
B. FEPA
C. ADEA
D. BFOQ

2. If the EEOC chooses not to bring suit, it issues a(n) _____ to the complainant.

A. affirmative defense
B. right to sue letter
C. filing date
D. document of claim

3. _____ discrimination occurs when an employer treats a specific individual less favorably than others because of that person's race, color, national origin, sex, or religion.

A. Disparate-treatment
B. Disparate-impact
C. Favored-treatment
D. Unfair-impact

4. Which of the following is true of employment discriminations defined under Title VII?

A. Disparate-treatment discrimination can be proven through statistical data about an employer's employment practices.
B. Disparate-impact discrimination occurs when an employer adopts a work rule that is neutral on its face but is shown to cause an adverse impact on a protected class.
C. Disparate-treatment discrimination occurs when an employer discriminates against an individual of a protected class.
D. Sexual harassment and refusal to hire physically challenged employees are illustrations of disparate-impact discrimination.

5. If a light-skinned member of a race refuses to hire a dark-skinned member of the same race, this will constitute as discrimination in violation of _____.

A. Title I of ADA
B. Title II of GINA
C. Title VII of the Civil Rights Act
D. Title IV of GINA

6. Which of the following best describes quid pro quo sex discrimination?

A. Employment discrimination because of pregnancy, childbirth or related medical conditions.
B. Discrimination where sexual favors are requested in order to obtain a job or be promoted.
C. Discrimination in hiring or promotion based on the gender of the employee under consideration.
D. Selective or partial treatment offered to an employee or a group of employees based on their gender.

7. Which of the following is true of sexual harassment?

A. Same-sex harassment is not covered under Title VII.
B. An employee being harassed at the workplace is not obligated to report it to the employer.
C. Sending offensive e-mail is considered sexual harassment.
D. Absence of a complaint policy makes an employer liable for disparate-impact discrimination.

8. Which of the following is true of religious discrimination?

A. Only monotheistic religions are covered under Title VII.
B. An employer need not accommodate religious observances or practices of its employees at the workplace.
C. An employee who claims religious discrimination cannot sue the employer for any other violation of Title VII.
D. Religious organizations can give preference in employment to individuals of a particular religion.

9. Why is proving a bona fide occupational qualification essential?

A. For discrimination to be legal.
B. To establish the employer's violation of Title VII.
C. To establish the employee's claim is fraudulent.
D. For an employee to claim being discriminated against by the employer.

10. A(n) _____ provides that certain job preferences will be given to members of minority racial and ethnic groups, females, and other protected-class applicants when making employment decisions.

A. retaliation
B. affirmative defense
C. affirmative action plan
D. reasonable accommodation plan

V. Answers to Objective Questions

Terms:

1. Equal opportunity in employment. The rights of all employees and job applicants (1) to be treated without discrimination and (2) to be able to sue employers if they are discriminated against. [p. 400]

2. Equal Employment Opportunity Commission. The Equal Employment Opportunity Commission (EEOC) is the federal agency responsible for enforcing most federal antidiscrimination laws. The members of the EEOC are appointed by the U.S. president. [p. 400]

3. Disparate Impact. A form of discrimination that occurs when an employer discriminates against an entire protected class. An example is discrimination in which a racially neutral employment practice or rule causes an adverse impact on a protected class. [p. 403]

4. Race, color, religion, national origin, sex. [p. 403]

5. Quid pro quo. Title VII also prohibits any form of gender discrimination where sexual favors are requested in order to obtain a job or be promoted. This is called quid pro quo sex discrimination. [p. 406]

6. Reasonable accommodation. The right of an employee to practice his or her religion is not absolute. Under Title VII, an employer is under a duty to reasonably accommodate the religious observances, practices, or beliefs of its employees if doing so does not cause an undue hardship on the employer. [p. 408]

7. Merit. Employers can select or promote employees based on merit. Merit decisions are often based on work, educational experience, and professionally developed ability tests. To be lawful under Title VII, such a requirement must be job related. [p. 409]

8. Bona fide occupation qualification. Discrimination based on protected classes other than race or color is permitted if it is shown to be a bona fide occupational qualification (BFOQ). Thus, an employer can justify discrimination based on gender in some circumstances. To be legal, a BFOQ must be both job related and a business necessity. [p. 409]

9. Affirmative action. A policy which provides that certain job preferences will be given to minority or other protected-class applicants when an employer makes an employment decision. [p. 416]

10. Reverse discrimination. The courts have held that if an affirmative action plan is based on pre-established numbers or percentage quotas for hiring or promoting minority applicants, then it causes illegal reverse discrimination. In this case, the members of the majority class may sue under Title VII and recover damages and other remedies for reverse discrimination. Some reverse discrimination cases are successful. [p. 416]

True/False:

1. True. If the EEOC sues the employer, the complainant cannot sue the employer. In this case, the EEOC represents the complainant. If the EEOC finds a violation and chooses not to bring suit, or does not find a violation, the EEOC will issue a right to sue letter to the complainant. This gives the complainant the right to sue his or her employer. [p. 401]

2. True. Under Title VII, a private complainant must first file a complaint with the EEOC. If the EEOC decides not to bring suit on behalf of the complainant, it will issue a right to sue letter. [p. 401]

3. False. A right to sue letter is issued by the EEOC when it decides not to bring suit on behalf of the complainant. [p. 401]

4. False. Both men and women are protected from sex discrimination under Title VII. However, women bring the vast majority of the cases. [p. 406]

5. True. Employers are not strictly liable for the sexual harassment of their employees. [p. 407]

6. False. Though many local ordinances do prohibit discrimination based on sexual preference, Title VII does not. [p. 407]

7. True. Discrimination based on protected classes other than race or color is permitted if it is shown to be a bona fide occupational qualification (BFOQ). Thus, an employer can justify discrimination based on gender in some circumstances. To be legal, a BFOQ must be both job related and a business necessity. [p. 409]

8. False. While back pay and liquidated damages are available remedies under the EPA, overtime pay is not. [p. 410]

9. True. The Age Discrimination in Employment Act (ADEA), which prohibits certain age discrimination practices, was enacted in 1967. The ADEA protects employees who are 40 and older from job discrimination based on their age.[p. 411]

10. True. An employer is under the obligation to make a reasonable accommodation to accommodate an individual's disability as long as such accommodation does not cause an undue hardship on the employer. [p. 413]

Multiple Choice:

1. A. The Equal Employment Opportunity Commission (EEOC) is the federal agency responsible for enforcing most federal antidiscrimination laws. [p. 400]

2. B. If the EEOC finds a violation and chooses not to bring suit, or does not find a violation, the EEOC will issue a right to sue letter to the complainant. This gives the complainant the right to sue his or her employer. [p. 401]

3. A. Disparate-treatment discrimination occurs when an employer treats a specific individual less favorably than others because of that person's race, color, national origin, sex, or religion. [p. 403]

4. B Disparate-impact discrimination is a form of discrimination that occurs when an employer discriminates against an entire protected class. An example is discrimination in which a racially neutral employment practice or rule causes an adverse impact on a protected class. [p. 403]

5. C. Title VII of the Civil Rights Act of 1964 was primarily enacted to prohibit employment discrimination based on race, color, and national origin. [p. 404]

6. B. Title VII also prohibits any form of gender discrimination where sexual favors are requested in order to obtain a job or be promoted. This is called quid pro quo sex discrimination. [p. 406]

7. C. Sometimes managers and co-workers engage in conduct that is offensive because it is sexually charged. Such conduct is often referred to as sexual harassment. This includes lewd remarks, offensive or sexually oriented jokes; name-calling, slurs, intimidation, ridicule, mockery, and insults or put-downs; offensive or sexually explicit objects, pictures, cartoons, posters, and screen savers; physical threats; touching; and other verbal or physical conduct of a sexual nature. [p. 407]

8. B. The right of an employee to practice his or her religion is not absolute. Under Title VII, an employer is under a duty to reasonably accommodate the religious observances, practices, or beliefs of its employees if doing so does not cause an undue hardship on the employer. [p. 408]

9. A. Discrimination based on protected classes other than race or color is permitted if it is shown to be a bona fide occupational qualification (BFOQ). Thus, an employer can justify discrimination based on gender in some circumstances. To be legal, a BFOQ must be both job related and a business necessity. [p. 409]

10. C. Employers often adopt an affirmative action plan, which provides that certain job preferences will be given to members of minority racial and ethnic groups, females, and other protected-class applicants when making employment decisions. Such plans can be voluntarily adopted by employers, undertaken to settle a discrimination action, or ordered by the courts. [p. 416]

VI. Answers to Essay Question

The passions involved in many of these antidiscrimination issues run deep. They are often founded on claims by both sides of being morally, economically, or politically correct. Here the alleged wrongful discrimination is based on a physical characteristic or condition, i.e., testing positive for HIV. The outbreak of AIDS has raised a raucous debate in this country about what body of law is applicable to persons afflicted with this physical condition.

On one side, many argue that it should be treated solely as a health problem. As such, laws with regard to communicable diseases should control. These measures would be based on the theory that certain prophylactic measures are necessary where there is a real and present danger to oneself and others from the disease.

On the other side, a number of commentators have argued that fear of HIV and AIDS-related afflictions have generated the worst sort of civil rights abuses against persons afflicted with those conditions. Discrimination in housing, jobs, education, health care, and insurance have all surfaced as a result of the fears raised by the disease. Where there is no provable risk of communication of the virus, civil rights, including job rights, should not be compromised.

The real answer probably lies somewhere in between. Society does have the right and responsibility to take reasonable measures to protect itself from deadly threats to public health. But, when measures are taken, society should also meet the burden of proof that the measures are reasonable and proper. It cannot and should not trample on civil rights based on panic and ill-founded fear.

In this case, Congress has sought to balance the needs of both society and persons afflicted with HIV through the Americans with Disabilities Act of 1990. Under that Act persons who have tested positive for HIV are classified as disabled persons because they are treated as such (the second definition of a disability). As such they are entitled to seek protection under the Act from discriminatory practices in the workplace.

Conversely, the employer is allowed to use the defenses listed in the statute. One of those defenses is the health and safety of others. Another is undue hardship to the employer. In both cases, the burden of proof is on the employer to show that the defenses are applicable. If the department store can show that a real health and safety hazard exists for the persons with whom "Santa" will have contact, it will prevail. In addition, if the department store can show that using this person in this setting would create an undue hardship, it again would prevail since a reasonable accommodation would be impossible. In either case, it must meet the burden of proof. Failure to do so will allow "Santa" to prevail under the Act. "Santa's" best strategy is to seek protection under the Americans with Disabilities Act of 1990. [p. 411-412]

Chapter 20
EMPLOYMENT LAW AND WORKER PROTECTION

Who needs protection—the employer or the employee?

I.   Overview

In the past, the dominant contractual form the employment relationship has taken has been found in the *employment at will* doctrine. This doctrine assumes that given equal bargaining power, and absent express or implied agreement to the contrary, either the employee or employer may end the relationship. This termination can come about at any time, for any reason, bilaterally or unilaterally. The doctrine has long been under fire because of being myopic on two main scores: it presumes equality of bargaining power between the employer and employee and that the employment relationship is a totally private contractual matter between the contracting parties.

Recent cases and legislative enactments have greatly eroded the doctrine. On the legislative front, a number of states have decided that public policy interests in favor of certain kinds of activities must take precedence over the employer/employee relationship. Examples would include voting rights, antidiscrimination measures, whistleblower protections, and employee health and safety protections. In addition, a number of courts have seen fit to interpret employer handbooks, written and oral job policies, and other acts as indicia of an implied contract between the employer and employee. So what may have appeared originally to be the employee's economic ball and chain has also become the employer's.

The simple truth is that there is a growing involvement of government at every step of the employer/employee relationship. It sets the ground rules for hiring, working conditions, paying for harm, termination, and ultimate payment of pensions and or death benefits. It all has come a long way from the simplistic and archaic notion that the employment contract is only the business of the immediate parties involved.

In fact, many statutes protect the employment relationship by insuring a minimum wage, a premium for overtime, safe working conditions and, hopefully, a drug free environment. Are these statutes good or bad for business? That remains to be seen.

II. Hypothetical Multi-Issue Essay Question

Mr. Quincy Harpie has a problem. As a matter of fact, he has a lot of problems. He is chronically complaining about all sorts of illnesses, both actual and perceived. His mother was never proud of him and kicked him out of the house at age thirty-two. Finally Mr. Harpie had to face reality and get a job.

He found his first job with Mega Widgets Corporation in Backwater as a crystal widget assembler. Two weeks into the job, he complained of severe backaches and sought worker compensation for his back problems. He was awarded his claim of partial disability and proceeded to stay at home while seeking other employment.

He did find other employment at Mini Widgets Corporation in the adjoining state of Massazona. He did not tell Mini Widgets about his employment history with Mega Widgets. Two weeks on the job as an assembler, guess what happened? His back flared up again. He successfully filed a worker compensation claim against Mini Widgets. He continued to also collect from Mega Widgets claiming that he was still disabled.

Mr. Harpie decided to try once more and moved to East Moncalla where he found employment with Micro Widgets Corporation. Micro had a strict employment at will policy and informed Mr. Harpie of that policy in writing. After two weeks of work on Micro's assembly line, Mr. Harpie again claimed a back injury. He filed yet a third claim under workers compensation. As in the prior incidents, he did not inform Micro of any of his prior job history.

Micro fought Mr. Harpie's claim and also fired him under the employment at will doctrine. Mr. Harpie claims that the doctrine is being wrongfully used against him. He is arguing that he was being fired only because he asserted his rights under the workers compensation law. At the time Micro did not know about Mr. Harpie's history with Mega and Mini Widgets Corporations. Should Mr. Harpie be reinstated at Micro Corporation?

III. Outline

Workers' Compensation
> Compensation paid to workers and their families when workers are injured in connection with their jobs

> Workers Compensation Insurance
>> Most states require employers to purchase insurance from private companies, state funds, or self-insurance

> Employment Related Injury
>> Claimant must prove that the injury arose out of and in the course of employment

> Exclusive Remedy
>> Workers cannot receive Workers' Compensation and sue an employer in court for damages
>>> Exception: If an employer intentionally injures and employee

Occupational Safety
> Occupational Safety and Health Act
>> A federal act enacted in 1970 that promotes workplace safety and established the Occupational Safety and Health Administration
> Occupational Safety and Health Administration
>> A federal agency within the Department of Labor that is empowered to enforce the act

> Specific duty standards
>> An OSHA standard that addresses a safety problem of a specific duty nature (ex. Safety guards)
> General duty standards
>> A duty that an employer has to provide a work environment free from recognized hazards that are causing or are likely to cause death or serious physical harm to employees
>>> OSHA can inspect the workplace and issue citations for violations

Fair Labor Standards Act
> A federal act enacted in 1938 to protect workers. It prohibits child labor and spells out minimum wage and overtime pay requirements.

> Child Labor
> 1. Children under 14 cannot work except to deliver newspapers

2. Children ages 14 and 15 may work limited hours in non-hazardous jobs

3. Children ages 16 and 17 may work unlimited hours in non-hazardous jobs

   Children who work in agricultural employment, child actors and performers are exempt

Minimum Wage

As of 2009, minimum wage is $7.25/hour

   Some states require hirer wages

   Students and apprentices may be paid less

Overtime Pay

Non-exempt employees must be paid one and one-half the regular rate of pay for any work over 40 hours performed in one week

Managerial, administrative, and professional employees are exempt from the FLSA wage and hour provisions

Other Worker Protection Laws

Consolidated Omnibus Budget Reconciliation Act (COBRA)

   A federal law that permits employees and their beneficiaries to continue their group health insurance after an employee's employment has ended

   To continue coverage, a person must pay the required group premium

Employee Retirement Income Security Act (ERISA)

A federal act designed to prevent fraud and other abuses associated with private pension funds

ERISA provides:

   1. Immediate vesting for each employee's own contributions to a pension plan; and

   2. It requires employer's contributions to be either (1) totally vested after five years (cliff vesting) or (2) gradually over a seven-year period

Family Medical Leave Act

A federal act that guarantees workers up to 12 weeks of unpaid leave in a 12-month period to attend to families and medical emergencies and other situations

   Employees must have worked 1250 hours in the previous 12 months

Government Programs

Unemployment Compensation

Federal Unemployment Tax Act (FUTA)

   A federal tax that requires employers to pay unemployment taxes and under which unemployment compensation is paid to workers who are temporarily unemployed

Social Security

A federal system that provides limited retirement and death benefits to covered employees and their dependents

   Benefits include:

   1. Retirement benefits

   2. Survivors benefits to family members of deceased workers

   3. Disability benefits

   4. Medical and hospital benefits (Medicare)

Federal Insurance Contributions Act (FICA)
> Employees must pay into social security and employers must pay a matching amount

Self Employment Contributions Act
> Self-employed individuals must pay the combined amount of employee-employer contributions to Social Security

IV. Objective Questions

Terms:

1. The administrative procedure created so that workers receive compensation for injuries that occur on the job is called _____.

2. The 1970 Occupational Safety and Health Act created the _____, a federal administrative agency empowered to administer the Act and adopt rules and regulations to interpret and enforce the Act.

3. The _____ forbids the use of oppressive child labor and makes it unlawful to ship goods produced by businesses that use oppressive child labor.

4. Compensation that is paid to workers who are temporarily unemployed is known as _____.

5. The _____ system is a federal system that provides limited retirement and death benefits to covered employees and their dependents.

True/False:

1. ____ Injuries that arise in the course of employment are not compensable.

2. ____ Workers' compensation is an exclusive remedy.

3. ____ Under the Fair Labor Standards Act, an employer cannot require nonexempt employees to work more than 40 hours per week unless they receive overtime pay.

4. ____ Employers are required to establish pension plans for their employees.

5. ____ ERISA provides for immediate vesting of each employee's own contributions to the plan.

6. ____ Employees do not pay unemployment taxes.

Multiple Choice:

1. How does the enactment of workers' compensation acts prove to be beneficial to workers?

A. These acts create an administrative procedure for workers to receive indemnification for injuries that occur on the job.
B. These acts reduce the total hours of mandatory labor and provide for a more flexible schedule.
C. These acts create an administrative procedure for workers to receive early retirement benefits.
D. These acts seek to insure workers against the perils of layoff.

2. Workers' compensation is an exclusive remedy. Which of the following can be deduced from this fact?

A. Workers' compensation acts do not bar injured workers from suing responsible third parties to recover damages.
B. All injuries that arise in the course of employment are remediable and compensable.
C. Workers cannot both receive workers' compensation and sue their employers in court for damages.
D. Workers are encouraged to sue their employers in court for damages.

3. If an employee is injured in an automobile accident while she is driving to an off-premises restaurant during her personal lunch hour, the injury is _____.

A. covered by workers' compensation insurance
B. not covered by workers' compensation
C. covered by workers' compensation
D. not covered by employee's medical insurance

4. The _____ is federal act enacted in 1970 that promotes safety in the workplace.

A. FLSA
B. ERISA
C. OSHA
D. FMLA

5. The _____ is an OSHA standard that requires an employer to provide a work environment free from recognized hazards that are causing or are likely to cause death or serious physical harm to employees.

A. provision of nonhazardous work environment
B. code of wellness
C. specific duty standard
D. general duty standard

6. According to the Department of Labor, children under the age of 14 can only be employed as _____.

A. newspaper deliverers
B. store assistants
C. waiters
D. stocking staff at stores

7. To be covered by the FMLA, an employee must _____.

A. have worked for the employer for at least six months
B. have performed more than 1,250 hours of service
C. not have claimed maternity leave in the past
D. be suffering from a serious injury or ailment

Statute Exercise:

Choose the correct statute or government program form the left column and match it to the explanation on the right column.

1. ERISA	A. Exclusive remedy for job-related injuries
2. Workers' Compensation acts	B. Minimum wage
3. Fair Labor Standards Act	C. Assistance for temporary loss at work
4. Family Medical Leave Act	D. Limited retirement and death benefits
5. COBRA	E. Protect private pension plans
6. OSHA	F. Continuation of health insurance post-employment
7. Social Security	G. Safety in the workplace
8. Unemployment Compensation	H. Unpaid time off for medical emergencies

V. Answers to Objective Questions

Terms:

1. Workers' compensation. The basic statutory scheme is designed to avoid the waste and expense of seeking compensation for work-related injuries through the courts. It is one of the earliest forms of contract-based strict liability. [p. 423]

2. Occupational Safety and Health Administration. This agency has power to promote and regulate safety in virtually all workplaces except federal, state, and local government workplaces. It is part of the Department of Labor, and it imposes a number of record-keeping and reporting requirements on employers. [p. 425]

3. Fair Labor Standards Act. This also deals with minimum wage and overtime pay. [p. 427-428]

4. Unemployment compensation. The federal government sets the guidelines for these benefits, but the actual administration of these employer-contributed taxes is handled by the individual states. [p. 431]

5. Social Security. In 1935, Congress established the federal Social Security system to provide limited retirement and death benefits to certain employees and their dependents. The Social Security system is administered by the Social Security Administration. [p. 432]

True/False:

1. False. For an injury to be compensable under workers' compensation, the claimant must prove that he or she was harmed by an employment-related injury. Thus, injuries that arise out of and in the course of employment are compensable. [p. 423]

2. True. Workers' compensation is an exclusive remedy. Thus, workers cannot both receive workers' compensation and sue their employers in court for damages. [p. 424]

3. True. Under the FLSA, an employer cannot require nonexempt employees to work more than 40 hours per week unless they are paid overtime pay of one-and-a-half times their regular pay for each hour worked in excess of 40 hours that week. Each week is treated separately. [p. 428]

4. False. Employers are not required to establish pension plans for their employees. If they do, however, they are subject to the record-keeping, disclosure, and other requirements of the Employee Retirement Income Security Act (ERISA). [p. 431]

5. True. Vesting occurs when an employee has a nonforfeitable right to receive pension benefits. ERISA provides for immediate vesting of each employee's own contributions to the plan. [p. 431]

6. True. Under the Federal Unemployment Tax Act (FUTA) and state laws enacted to implement the program, employers are required to pay unemployment contributions (taxes). [p. 431]

Multiple Choice:

1. A. States enacted workers' compensation acts in response to the unfairness of that result. These acts create an administrative procedure for workers to receive workers' compensation for injuries that occur on the job. [p. 423]

2. C. Workers' compensation is an exclusive remedy. Thus, workers cannot both receive workers' compensation and sue their employers in court for damages. [p. 424]

3. B. If an employee is injured in an automobile accident while she is driving to an off-premises restaurant during her personal lunch hour, the injury is not covered by workers' compensation. [p. 424]

4. C. In 1970, Congress enacted the Occupational Safety and Health Act1 to promote safety in the workplace. [p. 425]

5. D. The Occupational Safety and Health Act contains a general duty standard that imposes on an employer a duty to provide employment and a work environment that is free from recognized hazards that are causing or are likely to cause death or serious physical harm to its employees. [p. 426]

6. A. Under the FLSA, children under the age of 14 cannot work except as newspaper deliverers. [p. 428]

7. B. To be covered by the FMLA, an employee must have worked for the employer for at least one year and must have performed more than 1,250 hours of service during the previous twelve-month period. [p. 430]

Statute Exercise:

A. 2 [p. 431]
B. 3 [p. 423]
C. 8 [p. 427]
D. 7 [p. 430]
E. 1 [p. 431]
F. 5 [p. 425]
G. 6 [p. 432]
H. 4 [p.431]

VI. Answers to Essay Question

The employer/employee relationship between Mr. Harpie and Micro Widgets Corporation is clearly one of employment at will. The parties have agreed to this in writing. Under that doctrine, either party may terminate the relationship at any time for any reason, subject to limitations imposed as a matter of public policy, by statute or by court precedent.

There may be limitations imposed by the State of East Moncalla on the employment at will doctrine. Examples might include protection of whistleblowers or protection of persons who refuse to break the law at the behest of their employers. But none of these limitations are designed to protect the employee to the extent of shielding his or her own wrongdoing.

Worker's compensation fraud is one of the fastest growing and costliest crimes that today's employers face. States have not acted in concert to prevent this fraud as well as they might have. That failure to enforce against this sort of fraudulent behavior has made cases like Mr. Harpie's very common and very costly. Under the employment at will doctrine, unless Mr. Harpie can show that one of the exceptions applies based or public policy, case law, or statute, Micro Widgets can fire him. If they know haw bad an apple he really is, they should seek to have criminal charges filed also. Then maybe he can develop a bad back while punching out license plates. [p. 423-424]

Chapter 21
LABOR LAW AND IMMIGRATION LAW

Should strikes be stopped?

I. Overview

Organized labor has suffered from a long and steady decline in membership, power, and influence over the past forty years. Much of this slide has been of its own doing, traceable to poor union management, a fat cat image, and sometimes-silly work rules that have no economic justification in the face of changed technology. In spite of all this bad news for unions, consider the working conditions that existed before them. It is a hallmark of advanced industrialized economies that the work force is highly organized and has a strong bargaining power over its affairs. The immediate post-Civil War era of industrialization saw the possibilities for abuse of the work force not only become reality, but also a tragedy, when it came to workers' safety. Most modern social legislation, ranging from the minimum wage, to child labor laws, to workplace and antidiscrimination statutes are traceable not to the largess of employers but rather to hard fought collective bargaining agreements. It is no accident that union representation is low in areas of the world still noted for the exploitation of their labor force. Corollaries of low wages are low levels of worker protection, environmental callousness, and an overall diminished standard of living.

The basic employer/employee relationship is a contractual one. As with any contract, both parties are expected to enter into the relationship with their own best interests at heart. The quaint notion of a paternalistic employer who cares for his workers over and above his own interests is simply unrealistic in today's age of cutthroat economic competition. What is realistic is enlightened self-interest. Each side of the labor management relationship still looks out for itself. But in looking out for number one, both must realize their mutual interdependence on each other. Labor must realize that it cannot sustain its own survival on the backs of failed companies brought down by union imposed inefficiencies. Labor must adjust to "Real World 101" and make concessions to both the technological and economic realities of trying to compete in a global economy. Management, in turn, cannot forever continue to erode our economic consumer base at home by running overseas at every opportunity for lower wages and less restrictive hospitalities for doing business.

What will happen in the long run if we allow our home economy to become depleted of workers who earn real living wages? We cannot let our economy degenerate into one of only two classes: the very rich and minimum wage service workers. Our industrial base was built on a working partnership between management and labor. Like any marriage this partnership was not always easy to live with. But it did thrive on a mutual respect for the other's role in the larger scheme of things. What we have had instead for the past forty years is a willingness on the part of both sides to forgo the long-term societal benefits that can inure from good faith bargaining. The end result is that our economy is in danger of not only being nonunion, but also more noncompetitive, nonproductive, and nongrowth than ever. Unions and management both need to adjust before it's too late.

II. Hypothetical Multi-issue Essay Question

Major League baseball players have decided to strike after the end of the current contract. Management has told the rookies that if they honor the strike, they will be cut from the major and minor leaguer rosters. The union claims that the strike is necessary because management will not listen to salary or benefit demands and, in fact, will not speak to union representatives. Who has acted legally in this matter?

III. Outline

Labor Laws

American Federal of Labor (AFL) - formed in 1886 (skilled workers)
Congress of Industrial Organization (CIO) - formed in 1935 (semi-skilled and unskilled workers)

AFL-CIO – the combination of the AFL and CIO

Approximately ten-percent of private sector wage and salary workers belong to labor unions

Federal Labor Union Statutes

1. Railway Labor Act
2. Norris-LaGuardia Act
3. National Labor Relations Act (NLRA)
4. Labor Management Relations Act (Taft-Hartley)
5. Labor Management Reporting Act (Landrum-Griffin)

National Relations Labor Board

A five member administrative body that oversees union elections, prevents employers and unions from engaging in illegal and unfair labor practices, and enforces and interprets certain federal labor laws

Organizing a Union

Section 7 of the NLRA- provides employees a right to:

1. Self organize
2. Form, join or assist labor organizations
3. Bargain collectively through representatives of their own choosing
4. Engage in concerted activities for the purpose of collective bargaining or other mutual aid or protection

Bargaining unit – the group a union seeks to represent
This can be a single company or plant, group within a company, or entire industry

Types of Union Elections
30% or more of a bargaining unit must sign an election authorization card

1. Contested election (majority vote)
2. Consent election (employer does not challenge)
3. Decertification election (employees may vote to get rid of the union)

Union Solicitation on Company Property

Employers may restrict union solicitation activities on company time and property
Inaccessibility exception – a rule that permits employees and union officials to engage in union solicitation on company property if the employees are beyond the reach of reasonable union efforts to communicate with them

Illegal Interference with an Election
> Section 8(a) makes it an unfair labor practice for an employer to interfere with or coerce or restrain employees from exercising their statutory right to form and join unions

Collective Bargaining
The act of negotiating contract terms between an employer and the members of a union

Subjects of Collective Bargaining
1. Compulsory- wages, hours, and other terms and conditions of employment
2. Illegal- ex. Discrimination and closed shops
3. Permissive- may be bargained for if the parties agree to

Union Security Agreements
> Union shop- an employee must join the union within a certain number of days of being hired
> Agency shop- an employee does not have to join a union but must pay a fee equal to union dues

Right to Work Laws

Strikes
A cessation of work by union members in order to obtain economic benefits or correct an unfair labor practice

Cooling Off Period
> A mandatory 60 day notice before a strike can commence

Illegal Strikes
1. Violent strikes
2. Sit down strikes
3. Partial or intermittent strikes
4. Wildcat strikes

No Strike Clause
> An agreement between an employer and a union that the union will not strike during a particular period of time

Crossover and Replacement Workers
> Crossover workers- union members who choose not to strike
> Replacement workers- workers hired to replace striking workers

Employer Lockout
> An act of an employer to prevent employees from entering the work premises when the employer reasonably anticipates a strike

Picketing
Strikers walking in front of an employer's premises, carrying signs announcing the strike
> Picketing is lawful unless:
> 1. Accompanied by violence
> 2. Obstruction of customers entering the business
> 3. Prevents non-striking employees from entering the workplace

4. Prevents pickups and deliveries at the workplace

Secondary Boycott Picketing
> A type of picketing in which a union tries to bring pressure on an employer by picketing the employer's suppliers or customers

Internal Union Affairs
> Title I of the Landrum Griffin Act provides a "bill of rights" which gives each union member equal rights and privileges to nominate candidates for union office, vote in elections, and participate in membership meetings
>> Unions may discipline members for:
>> 1. A non-sanctioned strike
>> 2. Working for wages below union scale
>> 3. Spying for an employer
>> 4. Any other unauthorized activity that has an adverse economic impact on the union

Worker Adjustment and Retraining Notification Act (WARN)
> A federal act that requires employers with 100 or more employees to give their employees 60 days notice before engaging in certain plant closings or layoffs
>> See the Ethics Spotlight on page 390

Immigration Law
> Immigration Reform and Control Act of 1986 (IRCA)
>> A federal statute that makes it unlawful for employers to hire illegal immigrants

Employment Eligibility Verification
> Form I-9- a form that must be completed by each employee regardless of citizenship or national origin. The form provides verification that the employee is authorized to work in the United States.

H-1B Foreign Guest Visa
> This is a non-immigrant visa that allows U.S. employers to employ in the U.S. foreign nationals who are skilled in specialty occupations.
>> Foreign guest worker- a worker who is sponsored and employed by a U.S. employer pursuant to an H-1B visa

IV. Objective Questions

Terms:

1. If employees no longer want to be represented by a union, a(n) _____ must be held.

2. Wages and hours are _____ of collective bargaining.

3. In a(n) _____, an employee must join the union within a certain number of days after being hired.

4. The action of strikers walking in front of an employer's premises, carrying signs announcing their strike is known as _____.

5. A visa that allows U.S. employers to employ in the United States foreign nationals who possess exceptional qualifications for certain types of employment is known as a(n) _____.

True/False:

1. ____ Once a union is elected and certified, covered employees may negotiate individually with the employer regarding employment benefits.

2. ____ If a collective bargaining agreement cannot be reached, the union may call a strike.

3. ____ An employer may seek an injunction against picketing that prevents pickups and deliveries at the employer's place of business.

4. ____ Secondary boycott picketing is always permitted.

5. ____ The H-1B visa allows U.S. employers to employ in the United States foreign nationals who are skilled in specialty occupations.

Multiple Choice:

1. Which of the following is provided by the National Labor Relations Act of 1935?

A. To bargain collectively with employers
B. To regulate internal affairs of each union
C. To represent employees according to their sectors of employment
D. To equally represent every union member

2. Which act created the National Labor Relations Board?

A. Labor-Management Reporting and Disclosure Act.
B. Norris-LaGuardia Act.
C. National Labor Relations Act.
D. Labor-Management Relations Act.

3. A group of employees that a union is seeking to represent is known as a(n) _____.

A. combined conciliation unit
B. appropriate mediation unit
C. collective negotiation unit
D. appropriate bargaining unit

4. A _____ is a cessation of work by union members in order to obtain economic benefits or correct an unfair labor practice.

A. collective bargain
B. strike
C. crossover
D. persuasion

5. Picketing is lawful when it:

A. is accompanied by violence.
B. prevents nonstriking employees from entering the employer's premises.
C. does not obstruct customers from entering the employer's place of business.
D. prevents pickups and deliveries at the employer's place of business.

Statute Exercise:

Choose the statute from the left column and match it to the description in the right column.

1. Norris-LaGuardia Act	A. Labor's "bill of rights"
2. Wagner Act	B. Presidential injunction
3. Taft-Hartley Act	C. Covers railroad employees
4. Landrum Griffin Act	D. Collective bargaining
5. Railway Labor Act	E. Employees can organize

V. Answers to Objective Questions

Terms:

1. decertification election. If employees no longer want to be represented by a union, a decertification election will be held. [p. 438]

2. compulsory subjects. Wages, hours, and other terms and conditions of employment are compulsory subjects of collective bargaining. [p. 440]

3. union shop. A workplace in which an employee must join the union within a certain number of days after being hired is known as a union shop. [p. 441]

4. picketing. The action of strikers walking in front of an employer's premises, carrying signs announcing their strike is known as picketing. [p. 443]

5. EB-1 visa. A visa that allows U.S. employers to employ in the United States foreign nationals who possess exceptional qualifications for certain types of employment is known as a(n) EB-1 visa. [p. 446]

True/False:

1. False. Once a union has been elected, the employer and the union discuss the terms of employment of union members and try to negotiate a contract that embodies these terms. The act of negotiating is called collective bargaining. [p. 440]

2. True. The NLRA gives union management the right to recommend that a union call a strike if a collective bargaining agreement cannot be reached. [p. 442]

3. True. Picketing is lawful unless it (1) is accompanied by violence, (2) obstructs customers from entering the employer's place of business, (3) prevents nonstriking employees from entering the

employer's premises, or (4) prevents pickups and deliveries at the employer's place of business. An employer may seek an injunction against unlawful picketing. [p. 443]

4. False. Unions sometimes try to bring pressure against an employer by picketing the employer's suppliers or customers. Such secondary boycott picketing is lawful only if it is product picketing. [p. 443]

5. True. The H-1B visa allows U.S. employers to employ in the United States foreign nationals who are skilled in specialty occupations. These workers are called foreign guest workers. [p. 446]

Multiple Choice:

1. A. The NLRA establishes the right of employees to form and join labor organizations, to bargain collectively with employers, and to engage in concerted activity to promote these rights. [p. 437]

2. C. The National Labor Relations Act created the National Labor Relations Board (NLRB). [p. 438]

3. D. A group of employees that a union is seeking to represent is known as an appropriate bargaining unit. [p. 438]

4. B. A cessation of work by union members in order to obtain economic benefits or correct an unfair labor practice is called a strike. [p. 442]

5. C. Picketing is lawful unless it (1) is accompanied by violence, (2) obstructs customers from entering the employer's place of business, (3) prevents nonstriking employees from entering the employer's premises, or (4) prevents pickups and deliveries at the employer's place of business. [p. 443]

Statute Exercise:

A. 4
B. 3
C. 5
D. 2
E. 1 [p.437-438]

VI. Answers to Essay Question:

Management has engaged in unfair labor practices. They interfered with the operation of the union with the rookie threats and they refuse to bargain in good faith. These actions defeat the entire process.

Chapter 22

ANTITRUST LAW AND UNFAIR TRADE PRACTICES

Is competition really important?

I. Overview

Most people do not think of the trust device as a business tool. In another era the business trust was notoriously used as a device to eliminate competition. In the late 1800s, it was common to have key commodities and the industries related to those products controlled by large corporate enterprises. These entities would band together into a form of common trust ownership. The trustee, in turn, was able to control the prices, territories of distribution, and the like of the product. For example, prior to the enactment of antitrust laws, industries like oil, cotton, sugar, and whiskey were all dominated by such trusts. Probably the best known of these trusts was Standard Oil. In 1890 the Standard Oil Trust controlled over ninety percent of the market for oil products in the U.S. By the time the trust was "busted" in 1911, over thirty companies were ordered separated from the parent firm. This sort of monopolization of the marketplace led to the landmark antitrust legislation in 1890, the Sherman Antitrust Act. The act has two main objectives:

1. To prevent combinations in trust or otherwise, which act in restraint of trade, i.e.,illegal joining together to restrain trade.

2. To control markets thought to have a monopoly, i.e., illegal domination so strong as to *ipso facto* restrain trade.

These objectives are set out in Sections 1 and 2 of the Act and will be described in more detail below. What is interesting about this act is that Congress used very broad language to give the Justice Department maximum latitude in seeking enforcement of its provisions. This latitude has, in turn, not been consistently used. There appears to have been a constant shift in the enforcement strategies used by various administrations over the years. Those who favor strict enforcement essentially adhere to the notions originally proffered by Senator John Sherman and his cohorts. Under this traditional philosophy, competition is best served by having as many players in the arena of commerce as possible. Conversely, large concentrations of power in commerce are thought to be inherently bad.

On the other side of the enforcement spectrum, the more modern view says that large concentrations of economic power are not evil *per se* as long as they are efficient and are still fighting for a competitive position on a world-based economic playing field. Relatively recent administrative decisions have clearly favored this more lenient view as evidenced by the large number of mergers, acquisitions, leveraged buyouts, and consolidations that have taken place on Wall Street without objection.

The federal courts, in turn, have taken the middle road. Under their rules of interpretation, two main classifications of offenses have evolved. The *Per se Rule* is used to strike down restraints that courts deem to be so inherently anticompetitive that they cannot be allowed as a matter of law, regardless of any claimed justifications. On the other hand, the *Rule of Reason* has given courts latitude to accept restraints of trade on a case-by-case basis where legitimate concerns are overriding.

As strong and powerful a tool in the fight against monopolization and restraints of trade as the Sherman Act is, it has proven to be only a partial remedy to the problem. The Sherman Act sets the basic goals and objectives of keeping marketplaces open to competition. The Clayton Act and the Federal Trade Commission Act are designed to provide tools of implementation to those basic public policy objectives. As compared to the almost philosophical tenor of Sections 1 and 2 of the Sherman Act, the Clayton Act and more particularly, the Robinson-Patman Amendment to it, speak to much more specific objectives. These objectives arose out of discriminatory practices aimed at getting the little guy.

The biggest problem with the Clayton Act, and to a lesser extent with the FTC, is the government's commitment to enforcement combined with some very problematic aspects of the statutes themselves. On the issue of governmental level of commitment to enforcement, there is no question that things have changed in the geo-global scheme of economic competition. The market factors that were sought to be protected in the early part of the Twentieth Century are different as we have entered the Twenty-First Century. A free and open market is not measured now on regional or even national scales, but rather on worldwide competitive position. These changes have provided the philosophical underpinnings for the much more tolerant view taken by the government towards mergers, acquisitions, combinations, and the like. Yet the basic economic principles of monopolization, restraint of trade, and unfair trade practices have not changed. So government finds itself in a dilemma. It is trying to recognize the need to allow our economy to stay competitive on a worldwide playing field, but it must continue to keep the rules fair in that game.

The second factor involves questions that have been raised about the economic sense of the Clayton Act itself. Many critics of the act have argued that while provisions seeking to prevent price discrimination look good on the sheet music, they flop in the concert hall. The reason these particular measures have failed to live up to their billing is that some price volume cost incentives are all part of the competitive edge that all players are constantly looking for. To deny the reality of those competitive needs not only frustrates real competition, it may give noncompetitive parties an unwarranted edge against more efficient competitors by way of officious intermeddling on the part of government.

Where antitrust laws do not work, they actually become part of the problem. No one really wants to go back to the bad old days of robber barons and unmitigated jungle warfare in our economic system. Yet the time has probably come for a wholesale reexamination of our antitrust laws. This examination should focus on two main goals: (1) rewrite the laws so as to really provide a level playing field for all competitors and (2) get the government to act when needed.

All in all, antitrust law is still in a state of flux. Out of this debate, many are now arguing that the time has come for an overhaul of the entire antitrust law structure. Given the sporadic history of enforcement, who will enforce the law as intended no matter how it may be rewritten?

II. Hypothetical Multi-issue Essay Question

Spookey's Scareys specializes in Halloween costumes in Salem, Mazazona. Spookey's has 11 percent of a declining market. Its competitors are Ghosts and Goblins with 29 percent, Witches and Wanderers with 31 percent, Midnight Costumes with 20 percent, and several other Mom and Pop operations with the remaining 9 percent. On an average costume selling for $100, Spookey's has an overall cost of $90, including $75 paid to its main supplier, Bad Taste Haberdashery.

Because the market has been bad, Spookey's is looking for a buyer. It entered into a deal with Ghost and Goblins to sell a 51 percent interest in the store. Ghosts and Goblins would continue to operate both stores under their separate names. In addition, because of its combined buying power, the newly merged company is now able to get costumes from Bad Taste at $50 apiece and pass on the savings with lowered retail prices. Are there any antitrust problems with the above transactions?

III. Outline

Antitrust Laws

> A series of laws enacted to limit anticompetitive behavior in almost all industries, businesses and professions operating in the United States.
> Enforced by the Justice Department and the FTC.
> Penalties for violation include criminal sanctions, government sought civil damages (including treble damages).
> Section 4 of the Clayton Act permits private civil action with a possibility of treble damages.

Federal Antitrust Statutes
1. Sherman Act (restraint of trade and monopoly)
2. Clayton Act (regulates mergers and prohibits certain exclusive dealing arrangements)
3. Federal Trade Commission Act (prohibits unfair methods of competition)
4. Robinson-Patman Act (price discrimination)

Restraints of Trade: Section 1 of the Sherman Act

> Section 1 of the Sherman Act prohibits contracts, combinations, and conspiracies in restraint of trade
> It applies to two or more parties
>
> Rules of Reason and Per Se Rule
> Rule of Reason- holds that only unreasonable restraints of trade violate Section 1 of the Sherman Act
> Per Se- applies to restraints of trade that are considered inherently anti-competitive

Horizontal Restraint of Trade—between two or more competitors

> Horizontal Restraint of Trade- occurs when two or more competitors at the same level of distribution enter into a contract, combination, or conspiracy to restrain trade

Violation	Explanation	Analysis
Price-fixing	competitors' agreement to set prices → include quantity limitations and minimum/maximum prices	Per Se
Division of Markets (market sharing)	competitors' agreement to split a market	Per Se
Group Boycotts	competitors' agreement not to deal with others at another level of distribution	Rule of Reason/ Per Se
Other Horizontal Agreements	competitors' agreements at the same level → e.g., trade associations	Rule of Reason

Vertical Restraint of Trade—between customer/supplier		
Resale Price Maintenance	price schedule to set or stabilize prices	Per Se
Nonprice Restraints	example → franchises	Rule of Reason

Price Fixing
> A restraint of trade that occurs when competitors in the same line of business agree to set the price of goods or services they sell, thereby resulting in raising, depressing, fixing, pegging or stabilizing the price of the commodity or service

Division of Markets
> A restraint of trade in which competitors agree that each will serve only a designated portion of the market

Group Boycotts
> A restraint of trade in which two or more competitors at one level of distribution agree not to deal with others at another level of distribution

> Defense: Noerr Doctrine
> Two or more persons can petition the executive, legislative or judicial branch of the government or administrative agencies to enact laws or take other action without violating antitrust laws

> Defense: Unilateral Refusal to Deal
> (Colgate Doctrine) This is a unilateral choice by one party not to deal with another party. This does not violate Section 1 of the Sherman Act because there is no concerted action.

> Defense: Conscious Parallelism
> This defense provides that if two or more firms act the same but with no concerted action being shown, there is no violation of Section 1 of the Sherman Act

> Vertical Restraints of Trade
> This occurs when two or more parties on different levels of distribution enter into a contract, combination, or conspiracy to restrain trade

> Resale Price Maintenance (Vertical price-fixing)
> A per se violation of Section 1 of the Sherman Act that occurs when a party at one level of distribution enters into an agreement with a party at another level to adhere to a price schedule that either sets or stabilizes prices
>> Minimum resale prices is a per se violation
>> Maximum resale prices is examined under the rule of reason

> Non-Vertical Restraints
> These are restraints of trade that are unlawful under Section 1 of the Sherman Act if their anti-competitive effects outweigh their pro-competitive effects

Monopolization: Section 2 of the Sherman Act
> This is a section that prohibits monopolization and attempts or conspiracies to monopolize trade
>> Required proof:
>> 1. Relevant market
>>> a. Produce or service
>>> b. Geographical
>> 2. Monopoly power (power to control prices or exclude competition)
>> 3. Willful act of monopolizing
>>> Predatory pricing

Defenses to Monopolization
1. Innocent acquisition
2. Natural monopoly

Mergers: Section 7 of the Clayton Act
This section makes it unlawful for a person or business to acquire the stock or assets of another "where in any line of commerce or in any activity affecting commerce in any section of the country, the effects of such acquisition may be substantially to lessen competition or to tend to create a monopoly

Line of commerce- the relevant product or service market

Section of the country- relevant geographical market

Probability of a substantial lessening of competition- (deals in probabilities, not an actual showing of the lessening of competition)

Types of Mergers
1. Horizontal- a merger between two or more companies that compete in the same business or geographic market
2. Vertical- a merger that integrates the operations of a supplier and a customer
     a. Backward vertical- when a customer acquires a supplier
     b. Forward vertical- when a supplier acquires a customer
3. Market extension- a merger between two companies in similar fields where sales do not overlap
4. Conglomerate- a merger between firms in totally unrelated businesses

Defenses to Section 7 Actions
1. Failing company doctrine
2. Small company doctrine

Premerger Notification
Hart-Scott Rodino Antitrust Improvement Act
This act requires certain firms to notify the FTC and the Justice Department in advance of a proposed merger. Unless the government challenges a proposed merger within 30 days, the merger may proceed.

Tying Arrangements
Section 3 of the Clayton Act
This section prohibits arrangements involving sales and leases of goods
Tying arrangements- this is a restraint of trade in which a seller refuses to sell one product to a customer unless the customer agrees to purchase a second product from the seller

Price Discrimination: Section 2 of the Clayton Act
Section 2(a) of the Robinson-Patman Act
This section prohibits direct and indirect price discrimination by sellers of a commodity of a like grade and quality, where the effect of such discrimination may be to substantially lessen competition or to tend to create a monopoly in any line of commerce

Defenses to Price Discrimination
1. Cost justification
2. Changing conditions
3. Meeting the competitor

Exemptions from Antitrust Laws
     1. Statutory
     2. Implied
     3. State action

State Antitrust Laws
     Most states have enacted state antitrust laws

IV. Objective Questions

Terms:

1. Damages that may be awarded in a successful civil antitrust lawsuit, in an amount that is triple the amount of actual damages are known as _____.

2. A rule that holds that only unreasonable restraints of trade violate Section 1 of the Sherman Act is called the _____.

3. The standard that is applicable to those restraints of trade that are considered inherently anticompetitive is called the _____ rule.

4. A restraint of trade that occurs when two or more parties on different levels of distribution enter into a contract, combination, or conspiracy to restrain trade is called a(n) _____.

5. The doctrine that states that if two or more firms act the same but no concerted action is shown, there is no violation of Section 1 of the Sherman Act is called _____.

6. A merger between two or more companies that compete in the same business and geographical market is called a(n) _____ merger.

7. A merger that does not fit into any other category or a merger between firms in totally unrelated businesses is a(n) _____ merger.

8. A defense to a Section 7 action that says a competitor may merge with a failing company if (1) there is no other reasonable alternative for the failing company and (2) no other purchaser is available is called the _____.

9. A form of price discrimination that is less readily apparent than direct forms of price discrimination is known as _____.

10. The _____ establishes 3 statutory defenses to resulting liability from Section 2(a) of the Clayton Act.

True/False:

1. ____ All of the major federal antitrust acts have both civil and criminal sanctions.

2. ____ Under the *per se* standard of determining whether the Sherman Act prohibits conduct, there is no balancing of pro- and anticompetitive effects.

3. ____ Whether price fixing is a violation of Section 1 of the Sherman Act is determined by the Rule of Reason.

4. ____ To show a violation of the Sherman Act, two or more firms acting the same way must be acting in concert. That is, if each firm independently reaches the same decision, there is no violation.

5. ____ Under Section 2 of the Sherman Act, a plaintiff must show a defendant's specific intent to monopolize a market; the showing of mere deliberate or purposeful conduct is not sufficient to support a Section 2 action.

6. ____ A natural monopoly is a defense to the charge of monopolizing even if the natural monopoly operates in a predatory way.

7. ____ Under Section 7 of the Clayton Act, there must be proof of an actual decrease in competition for the court to forbid a merger.

8. ____ The merger of two grocery store chains that serve the same geographical market is an example of a horizontal merger.

9. ____ The unfair advantage theory is intended to prevent wealthy companies from overwhelming the competition in a given market.

10. ____ Under the meeting the competition defense to a Section 2(b) of the Robinsion-Patman Act charge, a seller can lower his selling price below that of his competitor to be competitive in a market.

Multiple Choice:

1. In 1890, Congress enacted the _____ in order to outlaw anticompetitive behavior.

A. Clayton Act
B. Sherman Act
C. Robinson-Patman Act
D. Federal Trade Commission Act

2. The two tests the U.S. Supreme Court has developed for determining the lawfulness of a restraint are the rule of reason and the _____.

A. *per se* rule
B. Noerr doctrine
C. *nolo contendere* rule
D. Colgate doctrine

3. Under the _____, the court must examine the pro- and anticompetitive effects of a challenged restraint.

A. *per se* rule
B. consent decree
C. Noerr doctrine
D. rule of reason

4. A restraint of trade in which two or more competitors at one level of distribution agree not to deal with others at another level of distribution is known as _____.

A. price fixing
B. resale price maintenance
C. group boycott
D. market sharing

5. Which of the following is an example of a vertical restraint of trade?

A. Division of markets
B. Resale price maintenance
C. Price fixing
D. Group boycott

6. The _____ holds that two or more persons can petition the executive, legislative, or judicial branch of the government or administrative agencies to enact laws or take other action without violating antitrust laws.

A. Colgate doctrine
B. *Nolo contendere*
C. Small company doctrine
D. Noerr doctrine

7. A monopoly power is characterized by _____.

A. a market share of below 20 percent
B. an inability to control prices in the market
C. an ability to exclude all competition from other sellers
D. a presence of multiple substitute goods at competing prices

8. A merger between two or more companies that compete in the same business and geographical market is known as a _____.

A. horizontal merger
B. vertical merger
C. conglomerate merger
D. market extension merger

9. _____ is a defense in a Section 2(a) action which provides that a seller's price discrimination is not unlawful if the price differential is due to "differences in the cost of manufacture, sale, or delivery" of the product.

A. Natural monopoly defense
B. Meeting the competition defense
C. Changing conditions defense
D. Cost justification defense

10. Which of the following businesses and activities enjoys a statutory exemption from antitrust laws?

A. Agricultural cooperatives
B. Airlines
C. Professional baseball
D. Professional sports

V. Answers to Objective Questions

Terms:

1. treble damages. Under Section 4 of the Clayton Act, single damages found by a jury are tripled in amount for antitrust violations. [p. 454]

2. rule of reason. If Section 1 of the Sherman Act were literally applied, it would prohibit many business contracts. In order to mitigate against that literal interpretation, the Rule of Reason is designed to allow the courts to weigh a number of factors when deciding if a contract question is in restraint of trade. [p. 455]

3. per se. Per se rule is a rule that is applicable to restraints of trade considered inherently anticompetitive. Once this determination is made about a restraint of trade, the court will not permit any defenses or justifications to save it. [p. 455]

4. vertical restraint. This restraint can take the form of a contract, combination, or conspiracy between the parties and is subject to the scrutiny of both the Rule of Reason and the *per se* rule interpretations of Section 1 of the Sherman Act. [p. 458]

5. conscious parallelism. Conscious parallelism is a doctrine which states that if two or more firms act the same but no concerted action is shown, there is no violation of Section 1 of the Sherman Act. [p. 460]

6. horizontal. This can involve a merger of one company with another company producing a similar product and selling it in the same geographic market. [p. 464]

7. conglomerate. Where the merger may not fit into any other category, it may still be a violation of Section 7 of the Clayton Act if it creates an unfair advantage, hurts potential competition, or creates potential reciprocity between competitors. [p. 465]

8. failing company doctrine. According to the failing company doctrine, a competitor may merge with a failing company if (1) there is no other reasonable alternative for the failing company, (2) no other purchaser is available, and (3) the assets of the failing company would completely disappear from the market if the anticompetitive merger were not allowed to go through. [p. 465]

9. indirect price discrimination. Indirect price discrimination is a form of price discrimination that is less readily apparent than direct forms of price discrimination. [p. 467]

10. Robinson-Patman Act. Cost justification, changing conditions, and meeting the competitors are the three defenses. [p. 467-468]

True/False:

1. False. The Sherman Act is the only federal antitrust act that has criminal sanctions. The other federal antitrust acts allow only civil sanctions. [p. 454]

2. True. The balancing of pro- and anticompetitive effects is used in the Rule of Reason test, not the *per se* standard of determining whether conduct is prohibited by the Sherman Act. [p. 455]

3. False. Price fixing is a *per se* violation of the Sherman Act. [p. 456]

4. True. Under the doctrine of conscious parallelism, two or more firms must be acting in concert to be in violation of the Sherman Act. [p. 460]

5. False. The showing of deliberate or purposeful conduct is sufficient to support a Section 2 action. Showing a defendant's actual specific intent to monopolize a market is not required. [p. 461]

6. False. Innocent acquisition and natural monopoly are defenses to the charge of monopolizing. These defenses are lost if the firm acts in a predatory or exclusionary way. [p. 462]

7. False. Under Section 7 of the Clayton Act, if a merger is likely to substantially lessen competition, the court may prevent the merger. Actual showing of the lessening of competition is not required. [p. 463]

8. True. A merger between two or more companies that compete in the same business and geographical market is known as a horizontal merger. [p. 464]

9. True. The unfair advantage theory holds that a conglomerate merger may not give the acquiring firm an unfair advantage over its competitors in finance, marketing, or expertise. This rule is intended to prevent wealthy companies from overwhelming the competition in a given market. [p. 465]

10. False. Under the meeting the competition defense, a seller can lower his selling price to match that of his competitor. However, the seller cannot set his price below that of his competitor. [p. 468]

Multiple Choice:

1. B. In 1890, Congress enacted the Sherman Act in order to outlaw anticompetitive behavior. [p. 455]

2. A. The two tests the U.S. Supreme Court has developed for determining the lawfulness of a restraint are the rule of reason and the per se rule. [p. 455]

3. D. Under the rule of reason, the court must examine the pro- and anticompetitive effects of a challenged restraint. [p. 455]

4. C. A group boycott (or refusal to deal) occurs when two or more competitors at one level of distribution agree not to deal with others at a different level of distribution. [p. 457]

5. B. Resale price maintenance (or vertical price fixing) occurs when a party at one level of distribution enters into an agreement with a party at another level to adhere to a price schedule that either sets or stabilizes prices. [p. 458]

6. D. The Noerr doctrine which says that two or more persons can petition the executive, legislative, or judicial branch of the government or administrative agencies to enact laws or take other action without violating antitrust laws. [p. 460]

7. C. Monopoly power is defined by the courts as the power to control prices or exclude competition. [p. 461]

8. A. A horizontal merger is a merger between two or more companies that compete in the same business and geographical market. [p. 464]

9. D. Cost justification defense is a defense in a Section 2(a) action which provides that a seller's price discrimination is not unlawful if the price differential is due to "differences in the cost of manufacture, sale, or delivery" of the product. [p. 467]

10. A. Statutory exemptions include labor unions, agricultural cooperatives, export activities of American companies, and insurance business that is regulated by a state. [p. 468]

VI. Answers to Essay Question

The basic policy presumes that competition is best protected in an open and fair marketplace. Monopolization and concentrations of economic controls are contrary to an open and fair marketplace and may be anticompetitive.

The main statutes that may be used are the Sherman Act of 1890, the Clayton Act of 1914, and the Robinson-Patman Act of 1930. In this case, the second two acts provide the best possibility for putting the actions of Spookeys and Ghost and Goblins to the antitrust law litmus test.

The partial acquisition of a competitor in the same geographical area may injure competition. In examining this horizontal merger, the Justice Department will use its Herfindal-Hirshman guidelines to see if the new arrangement will create an illegal concentration of costume sales in Salem in one controlled company. As a defense to this possible challenge, Ghost and Goblins can raise the argument that Spookey's was a failing company. That defense appears weak because there was no evidence of it losing money or that it was about to go bankrupt. Thus the merger could most likely be disallowed under Section 7 of the Clayton Act.

With regard to the new pricing arrangement with Bad Taste, the problems with Robinson-Patman become more apparent. Here the ultimate price charged to the consumer is lower and it would appear on its face (mask?) that competition is actually fostered by the new arrangement. The other costume stores in Salem might argue, however, that they have been discriminated against by predatory pricing. The best defense here would be to show that the new prices reflect efficiencies realized from higher volume purchases, i.e., lower costs. In addition, if Bad Taste can show that any buyer who purchased the higher volume would get that same lower price, price discrimination would be much more difficult to prove. From the problem as presented, it appears that no unfair trade practices were used.

Why should the buyer beware?

I. Overview

This chapter covers the set of remedies available to a wronged or injured consumer. First, there is criminal law. Victims of consumer fraud and similar offenses have always been able to seek state-supported sanctions against wrongdoers. This venue may provide some ephemeral satisfaction for the victim and may even, at least temporarily, protect society from further harm. But criminal law does not truly make the victim whole. As a matter of fact, most of the miscreants convicted of consumer fraud are also judgment proof, i.e., they have no assets from which civil judgments can be satisfied.

The second area of consumer protection is found in tort law and its permutations of intentional tort, negligence tort, and strict liability. These remedies can and do provide meaningful substance to civil correction of wrongdoing where the defendant is found to have some financial means. As seen in the prior discussions of these areas, tort law generally and products liability specifically are ripe with controversy and a great deal of uncertainty in today's legal environment. The major drawback to both the criminal law and tort law methods of consumer protection is that they represent *after-the-fact* remedies to harm already done. They are reactive remedies as opposed to proactive forms of prevention of harm. It has been argued that large civil judgments act as societal signals that are designed to discourage repetition of undesirable behavior.

The third side to our picture is found in contract. Contract law has the advantage of providing the consumer with the opportunity to anticipate any problems before they befall him or her. This notion is traditionally found in the doctrine of *caveat emptor,* which courts of another age used with cavalier abandon. Both the common law of contracts and its progeny, the Uniform Commercial Code, have come a long way from the days of "Let the buyer beware."

In spite of all this progress in the areas of crime, torts, and contract, the gap between consumer harm and consumer protection continues to remain unfilled. Legislators at all levels of government have sought to help fill this void with a number of consumer protection measures. These measures often incorporate elements from both civil and criminal areas of enforcement. In addition, these measures can and often do help prevent the many potential harms to the consumer. Unfortunately, another hallmark of many of these measures is that they are the end product of a trail of harm that had reached a crisis or disastrous level. Consider how long it took to take certain dangerous prescription drugs or unsafe toys off the market. Where these laws do provide a measure of safety, some consumer comfort may be found in "at least better late than never." Protection from harm has come a long way, but there is still no light at the end of the tunnel.

II. Hypothetical Multi-Issue Essay Question

Mr. and Mrs. Buyer owned a refrigerator that is in bad shape. They wanted to purchase another one but they are looking for a good deal. In the Sunday newspaper they noticed that Dime's Department Store was offering a new 25 cubic foot refrigerator that does everything from keep things cold to "completely revolutionizing the industry." The price quoted was less than half of any other comparable machine. They decided to buy one.

When the buyers arrived at the store on Saturday, they were greeted by John Salesman who explained that even though they had the refrigerators, he would not recommend them because they were really nothing special. He tried very hard to show the buyers items that were more expensive and, in his words, "more revolutionary." The buyers, however, insisted that they be shown the advertised item. When they inspected the refrigerator, they determined that it was a simple machine with a cold area and a freezer. In their opinion, it was "completely un-revolutionary."

The buyers need some help determining what the legal consequences of the store's actions were and so they ask you to advise them.

III. Outline

Introduction to Consumer Protection and Global Product Safety
> Consumer Protection Laws- federal and state statutes and regulations that promote product safety and prohibit abusive, unfair, and deceptive business practices
>> Caveat emptor- "let the buyer beware"

U. S. Department of Agriculture
> A federal administrative agency responsible for regulating meat, poultry, and other food products

> Food, Drug and Cosmetic Act
> This act regulates testing, manufacture, distribution, and sale of foods, drugs, cosmetics, and medicinal products and devices
>> The Food and Drug Administration enforces the act
>> See Landmark Law section on page 438

Food, Drug and Cosmetic Safety
> Regulation of food
1. The FDCA prohibits the shipment, distribution, or sale of unadulterated food
2. The FDCA prohibits false and misleading labeling of food products

> Food Labeling
> Nutritional Labeling and Education Act
>> A federal statute that requires food manufacturers to place on food labels a disclosure of nutritional information

> Regulation of Drugs
> The FDCA gives the FDA authority to regulate the testing, manufacture, distribution and sale of drugs
>> The Drug Amendment of the FDCA gives the FDA broad powers to license new drugs

> Regulation of Cosmetics
> The FDA definition of cosmetics includes substances and preparation or cleansing, altering the appearance of, and promoting the attractiveness of a person
> Regulation of Medicinal Devices
> The Medicinal Device Amendment to the FDCA gives the FDA authority to regulate medicinal devices, such as heart pace-makers, kidney dialysis machines, defibrillators, surgical equipment, and other diagnostic, therapeutic and health devices

Product Safety
> Consumer Product Safety Act (CPSA) - a federal statute that regulates potentially dangerous consumer products and that created the Consumer Products Safety Commission (CPSC)

CPSC- a federal administrative agency empowered to adopt rules and regulations to interpret and enforce the CPSA

Unfair and Deceptive Practices
Federal Trade Commission (FTC)
A federal administrative agency empowered to enforce the Federal Trade Commission Act and other federal consumer protection statutes
Section 5 of the FTC Act that prohibits unfair and deceptive practices:
1. False and Deceptive Advertising
Providing or omitting information likely to mislead a reasonable consumer
Making unsubstantiated claims
Opinions (sales talk) are not false or deceptive
2. Bait and Switch
The seller advertises low cost items, then tries to pressure the consumer to purchase a more expensive item when they are in the store
3. Door-to-door sales
Many states have enacted laws providing the consumer a period of time (usually 3 days) to rescind a contract made during a sale at the consumer's residence

IV. Objective Questions:

Terms:

1. The _____ is the federal agency responsible for regulating the safety of meat, poultry, and other food products.

2. The _____ requires certain uniform nutritional labeling.

3. The _____ prohibits the shipment, distribution, or sale of adulterated food.

4. The FDA's definition of _____ includes substances and preparations for cleansing, altering the appearance of, and promoting the attractiveness of a person.

5. The _____ is a federal statute that regulates potentially dangerous consumer products and that created the Consumer Product Safety Commission.

6. A type of deceptive advertising that occurs when a seller advertises the availability of a low-cost discounted item but then pressures the buyer into purchasing more expensive merchandise is known as _____.

7. To avoid unsolicited commercial phone calls, consumers can be placed on the federal _____.

True/False:

1. ____ The Consumer Product Safety Commission regulates the sale of medicinal devices.

2. ____ The FDA has broad powers to license new drugs.

3. ____ Under Section 5 of the Federal Trade Commission Act, actual deception must be proven to show deceptive or unfair advertising.

4. ____ Many states permit consumers three days to rescind contract made during a door to door sales contract.

5. ____Under Section 5 of the FTC Act, sales talk constitutes false and deceptive advertising.

Multiple Choice:

1. _____ laws are federal and state statutes and regulations that promote product safety and prohibit abusive, unfair, and deceptive business practices.
A. Profit-à-prendre B. Canon C. Consumer protection D Caveat emptor

2. The _____ is a federal administrative agency that is primarily responsible for regulating the safety of meat, poultry, and other food products.
A. U.S. Department of Agriculture B. Consumer Product Safety Commission C. Food and Drug Administration D. Federal Trade Commission

3. The _____ is a federal statute passed in 1990 that requires food manufacturers and processors to provide nutrition information on many foods and prohibits them from making scientifically unsubstantiated health claims.
A. Food, Drug, and Cosmetic Act B. Health Care and Education Reconciliation Act C. Patient Protection and Affordable Care Act D. Nutrition Labeling and Education Act

4. The U.S. Department of Agriculture places mandatory and consistent labeling requirements on _____.
A. Meat and poultry products B. Raw sea food C. Ready-to-eat meals D. Fresh fruits and vegetables

5. The Health Care Reform Act is an amendment of the _____ Act. A. Consumer Product Safety B. Patient Protection and Affordable Care C. Medical Device Amendment D. Federal Trade Commission

Deceptive Advertising Exercise:

State which of the following, if not accurate, could be deceptive (D), sales talk (S), or acceptable (A):

1. "This car is fast."	
2. "This car goes 150 MPH"	
3. A commercial showing a famous star wearing clothes they would not normally wear	
4. A commercial indicating that a particular medication is a cure for a migraine	
5. A car ad which shows a monthly payment rate which is very low but with an asterisk explaining, in a footnote, that this is a lease.	

V. Answers to Objective Questions

Terms:

   1. United States Department of Agriculture. The U.S. Department of Agriculture is a federal administrative agency that is responsible for regulating the safety of meat, poultry, and other food products. [p. 477]

   2. Nutrition Labeling and Education Act. There are standard definitions for common terms. [p. 478]

   3. FDCA. The FDCA prohibits the shipment, distribution, or sale of adulterated food. [p. 478]

   4. cosmetics. The FDA's definition of cosmetics includes substances and preparations for cleansing, altering the appearance of, and promoting the attractiveness of a person. [p. 479]

   5. Consumer Product Safety Act (CPSA). The Consumer Product Safety Act (CPSA) is a federal statute that regulates potentially dangerous consumer products and that created the Consumer Product Safety Commission. [p. 479]

   6. bait and switch. Remedies such as rain checks are designed to offset some of the harmful effects of these sorts of practices. [p. 483]

   7. Do Not Call Registry. Do-Not-Call Registry is a registry created by federal law on which consumers can place their names and free themselves from most unsolicited commercial telephone calls. [p. 483]

True/False:

   1. False. They are regulated by the FDA. [p. 477]

   2. True. The Drug Amendment to the FDCA, 3 enacted in 1962, gives the FDA broad powers to license new drugs in the United States. [p. 479]

   3. False. Under Section 5 of the FTCA, actual deception need not be proven to show deceptive or unfair advertising. [p. 483]

   4. True. The consumer must send notice of the cancellation to the seller. [p. 483]

   5. False. Statements of opinion and "sales talk" (e.g., "This is a great car") do not constitute false and deceptive advertising. [p. 483]

Multiple Choice:

   1. C. Consumer protection laws are federal and state statutes and regulations that promote product safety and prohibit abusive, unfair, and deceptive business practices. [p. 477]

   2. A. The U.S. Department of Agriculture is a federal administrative agency that is responsible for regulating the safety of meat, poultry, and other food products. [p. 477]

3. D. The Nutrition Labeling and Education Act (NLEA) is a federal statute that requires food manufacturers to disclose on food labels nutritional information about that food. [p. 478]

4. A. The Department of Agriculture adopted consistent labeling requirements for the meat and poultry products it regulates. [p. 478]

5. B. After much public debate, in 2010, Congress enacted the Patient Protection and Affordable Care Act (PPACA). This act was immediately amended by the Health Care and Education Reconciliation Act. The amended act is commonly referred to as the Health Care Reform Act of 2010. [p. 482]

Deceptive Advertising Exercise:

1. S – obvious exaggeration or an opinion, not a fact.

2. D – possibly false advertising.

3. S, D, A – does it materially mislead a reasonable customer?

4. D – possible false advertising.

5. A – not misleading as long as not intentionally hidden.
[p. 483]

VI. Answers to Essay Question

The initial response of the salesmen is bait and switch. They never really intended to sell the advertised item but would if forced. As far as the statement about being revolutionary, this is a term indicating a type of opinion or puffing. If it is attempted to mean something specifically that was not accurate then it would be false/deceptive advertising. This is probably not the case here. [p. 483]

Chapter 24
ENVIRONMENTAL PROTECTION

How can you pollute just a little?

I. Overview

A large chemical company recently aired a TV commercial to announce that it plans to use double-lined tanker ships to transport its products. In the ad, this news is shown being greeted with jubilation by all sorts of wildlife, while Beethoven's stirring Ninth Symphony swells in the background. The Twenty-First century ushered in a greater concern for environmental issues than ever before. One would hope this is not just the latest politically correct marketing fashion but rather a realization that our natural resources can no longer be taken for granted. Like it or not, our advances in technology have finally given us the power to permanently alter nature. This power has been used to feed millions and save lives. It has also been used to destroy endangered species, burn holes in the ozone, and uproot entire ecosystems.

The law of environmental protection attempts to balance the needs and desires for technological advancement with a realistic perspective of what natural limitations our environment places on these capacities. The age of growth *per se* as a good thing is changing to: "Is the growth worth it?" The environmental movement is not new. Conservationists have a long and proud history of protecting our natural resources. What is new are the threats raised by oil spills, hazardous wastes, nuclear accidents, and unmitigated depletion of irreplaceable resources. The emergence of environmental legislation which has a sense of urgency and response to these issues is only now in its third decade—a mere second on the ecological clock.

Because this legislation is so relatively new, the growing pains of new social engineering continue to be felt by business. These laws have especially impacted industries that have traditionally relied heavily on utilization of natural resources such as mining, oil, gas exploration, and timber. Consider also the auto industry. For years automakers outside the U.S. have complained about our pollution controls being too costly and cumbersome. It is no small point of pride that the world is catching up with us on this issue by finally adopting our standards for safety and emissions.

One thing, however, is abundantly clear—pollution exists. If we manufacture, we pollute. The key is how to balance this pollution with the damage to the environment. Pollution must go either into the air, into the water or into the land. What the law has tried to do, however, is to keep it at a minimum. We started with tort law which proved to be difficult to apply. In the 60's and 70's the statutory framework which we use today was therefore born. But again, even with this statutory help, how do we pollute just a little?

II. Hypothetical Multi-issue Essay Question

Bailout Bank of Metropolis is seeking to extend its operations to every corner of the great state of Louisiark. The state legislature just passed a law allowing branch banking Bailout to now open branches outside of Metropolis. Bailout's Vice-President in charge of real estate is Mr. Mortimer M. Misque. Mortimer's cousin, Ms. Sallie S. Spillaway, is Vice President in charge of real estate for Dryhole Oil Company. Dryhole's business has been terrible ever since it converted all its self-service operations into combination gas stations and mini-refineries. Dryhole thought it could save a lot of money by not having to ship gasoline from its out-of-state refineries to retail outlets.

Mortimer and Sallie hit upon a great idea. Why not sell the Dryhole gasoline refinery outlets to Bailout and convert them to branch banks? The deal went through, and Bailout proceeded to renovate the gas stations. The old refinery and pump facilities were simply capped into mothballs in case the bank ever decided to go into the business.

Unfortunately, several years after these renovations, Bailout's money began to take on a funny odor. In addition, the residents of the neighborhoods adjoining Bailout branches began to have trouble with their drinking water. What can be done?

III. Outline

Environmental Protection
 Environmental Protection Agency (EPA)
  A federal administrative agency created by Congress to coordinate the implementation and enforcement of the federal environmental protection laws
  National Environmental Policy Act (NEPA)
   A federal statute which mandates that the federal government consider the adverse impact a federal government action would have on the environment before the action is implemented
    Environmental Impact Statement (EIS)
     A document that must be prepared for any proposed legislation or major federal action that significantly affects the quality of the human environment
      An EIS must:
     1. Describe the affected environment
     2. Describe the impact of the proposed federal action in the environment
     3. Identify and discuss alternatives to the proposed action
     4. List the resources that will be committed to the action
     5. Contain a cost-benefit analysis of the proposed action and alternative actions

Air Pollution
 Pollution caused by factories, homes, vehicles and the like that affect the air
  Clean Air Act
   A federal statute that provides comprehensive regulation of air quality in the United States

 Sources of Air Pollution
 1. Stationary sources (industrial plants, oil refineries, etc.)
 2. Mobile sources (automobiles, planes, etc.)

 National Ambient Air Quality Standards
  Standards for certain pollutants set by the EPA that protect (1) human beings (primary level) and (2) vegetation, matter, climate, visibility and economic values (secondary level)

 Nonattainment Areas
 A geographical area that does not meet established air quality standards
  Categories: Marginal, moderate, serious, severe, extreme
  States must submit compliance plans that:
   1. Identify major sources of air pollution and require them to install pollution control equipment
   2. Institute permit systems or new stationary sources
   3. Implement inspection programs to monitor mobile sources

 Indoor Air Pollution
 - Sick building syndrome

Water Pollution
Pollution of lakes, rivers, oceans and other bodies of water
Clean Water Act
A federal statute that establishes water quality standards and regulates water pollution

Point Sources of Water
Sources of water pollution that are fixed and stationary

Thermal Pollution
Heated water or material discharged into waterways that upsets the ecological balance and decreases the oxygen content of water

Wetlands
Areas that are inundated or saturated by surface water or ground water that support vegetation typically adapted to life in such conditions

Safe Drinking Water Act
A federal statute that authorizes the EPA to establish national primary drinking water standards

Ocean Protection
Marine Protection, Research, and Sanctuaries Act
A federal statute that extends the limited environmental protection to the ocean
1. Requires a permit for dumping wastes and other foreign materials into ocean waters; and
2. Establishes marine sanctuaries in ocean water as far seaward as the Continental Shelf and in the Great Lakes
Oil Pollution Act
A federal statute that requires the oil industry to take measures to prevent oil spills and readily respond to and clean up oil spills
See Ethics Spotlight on page 499

Toxic Substances and Hazardous Waste
Toxic substances- chemicals used for agricultural, industrial, and mining uses that cause injury to humans, birds, animals, fish and vegetation
Hazardous Waste- solid waste that may cause or significantly contribute to an increase in mortality or serious illness or pose a hazard to human health or the environment if improperly managed

Toxic Substances Control
Toxic Substances Control Act
A federal statute that authorizes the EPA to regulate toxic substances
Toxic air pollutants- air pollutants that cause serious illness or death to humans

Insecticides, Fungicides, and Rodenticides
Insecticide, Fungicide, Rodenticide Act
A federal statute that requires pesticides, herbicides, fungicides, and rodenticides to be registered with the EPA; the EPA may deny, suspend or cancel registration

Hazardous Waste
> Land Pollution- pollution of the land that is generally caused by hazardous waste being disposed of in an improper manner
>> Resource Conservation and Recovery Act (RCRA)
>>> A federal statute that authorizes the EPA to regulate facilities that generate, treat, store, transport, and dispose of hazardous waste

Superfund
> See Landmark Law section
>> Comprehensive Environmental Response, Compensation and Liability Act (CERCLA)
>>> This is a federal statute that authorizes the federal government to deal with hazardous waste. The act creates a monetary fund to finance the cleanup of hazardous wastes sites.

Nuclear Waste
> Radiation Pollution
>> Emissions from radioactive wastes that can cause injury and death to humans and other life and can cause severe damage to the environment
>>> Nuclear Regulatory Commission
>>>> A federal agency that licenses the construction and operating of commercial nuclear power plants and that continuously monitors the operation

Endangered Species
> Endangered Species Act
>> A federal statute that protects endangered and threatened species of wildlife

State Environmental Protection Laws

Global Warming
> A hole in the ozone layer caused by greenhouse gases

IV. Objective Questions

Terms:

1. In 1970, Congress created the _____ that coordinates the implementation and enforcement of federal environmental protection laws.

2. The document that must be prepared for all proposed federal legislation that would significantly affect the quality of the human environment is called an _____.
3. The major source of mobile air pollution is the _____.

4. The EPA can establish water pollution control standards under the _____.

5. Areas that are inundated or saturated by surface or groundwater that support vegetation typically adapted for life in saturated soil conditions are called _____.

6. The act that extended environmental protection to the oceans is known as the _____ Act.

7. Asbestos, mercury, vinyl chloride, and benzene are examples of _____.

8. The act that provides for the creation of a fund to finance the cleanup of hazardous wastes is popularly known as _____.

9. Under the Superfund strict liability is imposed on _____.

10. Licenses for the construction and opening of commercial nuclear power plants are granted by the _____.

True/False:

1. _____ The Environmental Protection Agency has adjudicative powers to hold hearings, make decisions, and order remedies for violations of federal environmental laws.

2. _____ It is not necessary to prepare an environmental impact statement for all proposed legislation that may affect the environment.

3. _____ Although the states establish air quality standards, the EPA is responsible for their enforcement.

4. _____ States establish national ambient air quality standards for pollutants.

5. _____ Doctors have been more reluctant recently to attribute health symptoms to sick building syndrome.

6. _____ Municipal sewage plants are examples of point sources of water pollution.

7. _____ The Clean Water Act authorizes the U.S. government to clean up oil spills and spills of other hazardous substances in ocean waters within six miles of the shore.
8. _____ Pesticides must be registered with the EPA before they can be sold.

9. _____ The Resource Conservation and Recovery Act defines a hazardous waste as a solid waste that may cause or significantly contribute to an increase in mortality or serious illness or pose a hazard to human health or the environment if improperly managed.

10. _____ The EPA can order a responsible party to clean up a hazardous waste.

Multiple Choice:

1. The _____ is a federal administrative agency created by Congress to coordinate the implementation and enforcement of the federal environmental protection laws.

A. Ministry of Environmental Protection
B. Environmental Investigation Agency
C. Environmental Protection Agency
D. Global Environment Facility

2. Which of the following is a document required by the NEPA that must be prepared for any proposed legislation or major federal action that significantly affects the quality of the human environment?

A. environmental impact abstract
B. environmental impact statement
C. environmental impact design
D. strategic environmental assessment

3. Which of the following would be considered a stationary source of air pollution?

A. Aircrafts
B. Cargo ships
C. Oil refineries
D. Automobiles

4. The primary level of the NAAQS protect(s) _____.
A. human beings
B. climate
C. flora
D. water bodies

5. A geographical area that does not meet established air quality standards is designated as a _____.

A. limited pollution area
B. nonattainment area
C. zoned ordinance area
D. federal regulation area

6. Which of the following federal administrative agencies enacts the Clean Water Act?

A. Environmental Investigation Agency
B. Environmental Protection Agency
C. Ministry of Environmental Protection
D. Association of Environmental Professionals

7. Which of the following is primarily responsible for enforcing the provisions of the Clean Water Act regulations?

A. The federal government
B. Independent agencies
C. Not-for-profit organizations
D. State governments

8. The process by which heated water or material is discharged into waterways upsetting the ecological balance and decreasing the oxygen content is defined as _____.

A. thermal pollution
B. land pollution
C. radioactive pollution
D. air pollution

9. Areas that are inundated or saturated by surface water or ground water that support vegetation typically adapted for life in such conditions are called _____.

A. marine reefs
B. gullies
C. wetlands
D. reservoirs

10. The _____ is a federal statute that authorizes the EPA to regulate facilities that generate, treat, store, transport, and dispose of hazardous wastes.

A. Resource Conservation and Recovery Act
B. Clear Water Act
C. Toxic Substances Control Act
D. Comprehensive Environmental Response, Compensation, and Liability Act

V. Answers to Objective Questions

Terms:

1. Environmental Protection Agency. The EPA is growing in both economic and political importance. President Clinton has recommended that the office of EPA Administrator be raised to cabinet rank. [p. 494]

2. Environmental impact statement. Many states have followed suit and now call for local versions of these statements. [p. 494]

3. Automobile. An interesting footnote on this issue is that most auto-related pollution is being generated by the minority of autos built prior to the issuance of pollution guidelines. [p. 495]

4. Clean Water Act. This effort is coordinated with state and local water quality control authorities. [p. 496]

5. Wetlands. Arriving at a precise definition of land to qualify for this designation continues to be a political powder keg. [p. 498]

6. Marine Protection, Research and Sanctuaries. Much of the work done under this act is coordinated with state and local agencies. [p. 499]

7. Toxic pollutants. As thresholds of scientific discovery expand, this list gets longer every year. [p. 500]

8. Superfund. The actual title of this legislation is the Comprehensive Response Compensation and Liability Act. [p. 501]

9. Generator of waste, transporter of waste, owner at the time of disposal, current owner. This liability extends to all jointly and severally. [p. 501]

10. Nuclear Regulatory Commission. As compared to other environmentally sensitive activities, the federal government exclusively controls this activity. [p. 501-502]

True/False:

1. True. This pattern of powers is typical under the rights of the executive branch. [p. 494]

2. False. An environmental impact statement must be prepared. [p. 494]

3. False. Although the EPA establishes air quality standards, the states are responsible for their enforcement. [p. 495]

4. False. The EPA establishes NAAQS for pollutants. [p. 495]

5. False. See the Contemporary Environment- Indoor Air Pollution section on page 496.

6. True. Mines, manufacturing plants, paper mills, electric utility plants, and municipal sewage plants are examples of stationary sources of water pollution. [p. 497]

7. False. The distance is twelve miles off shore. [p. 499]

8. True. Insecticide, Fungicide, and Rodenticide Act requires pesticides, herbicides, fungicides, and rodenticides to be registered with the EPA; the EPA may deny, suspend, or cancel registration. [p. 500]

9. True. The Resource Conservation and Recovery Act defines a hazardous waste as a solid waste that may cause or significantly contribute to an increase in mortality or serious illness or pose a hazard to human health or the environment if improperly managed. [p. 501]

10. True. If the party refuses, the EPA may clean it up and sue for the cost of the cleanup. [p. 501]

Multiple Choice:

1. C. The Environmental Protection Agency (EPA) is a federal administrative agency created by Congress to coordinate the implementation and enforcement of the federal environmental protection laws. [p. 494]

2. B. The NEPA and EPA regulations require that an environmental impact statement (EIS) be prepared by the federal government for any proposed legislation or major federal action that significantly affects the quality of the natural and human environment. [p. 494]

3. C. Substantial amounts of air pollution are emitted by stationary sources of air pollution (e.g., industrial plants, oil refineries, public utilities). [p. 495]

4. A. The Clean Air Act directs the EPA to establish national ambient air quality standards (NAAQS) for certain pollutants. These standards are set at two different levels: primary (to protect human beings) and secondary (to protect vegetation, matter, climate, visibility, and economic values). [p. 495]

5. B. A geographical area that does not meet established air quality standards is called a nonattainment area. [p. 496]

6. B. The Clean Water Act is administered by the EPA. [p. 496]

7. D. States are primarily responsible for enforcing the provisions of the Clean Water Act and EPA regulations adopted thereunder. [p. 496]

8. A. Heated water or material discharged into waterways that upsets the ecological balance and decreases the oxygen content is known as thermal pollution. [p. 498]

9. C. Wetlands are defined as areas that are inundated or saturated by surface water or ground water that support vegetation typically adapted for life in saturated soil conditions. [p. 498]

10. A. The Resource Conservation and Recovery Act (RCRA) is a federal statute that authorizes the EPA to regulate facilities that generate, treat, store, transport, and dispose of hazardous wastes. [p. 500]

VI. Answers to Essay Question

The jurisdiction over environmental issues is generally given to the Environmental Protection Agency (EPA). On a number of issues, the EPA shares this jurisdiction with other federal or state and local agencies. One of the primary regulatory aspects of the EPA function is to gather information on key environmental concerns. State and local agencies often have similar information gathering functions.

One common method of gathering such information is through the use of environmental impact statements. Normally the EPA will not require such a statement on proposed projects not covered by the National Environmental Policy Act, but most state and local governments do require such disclosures. Here there appears to be no evidence of Bailout or Dryhole having provided such a statement to any government agency. They may be held liable for such a failure.

It appears that there may be some damage to the water table in the areas underneath the former gasoline outlets. This sort of problem has become relatively common around the country as older gasoline outlet facilities are closed or converted to other uses. The old tanks are often left in the ground and allowed to rust. As they rust out, toxic chemicals are released from them into the ground water table. These emissions are often in violation of the Clean Water Act. Various state and local agencies may seek both equitable injunctive relief and money damages for the cost of cleanup and possibly even criminal sanctions, where appropriate, for the violation of these statutes.

In addition to the violation of the Clean Water Act, this situation may involve imposition of the provisions of the Comprehensive Environmental Response Compensation and Liability Act (Superfund). Under this Act, the costs of cleaning up a designated site may generally be passed on to any owners of the property who had an active part in the management of the property. Bailout Bank became an active owner of the property when it decided to convert the stations to branch banks. As such, it is subject to joint and several liability with Dryhole Oil to pay for the cost of the cleanup. The EPA can order them to clean it up directly. If they fail to do the cleanup, the EPA can clean it up and seek recovery of the cost from Bailout, Dryhole, or both. Interestingly enough, both Mortimer and Sallie are now in other lines of work. They took jobs at nuclear power plants.

Chapter 25
LAND USE REGULATION AND REAL PROPERTY

What do I really own?

I. Overview

Students find it important to learn how to plan their personal affairs through the law. The laws of contracts, property, and torts play significant roles in business and vital roles in how one arranges his or her personal affairs. Personal property is one such key area.

The study of personal property revolves around being able to answer three key questions:
1. How is this property classified?
2. How is this property acquired or transferred?
3. What are the legal consequences of the answers to questions 1 and 2?

All personal property falls into one classification or another. The type of classification used will determine how property will be treated in the eyes of the law. For example, consider the basic distinction between real and personal property. Sales of real property transactions generally come under the purview of the common law of contracts. Sales of goods, however, are generally covered by the UCC. If you are selling trees on the land, that property is classified as real, and the common law of contract controls. If the trees have been cut and are being sold to a mill, the UCC will now call the shots. If that lumber becomes part of a house, the common law of contracts again controls because the house is treated as real property.

In addition to classification, the acquisition and transfer of rights and duties to property are of key personal and business importance. Most property is transferred by way of contract with some sort of reciprocal exchange of consideration. You work, get paid, and that money is exchanged for property. You may be lucky, however, and find it, inherit it, or just have it given to you. In all these events, the acquisition or transfer must be made in compliance with the elements required by law. Once you have acquired the property, what are the rights and duties that arise out of that ownership? What if you found it? What if others have claims against it? These issues are of key importance in both business and private lives.

This chapter is in part, designed to introduce students to the law of real property from two key perspectives: first, ownership and the rights and duties that arise out of the ownership of real property, and second, use of real property and the respective rights and duties that can arise out of that use.

Real property represents the largest single outlay most people make in the course of their earning years. Even if they choose to rent, the price of keeping a roof over one's head will still probably be their biggest expense. Real estate is not only necessary as a matter of physical survival, it is critically important to our economic system because of this large dollar outlay. One of the most basic terms used in the law of real estate is "fee simple absolute." It connotes the highest form of recognized ownership in real property. The term is originally derived from the words *feud* or *fief* and *fief d'haubert* meaning a fee held by tenure of a knight's service to the lord of the manor. It is infinite, with no limitation on inheritability, and does not end upon the happening of any event. Think of fee simple as the whole pie. That pie, in turn, may be sliced and diced into all sorts of smaller morsels.

Another way to look at real estate is as a circular object in the physical shape of the earth. It is round, and each ownership of land has a unique wedge-shaped slice of that round body. The basic parameters of that ownership start with the surface rights as defined by the surveyed metes and bounds in the legal description. In addition to those rights, real estate extends theoretically to the center of the earth in minerals below the surface and in development of air rights. Both these rights are subject to use limitations and the rights of other owners of adjoining properties.

The other interesting aspect of this chapter goes into more detail on forms of co-ownership of property and the landlord-tenant relationship. Most of us, sooner or later, will get involved with co-ownership of property in one way or another. Anyone who is married is a likely co-owner. Anyone who shares property interests by gift, inheritance, or earnings is likely to be a co-owner. Even if one's property is entirely his or her own, he or she will need to know the rules of the co-ownership game for purposes of credit, finance, business planning, and the like. How, when, and where co-ownership rights and duties are created is as important as the basic terms of real property law itself. Most of us also will rent at some time in our lives. The various aspects of renting are also very important and are dealt with in this chapter.

II. Hypothetical Multi-Issue Essay Question

Bloke and Crissy Carrington have been married for the past 50 years (the first 20 in California) and live on the Worthmore Ranch in Aspen, Colorado. Bloke met Ms. Misty Blue (age 21) at the annual cookout on the ranch. He decides it's now or never for his mid-life crisis and runs off with Misty to Miami, telling Crissy: "My lawyer will call your lawyer about the divorce." Three days later Bloke dies on the beach. He did not leave a will but told Misty just before he died, "I leave you everything!"

Crissy comes to you for advice as to the disposition of the ranch.

The following properties have been acquired during the marriage:

    1. The Worthmore Ranch, held as tenancy in the entirety.

    2. Bank accounts in California and Colorado. They had been held in joint tenancy, but Bloke tried to wire the money to Miami the day before he died. The money had not yet been wired to Miami.

    3. Jewelry worth over $1 million that Bloke had handed to Misty on the plane to Miami. Please advise.

III. Outline

Real Property

    The land itself as well as buildings, trees, soil, minerals, timber, plants, and other things permanently affixed to the land

Land and Buildings (

    Land

    Buildings → constructed on land

    Subsurface Rights →located beneath land surface

    Plant Life and Vegetation → growing in or on the land surface

    Fixtures → affixed to real estate so as to become part of it

Estates in Land—ownership rights

    Freehold Estates—present possessory, interest

    Estates in Fee

        Fee simple absolute

            Highest form of ownership of real property

            Ownership is infinite in duration, has no limitation on inheritability, and does not end upon the occurrence or nonoccurrence of any event

        Fee simple defeasible

            Grants owner all of the incidents of a fee simple absolute except that it may be taken away if a specified condition occurs or does not occur

Life estate
Interest in property for the life of a specified person
A life estate terminates upon the death of the named person and reverts back to the grantor or his or her estate or other designated person

Concurrent Ownership—two or more persons owning a piece of real property together (co-ownership)
Joint tenancy—right of survivorship
Deceased tenant's interest automatically passes to co-tenants
Tenant may transfer his or her interest without consent of co-tenants; transfer severs joint liability
Tenancy in common
Deceased tenant's interest passes to his or her estate
Tenant may transfer his or her interest without the consent of co-tenants; transfer does not sever tenancy in common
Tenancy by the entirety—right of survivorship
Deceased tenant's interest automatically passes to his or her spouse
Neither spouse may transfer his or her interest without the other spouse's consent
Community property—only in some states
Surviving spouse automatically receives 1/2 of the income of both spouses and the assets acquired during the marriage
Neither spouse may transfer his or her interest without the other spouse's consent
Condominiums
Usually in multiple-dwelling buildings and sometimes in office buildings.
Purchasers have title to individual units and can be transferred.
Common areas are owned as tenants in common with monthly fees.
Cooperatives
Multiple-dwelling buildings
Corporation owns building. Residents own share of corporation and lease a unit from the corporation with special lease.

Future Interests—right to possess property in the future
The interest that the grantor retains for himself or herself or a third party
Reversion
Right to possession of real property returns to the grantor after the expiration of a limited or contingent estate
Remainder
Right to possession of real property goes to a third person or remainderman upon the expiration of a limited or contingent estate

Transfer of Ownership of Real Property
Sale (Conveyance)
Deed
A writing that describes a person's ownership interest in a piece of real property
Warranty deed has greatest number of warranties.
Quitclaim deed conveys only ownership interest owner has.
Recording statute
A state statute that requires the mortgage or deed of trust to be recorded in the county recorder's office of the county in which the real property is located. Gives constructive notice of owner's interest. Quiet Title Action may be bought to determine the extent of a party's ownership rights.
Adverse possession—wrongful possession for a set time that is open, visible, notorious, actual, exclusive, continuous, peaceful, hostile, and adverse
Marketable title is required. Title insurance may be a good idea.

Nonpossessory Interests in Real Property
Easement—right to make limited use of other's property without owning or leasing it. Given by grant or reservation. May be implied or by necessity.

Landlord – Tenant Relationship
Landlord or lessor transfers right of temporary possession to tenant or lessee who does not receive title. Tenant's interest is a leasehold.
Types:
Tenancy for Years → specific duration is agreed upon.
Periodic Tenancy → payments due at certain intervals but no specification of length of lease
Tenancy at Will → may be terminated by either at any time
Tenancy at Sufferance → tenant retains possession at end of lease without owner's consent
Rental agreement is called the lease.
Implied warranty of habitability provides that the leased premises must be fit, safe and suitable for ordinary residential use. Failure allows tenant usually to withhold rent, repair defect, cancel the lease or sue for damages.

Civil Rights Act
A federal statute that prohibits racial discrimination in the transfer or real property

Fair Housing Act
A federal statute that makes it unlawful for a party to refuse to rent of sell a dwelling to any person because of his race, color, national origin, sex or religion

Title III of the American with Disabilities Act
A federal statute that prohibits discrimination on the basis of a disability in places of public accommodation by private entities

Zoning
Zoning ordinances- local laws that municipalities and local governments adopt to regulate land use within their boundaries
Ordinances generally:
1. Establish use districts
2. Restrict height, size and location of buildings
3. Establish aesthetic requirements or limitation for the extension or buildings
Zoning commission- usually formulates zoning ordinances, conduct public hearings, and make recommendations to the city council
Variance- an exception that permits a type of building or use in an area that would not otherwise be allowed
Nonconforming uses- use and buildings that already exist in a zoned area that are permitted to continue even though they do not fit within new zoning ordinances

Eminent Domain and "Taking"
Eminent Domain- the government's power to take private property for public use, provided that just compensation is paid to the private property holder
Just Compensation Clause- a clause in the United States Constitution that requires the government to compensate a property owner, and possibly others, when government takes property under eminent domain.
"Taking"- government acquisition of private property for public use, pursuant to its power of eminent domain

IV. Objective Questions

Terms:

1. Property that consists of tangibles such as automobiles, furniture, and jewelry, or any other property that is movable can be classified as _____.

2. Subsurface rights are also called _____.

3. Property is usually classified as either _____ or personal property.

4. Kitchen cabinets, carpets, and doorknobs are _____.

5. A(n) _____ is defined as the bundle of legal rights that the owner has to possess, use, and enjoy the property.

6. A(n) _____ is treated as the owner of the property during the duration of a life estate.

7. When property is owned by two or more persons at the same time, there are four types: (1) joint tenancy, (2) tenancy in common, (3) tenancy by the entirety, and (4) community property. All these are forms of _____.

8. The two most prominent forms of future interests are called _____.

9. The party who transfers an ownership interest in real property is called a(n) _____.

10. A deed in which a grantor of real property transfers whatever interest he or she has in the property to a grantee is known as a(n) _____.

True/False:

1. _____ A bridge would be an example of real property.

2. _____ Subsurface rights cannot be sold separately from surface rights.

3. _____ The person who is given a life estate is called the life tenant.

4. _____ A life tenant is treated as the owner of the property even after the duration of the life estate.

5. _____ A joint tenant does not have the right to sell or transfer his or her interest in the property.

6. _____ A surviving spouse in a tenancy by the entirety has the right of survivorship.

7. _____ The Statute of Frauds requires the real estate sales contracts to be in writing.

8. _____ In a special warranty deed, the seller is liable for defects in title that existed before the seller obtained the property.

9. _____ To obtain title under adverse possession, the adverse possessor must physically occupy the property.

10. _____The Fair Housing Act specifically prohibits discrimination against disabled individuals in employment, public services, public accommodations and services.

Multiple Choice:

1. Land, and buildings, constructed on land are examples of _____.

 A. chattel
 B. intangible property
 C. personal property
 D. real property

2. The rights to the earth located beneath the surface of the land are defined as _____.

 A. chattel rights
 B. IP rights
 C. mineral rights
 D. joint rights

3. The legal rights that the owner has to possess, use, and enjoy the property are known as _____.

 A. future interests
 B. estate in land
 C. easement rights
 D. estoppel by deed

4. A(n) _____ is an estate in which the owner has a present possessory interest in the real property.

 A. estate pour autre vie
 B. future interest
 C. easement
 D. freehold estate

5. _____ is a type of ownership of real property that grants the owner the fullest bundle of legal rights that a person can hold in real property.

 A. Fee simple absolute
 B. Life estate
 C. Servient estate
 D. Fee simple defeasible

6. A(n) _____ grants the owner all the incidents of a fee simple absolute except that ownership may be taken away if a specified condition occurs or does not occur.

 A. servient estate
 B. future interest
 C. fee simple defeasible
 D. easement estate.

7. A life estate that is measured by the life of a third party is referred to as _____.

    A. servient estate
    B. estate pour autre vie
    C. community property
    D. future interest

8. Which of the following provisions protects the interest of a joint tenancy upon the death of a joint tenant?

    A. Quiet title action
    B. Estate in land
    C. Quitclaim deed
    D. Right of survivorship

9. _____ is a form of co-ownership of real property that can be used only by married couples.

    A. Tenancy by the entirety
    B. Joint tenancy
    C. Tenancy in common
    D. Cooperatives

10. A _____ is a right of possession that returns to the grantor after the expiration of a limited or contingent estate.

    A. remainder
    B. reversion
    C. quiet title action
    D. nonconforming use

V. Answers to Objective Questions

Terms:

1. personal property. Technically, personal property is any property that cannot be classified as real property. Remember, however, that property that may have started as personal may be converted to real (such as a fixture) or vice versa (such as timber which has been severed from the land). [p. 509]

2. mineral rights. These rights can be very valuable. [p. 509]

3. real. Some jurisdictions refer to this dichotomy as movables vs. immovables. [p. 509]

4. fixtures. Unless otherwise provided, if a building is sold, the fixtures are included in the sale. [p. 510]

5. Estate. An estate is defined as the bundle of legal rights that the owner has to possess, use, and enjoy the property. [p. 510]

6. life tenant. . The person who is given a life estate is called the life tenant. [p. 511]

7. concurrent ownership. Coownership can take place over both real and personal property. It can be between only two persons, such as a marital community property, or between thousands of persons, as seen in large publicly traded companies. [p. 512]

8. reversions and remainders. The two forms of future interests are reversion and remainder. [p. 515]

9. grantor. A party who transfers an ownership interest in real property is known as a grantor. [p. 516]

10. quitclaim deed. A deed in which a grantor of real property transfers whatever interest he or she has in the property to a grantee is known as a quitclaim deed. [p. 517]

True/False:

1. True. Real property is immovable. [p. 509]

2. False. Subsurface rights may be sold separately from surface rights. [p. 509]

3. True. The person who is given a life estate is called the life tenant. [p. 511]

4. False. Upon the death of the life tenant, the life estate terminates, and the property reverts to the grantor or the grantor's estate or another designated person. [p. 511]
5. False. Each joint tenant has a right to sell or transfer his or her interest in the property, but such conveyance terminates the joint tenancy. [p. 512]

6. True. In tenancy by the entirety, a surviving spouse has the right of survivorship. [p. 513]

7. True. The Statute of Frauds in most states requires this contract to be in writing. [p. 516]

8. False. In a special warranty deed, the seller is not liable for defects in title that existed before the seller obtained the property or for encumbrances that were present when the seller obtained the property. [p. 517]

9. True. The adverse possessor must physically occupy the premises. The planting of crops, grazing of animals, or building of a structure on the land constitutes physical occupancy. [p. 518]

10. False. Fair Housing Act of 1968 is a federal statute that makes it unlawful for a party to refuse to sell, rent, finance, or advertise housing to any person because of his or her race, color, national origin, sex, religion, disability, or familial status (e.g., pregnant women, a family with children under 18 years of age). [p. 522]

Multiple Choice:

1. D. Real property is immovable or attached to immovable land or buildings. Land is the most common form of real property. Buildings constructed on land are real property. [p. 509]

2. C. Rights to the earth located beneath the surface of the land are known as subsurface rights or mineral rights. [p. 509]

3. B. Estate in land (estate) refers to ownership rights in real property; the bundle of legal rights that an owner has to possess, use, and enjoy the property. [p. 510]

4. D. A freehold estate is an estate in which the owner has a present possessory interest in the real property. [p. 510]

5. A. A fee simple absolute (fee simple) is a type of ownership of real property that grants the owner the fullest bundle of legal rights that a person can hold in real property. [p. 511]

6. C. A fee simple defeasible type of ownership of real property grants the owner all the incidents of a fee simple absolute except that it may be taken away if a specified condition occurs or does not occur. [p. 511]

7. B. Estate pour autre vie refers to a life estate that is measured by the life of a third party. [p. 511]

8. D. The right of survivorship is a legal rule which provides that upon the death of one joint tenant, the deceased person's interest in the real property automatically passes to the surviving joint tenant or joint tenants. [p. 512]

9. A. Tenancy by the entirety is a form of co-ownership of real property that can be used only by married couples. [p. 513]

10. B. Reversion is a right of possession that returns to a grantor after the expiration of a limited or contingent estate. [p. 515]

VI. Answers to Essay Question

First, the properties in question must be generally classified. The ranch is clearly classified as real property. This classification would include the surface, mineral, and air rights associated with land. It would also include any permanent improvements on the land, including buildings, fixtures, and the like.

The bank accounts would be classified as personal property. Because the accounts may be represented by passbooks or some other indicia of ownership such as a certificate of deposit, these assets would be classified as intangibles in that the real value of the property is found in what these documents represent, i.e., monies deposited with the financial institution. The jewelry is classified as tangible personal property. All the property involved is privately held.

Because all the properties were presumed to be acquired during a fifty-year marriage, it must be assumed that in the hands of Bloke and Crissy, the property was either purchased or somehow otherwise legally acquired by them. The more important immediate issue is: was any of the property in question transferred to Misty in the problem as presented? Of overriding concern is the attempt by Bloke to deprive Crissy of her legitimate marital claims to the properties. Here the laws of Colorado, Florida, and California will all come into play to one extent or another.

With regard to the ranch, under the laws of tenancy by the entirety, the property will pass automatically at death to the surviving spouse. This right of survivorship is by operation of law, and the property will not pass by way of probate, with or without a will. Transfer of the property must have been made with the consent of both tenants and must be evidenced by some sort of symbolic written document, i.e., a deed. None of those occurred here. Some states sever the tenancy by entirety in case of divorce. Here the divorce had not yet taken place, so Crissy takes the ranch as surviving tenant by the entirety.

Chapter 26
INTERNATIONAL AND WORLD TRADE LAW

*What do you do if you want to do business in
another country and their laws conflict with ours?*

I. Overview

The word oxymoron is defined as a combination of contradictory or incongruous words or phrases. To many, the term international law represents one such example. At best, defining international law along the traditional domestic lines of a body of rules of behavior and mechanisms designed to enforce those rules cannot work as well when the protagonists are sovereign nations. By definition, sovereignty incorporates the notion of freedom from external controls and supreme power over one's own affairs. Perhaps that might be a starting point to resolve this oxymoronic dilemma. A nation does need to have control over its internal affairs, but its national interests and the welfare of its citizens do not end at its borders. Nations, just like individuals, can only find protection for their own rights when they are willing to honor the rights of others. Law eventually works its way through to a system of cooperative behavior for the larger mutual good. All law calls for some sacrifice of individual freedoms for the betterment of the corporate body. This is the fundamental reality upon which all law is ultimately based. Consequences of failures to honor that reality at the global level are readily apparent to all of us. If the role of law is to act as a mechanism for civilization that makes violence the last resort, then international law is a goal worth striving for by all nations.

International law, however, involves, by definition, a sense of compromise which is only effective if the parties involved are truly willing. There are many customs, conventions, and treaties that require that their participants be bound because of certain threats of discipline. In the end, however, this discipline is virtually voluntary and self-imposed. Compromise is the answer but voluntary compromise is often the problem.

The second interesting aspect of any comparison between international law of nations and international commerce is the sheer breadth and scope of commerce. International trade has become the lifeblood of nations, and international business entities are its circulatory system. In quite blunt terms, the scale and power attained by many large multinational banks, manufacturers, and diversified business organizations have simply surpassed the ability of any one country to control them. That is not to say that these are renegade free agents with no accountability. It is to say, however, that the worldwide staging area of economic competition is such that these players are big enough and strong enough to have the rules written in their favor. Witness the worldwide and sometimes fawning competition by countries for new plants and financial investments created by these entities.

This chapter seeks to outline some of the basic terminology used in international law. It also describes some of the key players on that stage. Like any good play, this stage is filled with intrigue, pathos, and sometimes-epic Greek tragedy. The failures of whole nations only magnify our own fallibilities, because international law is the most fragile of all legal systems. Yet in an age of possible nuclear self-destruction, do we have any choice? Like it or not, as William James said: "The things we cherish most are at the mercy of the things we cherish least."

II. Hypothetical Multi-issue Essay Question

Mario LaFast is a U.S. resident who has finally made it to the top of the auto-racing world. He just signed a three-year contract to drive for Enzo Frank and his Formula One Supercharged Turbo Racing Team in Italy. Mario's retainer is over $10 million annually plus a percentage of the winning purse if he finishes third or higher. The Formula One race calendar starts in South America in late spring and finishes in late fall in Australia. The races are held in a total of sixteen different countries.

All of the host countries have their own tax systems, and they all seek to tax, as income, winnings from auto races. In addition, many of these tax laws measure income on a worldwide basis. Thus income earned in a race in Italy may be reportable on Mario's tax returns filed in New York. If all the possible taxes are independently and fully imposed by every nation in which Mario won, his tax bill would exceed his income because of "double-taxation" on the same income by more than one taxing entity. What can Mario do?

III. Outline

International Law—governs affairs between nations and regulates transactions between individuals and businesses of different countries
> No single source
> No single court (many voluntary courts)
> No executive branch for enforcement

United States and Foreign Affairs
> Foreign Commerce Clause
>> Vests Congress with the power "to regulate commerce with foreign nations" (Article I, section 8, clause 3)
> Treaty Clause
>> States that the President "shall have power, by and with the advice and consent of the Senate, to make treaties, provided two-thirds of the senators present concur" (Article II, section 2, clause 2)
>> - Treaty- an agreement or contract between two or more nations
>> - Convention- a treaty that is sponsored by an international organization

United Nations
> An international organization created by a multilateral treaty in 1945 to maintain peace and security in the world, provide economic and social cooperation, and protect human rights.
> Is governed by:
>> The General Assembly---composed of all member nations as the legislative group
>> The Security Council—composed of 15 member nations to maintain peace
>> The Secretariat---administers day-to-day operations
>> International Court of Justice—the judicial branch of the United Nations, also called the World Court

International Regional Organizations
> European Union—countries of Eastern and Western Europe
> North American Free Trade Agreement (NAFTA) – U.S., Canada and Mexico
> Association of Southeastern Asian Nations (ASEAN)
> Organization of the Petroleum Exporting Countries (OPEC)

World Trade Organization
- An international organization of more than 130 member nations, created to promote and enforce trade agreements among member nations

National International Law
  National Courts- courts of individual nations
  Jurisdiction
  - Choice of forum clause
  - Choice of law clause
  -
Act of State Doctrine and Sovereign Immunity Compared
  Act of state
  An act of a government in its own country that is not subject to suit in another country's courts. Judges in one country cannot question the validity of an act committed by another country within that other country's borders.
  Sovereign immunity
  Act of a government in a foreign country that is not subject to suit in the foreign country. Exceptions include waiver or commercial activity.

IV. Objective Questions:

Terms:

1. The power of Congress to regulate commerce with foreign nations is granted by the _____.

2. An agreement or contract between two or more nations that is formally signed by an authorized representative and ratified by the supreme power of each nation is called a _____.

3. The most important of all international organizations is the _____.

4. This international court is located in The Hague and is the judicial branch of the United Nations. It is called the _____ or the _____.

5. Canada, Mexico, and the United States entered into an international trade agreement that created the largest free trade area in the world. This treaty is called the _____.

6. The major trading block of Eastern and Western Europe is the _____.

7. The influence of this economic group is inexorably tied to the worldwide supply and price of oil. It is the _____.

8. The doctrine which provides that judges of one country cannot question the validity of an act committed by another country within that other country's own borders is known as the _____.

9. A clause in an international contract that designates which nation's laws will be applied in deciding a dispute is known as a _____.

10. A doctrine which states that countries are granted immunity from suits in courts of other countries is the doctrine of _____.

True/False:

1. ____ Under the Treaty Clause of the U.S. Constitution, states may enter into treaties with foreign nations.

2. ____ The President is the agent of the United States in dealing with foreign nations.

3. ____ The United Nations was created by a multilateral treaty on October 24, 1945.

4. ____ Individuals or businesses may have cases decided by the International Court of Justice.

5. ____ The International Court of Justice is composed of 15 judges who serve nine-year terms.

6. ____ The FTAA is a proposed extension of NAFTA.

7. ____ A forum-selection clause designates the judicial or arbitral forum that will hear and decide a case.

8. ____ The United States grants absolute immunity to foreign governments from suit in U.S. courts.

9. ____ An action based on a commercial activity carried on in the United States will not make a foreign nation immune from suit in U.S. courts.

10. ____ Jewish law is decided by rabbis, who are scholars of the Torah and other Jewish scriptures.

Multiple Choice:

1. If a state enacts a law that increases its tax on imported automobiles but not on American-made automobiles, it violates the _____ of the U.S. Constitution.

A. Equal Protection Clause
B. Foreign Commerce Clause
C. Supremacy Clause
D. Due Process Clause

2. An agreement between two or more nations that is formally signed by an authorized representative of each nation and ratified by each nation is defined as a(n) _____.

A. statute
B. charter
C. treaty
D. arraignment

3. Which of the following branches of the United Nations is primarily responsible for maintaining international peace and has authority to use armed force for this purpose?

A. the General Assembly
B. the Secretariat
C. the Security Council
D. the International Court of Justice

4. The _____ is a staff of persons that administers the day-to-day operations of the UN.

A. Council of Ministers
B. Security Council
C. General Assembly
D. Secretariat

5. The World Bank is _____.

A. an autonomous agency under the aegis of the European Union
B. an agency that monitors the financial collaborations taking place in the eurozone
C. primarily responsible for promoting sound monetary, fiscal, and macroeconomic policies worldwide
D. primarily responsible for providing money to developing countries to fund projects for humanitarian purposes

6. Which of the following statements is true of the NAFTA?

A. It allows a member country to reimpose tariffs if imports are hurting that country's economy or its workers.
B. It disallows any special protection being extended to specific industries.
C. It disallows NAFTA members from trading with other countries unless a unanimous permission is obtained.
D. It has been hailed by economists to be a perfect example of a free trade pact.

7. Which organization has been referred to as the "Supreme Court of World Trade?"

A. UN
B. ICJ
C. WTO
D. IMF

8. _____ is a clause in an international contract that designates which nation's court has jurisdiction to hear a case arising out of the contract.

A. Forum-selection clause
B. Treaty Clause
C. Foreign Commerce Clause
D. Choice of law clause

9. Which of the following is an exception to the Foreign Sovereign Immunities Act?

A. sham exception
B. managed trade exception
C. diversity of citizenship exception
D. commercial activity exception

10. Islamic law is derived from:

A. the Torah
B. the Koran
C. Hindu law
D. British Common law

V. Answers to Objective Questions:

Terms:

1. Foreign Commerce Clause. Only the federal government may enter into treaties with other nations, and these treaties become part of the law of the land. [p. 533]

2. treaty. Treaties can be classified as bilateral, multilateral, and/or conventions. [p. 534]

3. United Nations. This organization, created after World War II, is the spiritual successor to the League of Nations, which was dissolved in April 1946. [p. 535]

4. International Court of Justice or World Court. The decisions of this court are only binding if a nation agrees to be bound. [p. 536]

5. North American Free Trade Agreement. This treaty creates the largest free trade area in the world. It was ratified after much heated debate over jobs, environmental issues, and immigration issues. [p. 538]

6. European Union. The EU represents more than 500 million people. [p. 538]

7. Organization of Petroleum Exporting Countries. The influence of this group will never be insignificant, but it has been reduced by the discovery of oil in areas like the North Sea and Alaska. [p. 541]

8. act of state doctrine. The underlying reasoning for this doctrine is restraint on the part of the judiciary that permits the executive branch to arrange affairs with foreign governments. [p. 543]

9. choice of law clause. This clause may resolve issues related to jurisdictional matters. [p. 543]

10. sovereign immunity. This is one of the oldest principles of international law. [p. 545]

True/False:

1. False. Only the federal government can enter into treaties. [p. 534]

2. True. Under the Supremacy Clause of the Constitution, treaties become part of the "law of the land," and conflicting state or local law is void. [p. 534]

3. True. This organization has grown dramatically over the past half century, yet many analysts say it has still fallen short of achieving its original goals. [p. 535]

4. False. Only nations can have cases decided by the International Court of Justice, but nations may bring a case on behalf of an individual or business. [p. 536]

5. True. The ICJ hears cases that nations refer to it as well as cases involving treaties and the UN Charter. [p. 536]

6. True. This will include all countries of North, Central, and South America. [p. 541]

7. True. It is a clause in an international contract that designates which nation's laws will be applied in deciding a dispute arising out of the contract. [p. 543]

8. False. The U.S. grants qualified or restricted immunity to foreign governments, as outlined in the Foreign Sovereign Immunities Act of 1976. [p. 545]

9. True. One of the exceptions to absolute foreign immunity provided by the Foreign Sovereign Immunities Act of 1979 allowing for a suit to be brought on the basis of commercial activity. [p. 545]

10. True. Jewish law is a complex legal system based upon the ideology and theology of the Torah. [p. 546]

Multiple Choice:

1. B. Article I, Section 8, Clause 3 of the U.S. Constitution—the Foreign Commerce Clause—vests Congress with the power "to regulate commerce with foreign nations." [p. 533]

2. C. Bilateral treaties are between two nations; multilateral treaties involve more than two nations. [p. 534]

3. C. The UN Security Council is composed of fifteen member nations, five of which are permanent members (China, France, Russia, the United Kingdom, and the United States), and ten other countries selected by the members of the General Assembly to serve two-year terms. [p. 535]

4. D. It is headed by the secretary-general, who is elected by the General Assembly. [p. 535]

5. D. The World Bank is a United Nations agency that comprises more than 180 member nations. [p. 536]

6. A. The treaty creates a free trade zone stretching from the Yukon to the Yucatan, bringing together more than 400 million people in the three countries. [p. 538]

7. C. The entity was created to promote and enforce trade agreements among member nations. [p. 542]

8. A. Many international contracts contain a choice of forum clause (or forum-selection clause) that designates which nation's court has jurisdiction to hear a case arising out of a contract. [p. 543]

9. D. With commercial activity, the foreign sovereign is subject to suit in the United States; without it, the foreign sovereign is immune to suit in this country. [p. 545]

10. B. Islamic law is derived from the Koran, the Sunnah, and Islamic scholars. [p. 546]

VI. Answers to Essay Question:

Mario certainly has a mixed blessing in having made it to the top of the racing world. On the plus side, he is a world celebrity who really does live out the fantasy of "life in the fast lane!" The down side of all this is that life has gotten far more complicated since the days when he was drag racing behind the high school parking lot.

Under our taxing structure, both the federal and state governments can impose income taxes. Some taxes paid to the states can be taken as either a business expense above the line for arriving at adjusted gross income or as a personal itemized deduction after having arrived at adjusted gross income. This would all be well and good if Mario's racing activities were limited to the confines of the U.S.

But his income source will not only be the U.S. Because our tax laws seek to impose a tax on world-based income, Mario must seek ways to avoid double taxation. The federal government will be the source of any protection that may be afforded to him on this issue in the U.S. He must look at the national governments of other nations seeking to impose their taxes. Those national policies will preempt any state laws that may be in conflict with the national policies enumerated in the tax laws.

The best source of protection available to Mario will be tax treaties. These are either bilateral or multilateral agreements entered into by various nations that are designed to allow each other to tax a "fair share" of Mario's overall worldwide income without creating confiscatory double taxation. Under these treaties, each nation decides how to defer taxation to other nations where that income is already earned and taxed in the other nation. By use of certain agreed upon parameters of exclusions from income or credits for taxes paid to other countries, the net intended effect is to allow taxation of the same income only once in each country where it is earned.

All this is easier said than done. The world of international taxation is one of the most difficult areas of law, accounting, and business practice. It takes years just to learn the ropes and is extremely technical in nature. Mario should seek advice and counsel from professionals trained in these matters.

In case two or more of the countries seeking to tax Mario reach an impasse on how his income should be taxed, they may choose to voluntarily submit their disagreement to the one of the international tribunals such as the U.N. International Court of Justice. As an alternative, the countries may choose to seek a voluntary form of arbitration. If arbitration is chosen, enforcement will still be an issue if they are not signatories to an arbitration enforcement convention.

In any event, Mario's best route on this issue is to have his contract set out, at the beginning, a choice of law and choice of jurisdiction. Even there, remember, each country as a sovereign can still ultimately control the taxation of income earned within its own borders.

Mario has decided to move to Monaco because of the favorable tax laws there. Even if he is still taxed elsewhere, he will do just fine, thank you, at the casinos in Monte Carlo.